From Disciple to Friend

The Middle of a Celtic Journey
through
The Spiritual Exercises of Saint Ignatius of Loyola

Timothy J. Ray

Copyright © 2021 Timothy J. Ray
All rights reserved.
ISBN: 9798485586072

To
Laurens van der Werf, SJ

who taught me to walk confidently with Christ
in the presence of the poor

Table of Contents

Finding Your Place of Resurrection: a foreword	i
Preface for *From Disciple to Friend*	iii
Acknowledgements	v

Companioning the King of Heaven

Companioning the King of Heaven	3
A Contemplation of the Kingdom of Jesus Christ	4

From Disciple to Friend

Considerations	9
Prelude: Praying with Jesus and St. Brigid	13
1. The Incarnation	15
1.1a Let Thanks Arise On Every Side	16
1.1b Preparation for Prayer	22
1.2 A Meditation on the Incarnation	24
1.3 Luke 1:26-38	26
1.4 Luke 1:39-56	29
1.5 Repetition of Luke 1:26-38	32
1.6 An Application of the Senses	35
1.7 Review of Prayer	37
2. The Nativity and Childhood of Jesus	39
2.1a Behold The Lamb! He Comes.	40
2.1b Preparation for Prayer	46
2.2 Luke 2:2-20	48
2.3 Matthew 2:2-15	51
2.4 Luke 2:22-40	54
2.5 Repetition of Luke 2:2-20	57
2.6 An Application of the Senses	60
2.7 Review of Prayer	62
3. The Hidden Life of Jesus	65
3.1a Gentle Jesus, Fount Of Healing	66
3.1b Preparation for Prayer	72
3.2 Luke 2:41-52	74
3.3 Romans 12:9-21, using Luke 2:52	77
3.4 Romans 14:13-23, using Luke 2:52	80
3.5 A Consideration of Jesus' "Hidden Life"	83

	3.6	An Application of the Senses	85
	3.7	Review of Prayer	87
4.	Jesus' Baptism and the Temptation in the Desert		89
	4.1a	Dear Redeemer, Loved And Loving	90
	4.1b	Preparation for Prayer	96
	4.2	Matthew 3:1-17	98
	4.3	Luke 4:1-13	101
	4.4	Luke 4:14-22	104
	4.5	Repetition of Luke 4:14-22	107
	4.6	An Application of the Senses	110
	4.7	Review of Prayer	112
5.	The Call of Christ		115
	5.1a	Hear Me, Christ, My King	116
	5.1b	Preparation for Prayer	122
	5.2	John 1:35-51	124
	5.3	Luke 5:5-11	127
	5.4	Luke 5:27-38	130
	5.5	Repetition of Luke 5:27-38	133
	5.6	An Application of the Senses	136
	5.7	Review of Prayer	138
6.	Committing Oneself to Christ		141
	6.1a	The Victor, Christ, With Flag Unfurled	142
	6.1b	Preparation for Prayer	148
	6.2	Meditation concerning the 2 Standards	150
	6.3	Meditation concerning the 3 Classes of Persons	152
	6.4	The 3 Modes of Humility	154
	6.5	Galatians 5:16-25	156
	6.6	An Application of the Senses	159
	6.7	Review of Prayer	161
7.	Following Jesus as a Disciple		163
	7.1a	You Are, O Christ, My Health And Light	164
	7.1b	Preparation for Prayer	170
	7.2	Matthew 14:13-21	172
	7.3	Luke 18:35-43	175
	7.4	Matthew 17:1-9	178
	7.5	2 Peter 1:3-11	180
	7.6	An Application of the Senses	183
	7.7	Review of Prayer	185
8.	Following Jesus as a Companion		187
	8.1a	Oh, Kind Creator Of The Skies	188

	8.1b Preparation for Prayer	194
	8.2 Luke 7:36-50	196
	8.3 Luke 10:25-37	199
	8.4 Matthew 5:1-16	202
	8.5 Colossians 3:12-17	205
	8.6 An Application of the Senses	207
	8.7 Review of Prayer	209
9.	Following Jesus as a Friend	211
	9.1a To The Fount Of Life Eternal	212
	9.1b Preparation for Prayer	218
	9.2 John 15:12-17	220
	9.3 John 11:1-37	222
	9.4 John 11:38-45	225
	9.5 1 Corinthians 13:1-13	228
	9.6 An Application of the Senses	231
	9.7 Review of Prayer	233

Embracing the Adventure of Jesus' Friendship

Embracing the Adventure of Jesus' Friendship	237
A Contemplation of the Friendship of Jesus Christ	238

Living as a Citizen of Heaven

Introduction	243
Spiritual Practices	245
Traditional Irish Prayers	247
Meeting a Soul Friend	254
Laments, Litanies and Loricas	259
Sacred Citizenship	273
Brigid of Kildare – The Flame of Justice	275
Selections from Cogitosus' *Life of Saint Brigid*	280
Articulate Witness	285
Defining Your Style	287

Textual Resources

From Saint Ignatius' *Spiritual Exercises*	299
A Contemplation of the Kingdom of Jesus Christ	299
A Meditation on the Incarnation	300

The Two Standards	302
Anima Christi	303
The Three Classes of Persons	304
The Three Modes of Humility	305
Rules for the Discernment of Spirits, Week 2	305
From Celtic Sources	**309**
A Description of Saint Brigid	309
Stories about Saint Brigid	309
A Prophecy about the Unborn Brigid	309
The Birth of Brigid	310
Brigid Returns to Her Father	311
Brigid's Father Attempts to Sell Her	311
Brigid and the Religious Scholar	312
Brigid and the Two Lepers	312
Two Miracles Performed by Brigid	313
Brigid and the Silver Chain	313
Brigid Discusses a Vision with Patrick	314
The Things Brigid Wished For	314

Finding Your Place of Resurrection: a foreword

A commitment to the spiritual life involves a journey of unfolding possibilities and new awarenesses. Each new discovery in our relationship with God reveals a deeper experience of divine love as well as further opportunities to serve God through our involvement with other people and various causes in our world, which in turn invites further prayer and reflection about these new expressions of God's activity in our lives. This is a journey into ever-deepening awareness of God's love for us and our need to respond in kind – a love that invites a reciprocal response of love. It is an unending pilgrimage into the mystery of creation that does not end until we find our rest within God's loving consciousness.

For the ancient Celtic saints, this pilgrimage is a journey towards the individual's "place of resurrection" – that place in the world where a person discovers his or her relationship to God and their purpose in life. For the ancient Celts, this was an actual location a man or woman sought out through prayer (and often quite dangerous travel) where he or she would wait for death and subsequent resurrection while committing themselves to rigorous spiritual disciplines and prayers. In the modern world, this "place of resurrection" might better be understood as an earthly situation or type of ministry where a person feels closest to God through prayerful and social activities intended to foster the renewal of God's creation (both human and nonhuman) and the establishment of the kingdom of God.

Centuries later, Saint Ignatius of Loyola would create in his *Spiritual Exercises* an ordered set of meditations designed to help men and women open themselves with ever-increasing generosity to the love God demonstrates towards them and the world around them. At the heart of these Ignatian exercises lies an ideal that Ignatius called *"magis"*, "the more" by which God invites an individual – through an incremental and ongoing process of revelation and invitation – to greater and more challenging opportunities to become instruments of God's love in the world. Like the Celtic saints before him, Ignatius understood the spiritual life as an unfolding journey of possibilities to be embraced in response to the individual's tangible experience of God's love in his or her life.

The recognition of this shared vision between the ancient Celtic saints and St. Ignatius of Loyola forms the foundation for the books in this series. Each book presents a self-directed retreat addressing a portion of *The Spiritual Exercises of Saint Ignatius of Loyola* accompanied by materials by or about a particular Celtic saint whose vision complements Ignatius' exercises. Each book in the series also provides resources from both the Celtic and Ignatian spiritual traditions to facilitate further prayer and reflection as well as exercises developed from Celtic spiritual practices related to the themes of each retreat. Used together, these retreats and their companion materials cultivate habits of prayer and action intended to nurture a holistic spirituality embracing spiritual discipline, sacred citizenship and articulate witness in the world.

So, as you begin this pilgrimage of faith and love, you should walk with confidence in the knowledge that many have walked before you and others will follow after you. You are being invited into an intimate relationship with God through which your faults and failings are forgiven as you become an instrument of love and reconciliation in a world often bereft of hope. The examples of the ancient Celtic saints and the followers of the Ignatian spiritual tradition offer you a supportive companionship as you strive to find your own "place of resurrection" – embracing the increasingly wonderful gifts God presents to you and expressing your gratitude through generous acts of self-giving service to God's other children and creatures.

Preface for *From Disciple to Friend*

Through your prayers and reflections in *From Loss to Love*, you received an invitation to participate in God's loving plan of redemption. Since you are reading these words, you have chosen to explore the forms of service God might offer you through a deeper and more intimate relationship with Jesus Christ. This decision reflects gratitude for what you experienced during your previous retreat and reflections as well as faith in God's commitment to remain with you as you travel toward an unknown future. Your choice to enter deeper into the mystery of a transformative and empowering friendship with God reflects hope inspired by God's demonstrations of love in the past as well as trust evoked by God's promises of a future offering you ever-increasing possibilities of loving service to God.

From Disciple to Friend presents the second of a three-part journey through *The Spiritual Exercises of Saint Ignatius of Loyola*. It explores God's decision to intervene in human history and to invite men and women to share in the redemptive mission of Jesus. It also presents a call to discipleship as well as an invitation to increasing intimacy with Jesus Christ. This book includes a self-guided journey through the early life of Jesus, the call of his first disciples and his public ministry. Like *From Loss to Love*, both the retreat and its companion reflection materials draw upon the stories and prayers of a Celtic saint, Brigid of Kildare, and other materials that would have been easily recognizable to her in order to provide a broader context to the issues you will engage during your journey through the Ignatian exercises.

In *From Disciple to Friend*, you will encounter the call to discipleship offered to Jesus' first followers and experience the same offer of friendship with Jesus these men and women received. These invitations provide a context in which to express the gratitude you feel after recognizing in *From Loss to Love* that you are a "loved sinner", a state of being made possible only through Jesus' redemptive mission. It is a reciprocal offer of love for the love you have received from God through Jesus Christ. So, you might find it helpful to review your consideration of the Two Kings at the end of your first retreat to understand the significance of the new offerings of love – and opportunities for service – you will receive through your prayers and reflections with this book.

As you begin your journey with Jesus through his life and public ministry, it is also important that you remember your need to remain grounded in the present moment and not to look forward to what may come in the future. As a Christian, you are aware that Jesus' ministry leads to the cross and the empty tomb – the subject matter of the final book in this series. Because of this, you may be tempted to look beyond the very important and transformative moment that comes when you are first called to be of disciple and friend of Jesus Christ. You should avoid this temptation by focusing only on what you are asked to consider through prayer and reflection in this book, trusting in the knowledge that God will reveal your "place of resurrection" through an unfolding sequence of invitations to greater participation in the divine plan for creation.

So, just as you did in your journey through *From Loss to Love*, you should pray for the patience to learn the disciplines of prayer and to persevere as the seeds planted in this book mature and bear fruit over time – carrying with you the promise offered by God through Isaiah 55:10-11:

> *For as the rain and the snow come down from heaven,*
>   *and do not return there until they have watered the earth,*
> *making it bring forth and sprout,*
>   *giving seed to the sower and bread to the eater,*
> *so shall my word be that goes out from my mouth;*
>   *it shall not return to me empty,*
> *but it shall accomplish that which I purpose,*
>   *and succeed in the thing for which I sent it.*

Acknowledgements

This book represents a personal journey that would not have been possible without the companionship of my friends and spiritual companions who, to varying degrees and for different lengths of time, supported and encouraged me to persevere in this pilgrimage.

Among these friends, I remain especially grateful to Kathleen Deignan, Edward Egros, Rosalyn Knowles Ferrell, Douglas Galbraith, Patrick Henry, Susan Rakoczy, Jim Swonger and George Theodoridis.

In addition, I am very grateful for:
- the permission of *The Capuchin Annual* and the King estate to reproduce Richard King's image of Saint Brigid on the cover of this book.
- the permission of Four Courts Press to excerpt selections from Liam de la Paor's translation of Cogitosus' "Life of Saint Brigid" in *Saint Patrick's World* (Dublin, Four Courts Press, 1993).
- the permission of Johnston McMaster to excerpt "Brigid of Kildare – The Flame of Justice" from his *A Passion for Justice: Social Ethics in the Celtic Tradition* (Edinburgh: Dunedin Academic Press Ltd., 2008).

The prayer sequences presented in this book were developed using ancient Christian hymns and traditional Irish prayers from the following public domain books, all of which are available on the Internet Archive:
- *Early Christian Hymns; translations of the verses of the most notable Latin writers of the early and middle ages* (1908), edited by Daniel Joseph Donahoe.
- *Early Christian Hymns, Series II: translations of the verses of the early and middle ages* (1911), edited by Daniel Joseph Donahoe.
- *Hymns of the Early Church* (1896), edited by John Brownlie.
- *The Irish "Liber hymnorum", Volume 2* (1908), edited by John Henry Bernard Robert Atkinson.
- *The Religious Songs of Connacht: A collection of poems, stories, prayers, satires, ranns, charms, etc., Volume One* (1906) by Douglas Hyde.
- *The Religious Songs of Connacht: A collection of poems, stories, prayers, satires, ranns, charms, etc., Volume Two* (1906) by Douglas Hyde.

• *The Story of Iona* (1909) by Edward Craig Trenholme.
These prayer sequences are adaptations of these sources – not transcriptions or translations – so any fault in their literary quality lies with the author.

Also, excerpts from the following public domain books have been included in this retreat, its reflection materials, and its resources:
• *A book of saints and wonders put down here by Lady Gregory according to the old writings and the memory of the people of Ireland* (1907), edited by Lady Augusta Gregory.
• *The Spiritual Exercises of Saint Ignatius of Loyola* (1847), edited by Charles Seager.
• *Three Middle-Irish homilies on the lives of Saints Patrick, Brigit and Columba* (1877), edited by Whitley Stokes.
All these books are available on the Internet Archive.

Finally, some material in this book has been excerpted (with adaptations) from the author's earlier *Nurturing the Courage of Pilgrims*.

Companioning the King of Heaven

Companioning the King of Heaven

While it is very easy to understand a person's desire to follow a worthy leader or to aid a noble cause, it is far more difficult to understand what makes that person appealing to the person they hope to emulate or serve. From Jesus' public ministry, for example, we know some people (such as the rich young man in the 10th chapter of Mark's gospel) did not accept Jesus' invitation to follow him. However, it is also clear that many of the people Jesus helped through miracles or acts of kindness were not asked to become disciples or to become Jesus' intimate friends – inviting reflection on the qualities a person must possess or demonstrate in order to be called to discipleship.

On one level, the answer to this dilemma involves human practicality. The value of a disciple depends on their capabilities to serve the cause they wish to serve. So, the individuals chosen as disciples possess capabilities and dispositions that suit them to particular tasks or challenges. For example, in the ancient Celtic church, a monk might be highly talented at preparing illuminated manuscripts in an abbey's scriptorium but not appropriate as a traveling companion when a highly respected Celtic saint (such as Brendan, Brigid or Columba) left their abbey on a pilgrimage or mission. It is the leader who must decide the best use of a disciple's abilities, and a disciple must trust that the leader is using his or her talents in the proper manner and place.

On a more intimate level, a leader may recognize personal qualities he or she values in a person and welcome that individual to share in a common purpose. In this way, the invitation to become a disciple expresses a desire for companionship that is almost as important to the leader as to the follower. This is certainly true in the vision of discipleship presented by Saint Ignatius in his *Spiritual Exercises*, where God actively seeks out and welcomes men and women to join in the cosmic struggle to redeem creation. Through a person's intimate encounters with the life and ministry of Jesus, witnessing both its human and divine aspects, an individual experiences a deeply personal call to offer his or her whole self in service to God through Christ.

Finally, the invitation to discipleship may emerge from a demonstrated openness to be transformed into a new type of person. On the human level, this willingness be completely changed for a person or cause may become dangerous and delusional. However, these uncertainties do not exist when a person offers all of himself or herself to a loving and all-knowing God. Instead, with each act of self-offering, God summons a new man or woman into being by revealing hidden capabilities already within the person or creating new ones through divine action. In this way, God's desire to see the fullness of a person be fully manifested creates new companions out of love.

A Contemplation of the Kingdom of Jesus Christ

So, through the following exercise, consider the qualities you present to Jesus Christ that would lead him to call you into his service:

At this point, you may want to read the text of this exercise as Ignatius presented it is in his Spiritual Exercises *(see page 299). This review might offer you different perspectives on various aspects of this exercise, illuminate your reflections and open you to a broader awareness of God's activity during your prayer. However, you should feel free to ignore this suggestion if it distracts you from your prayers.*

[1]   Focus on this specific time and place as you allow all other concerns to fall away. As you become still, become aware of your desires during this moment of prayer. Ask of Jesus Christ that you may not be deaf to his call but that you remain alert and eager to fulfill his most holy will to the best of your ability. Ask also that you might fully understand the qualities in you that Jesus, the King of Heaven, wishes to nurture and cultivate in his service.

As these desires fill your consciousness, let all other concerns fall aside as you focus on this specific time and place of prayer.

[2]   Then, slowly and deliberately, consider the invitation of Jesus Christ to become his companion.

• In your imagination, allow yourself to see a human king, queen or other leader chosen by God. Take a moment to look at this person, making a mental note of his or her physical appearance and demeanor. Watch as this person interacts with others, commanding their respect and service. Listen to the way this leader takes individuals apart from the crowd, discussing in private with each their noble attributes as well as specific deficiencies (e.g., personality issues, skills, etc.) the leader hopes to improve in them. See how the followers respond with humility, gratitude and deference as the leader speaks. Watch and listen as this leader speaks directly to you, speaking in a nurturing manner both of the strengths and of the weaknesses you present to the success of the leader's cause.

Linger for a time in this moment, becoming aware of all the emotions and thoughts evoked by your conversation with this great human leader. Then, allow this moment to fade from your consciousness while retaining an awareness of the love and support you have received from your friend.

- When you are ready, allow yourself to see Jesus Christ standing in front of you with a few of his companions. Take a moment to look at Jesus and those around him, noting their physical appearance and demeanor. Watch as Jesus interacts with his companions and witness the respect these companions have for Jesus and their joy in being his companion. Listen to Jesus as he speaks privately with his various companions about their various strengths and weaknesses, assuring each person of his unconditional love and support. Then, watch and listen has Jesus speaks directly to you about your own noble attributes and capabilities – as well as your deficiencies – before assuring you of his unconditional love and support.

Again, linger in this moment and become aware of all the emotions and thoughts evoked by this conversation with Jesus. Then, allow this moment to fade from your consciousness while retaining an awareness of the many expressions of Jesus' love you have received during your life.

- Afterward, allow the various words and images of your prayer to flow freely in your consciousness without being controlled. Become aware of those aspects of your prayer that arouse holy desires in you, toward God and toward others (including nonhuman creatures). Become aware of those aspects of your prayer that make you feel shame for those times you fall short of these holy aspirations.

- Gradually allow these thoughts and images to fade from your consciousness and become aware of the return of Jesus, standing or sitting with you in this moment. Then, have open and informal conversation about your experiences during this meditation. Speak about how these experiences express your own desires and fears, giving space for Jesus to explain the love that motivates the call to serve in building his kingdom. At the end of this conversation, ask Jesus to help

you reform those aspects of your personality and life that impede your ability to respond to his invitation to service and companionship.
- Then, gradually allow your thoughts to recede as you focus on Jesus' continuing presence in your life and in the world around you.

[3] Conclude by offering this prayer adapted from a Christian song collected in Daniel Joseph Donahoe's *Early Christian Hymns* (Series II):

> *Hear me, Christ, my King,*
> *Hear you the praise I bring,*
> *And lead me on;*
> *In tender mercy bend,*
> *My soul from harm defend,*
> *And let my hopes ascend*
> *Unto your throne.*
> *Upon the road of life*
> *Keep me from stain and strife*
> *In your sweet care;*
> *Extend your right hand, Lord,*
> *your gracious aid afford,*
> *Be you my watch and ward;*
> *Lord, hear my prayer. Amen.*

[4] Afterward, take 10-15 minutes in a quiet space to reflect on the most significant moments from your prayer and record your reflections in your retreat journal.

From Disciple to Friend

Considerations

As with your retreat in *From Loss to Love*, you need to consider the requirements of your upcoming retreat. Unlike your previous spiritual journey, the value of your prayer in the coming days or weeks may be diminished if you do not continue to the third retreat in this series. So, you need to carefully review your experiences during your previous prayers in order to properly prepare yourself for the needs of this retreat and the one that will follow it.

With this in mind, you need to decide whether you will approach this retreat in the same manner as the previous one or change your process during this part of your journey. You again need to decide whether you will conduct this retreat in daily life or in seclusion and whether you will invite others to join you in your upcoming journey prayer or travel that path alone. By considering the following questions, you can build upon the successes of your previous retreat and learn from the challenges you faced during your earlier experiences:

If your previous retreat was in daily life:

• **How might you improve the quality and consistency of your prayer?** To answer this question… Reflect upon the times that were most consoling during your previous prayer and those times you found most challenging. If it is not clear to you why these moments have these qualities, ask God in prayer to illuminate your heart and mind so that you may better be present to the spiritual leadings of your upcoming retreat.

• **How might you better preserve the sacred character of the place where you pray?** To answer this question… Consider the aspects of your prayer space that were most comforting and those which were most distracting. Think about ways to adjust the place in which you pray to alleviate or enhance these various experiences and ask God to confirm your decisions.

• **How successful were you in avoiding distractions while praying at or near your home?** To answer this question… Examine the record of your previous prayers in your retreat journal and try to determine any commonalities in those situations which were either most prayerful or most distracting. As with the previous question, think about ways to adjust the habits of your prayer to alleviate or enhance these various experiences and ask God to confirm your insights.

If your previous retreat was in seclusion:

•	**What were the most affirming and challenging aspects of your experience?** To answer this question… Visualize the good and bad experiences of your time in seclusion. Try to find commonalities within each type of experience and ask God to help you understand the ways through which you might be able to alleviate the negative and enhance the positive aspects of your experience.

•	**How successful were you in maintaining a calm environment for your prayer throughout the day?** To answer this question… Think about those moments when you were most distracted and contemplate the commonalities of these different times during your previous retreat before asking God how you might better preserve a calm atmosphere in your upcoming retreat.

•	**What issues or distractions diminished the quality of your prayer during your retreat?** To answer this question… Visualize the good and bad experiences of your time in seclusion as well as review your journal notes from the previous retreat. Then, isolate those moments when you were most distracted and determine whether they were movements of prayer that you found difficult emotionally or external distractions that took you away from prayer. Finally, ask God to help you improve your spiritual focus and stamina when you approach these types of moments during your upcoming prayer.

•	**How successful were you and avoiding distractions either at your home or away from home during your retreat?** To answer this question… Consider the activities that surrounded your prayer during your retreat and determine those which disrupted the prayerful environment you hope to create. Again, consider the adjustments you need to make in your environment to reduce these problems and ask God to help you remain focused when new distractions come during your upcoming retreat.

If you were alone during your previous retreat:

- **What were the liberating aspects of being in solitude with God during your retreat?** To answer this question... Visualize the good and bad experiences of your retreat and review your retreat journal, finding those moments when you found pleasure in being alone with God and express your gratitude for these times.

- **What aspects of being in solitude left you feeling alone or easily distracted during your retreat?** To answer this question... Again visualize the good and bad experiences of your retreat and review your retreat journal, finding those moments when you felt completely alone and ask God to illuminate the reasons for these feelings as well as the loving presence you failed to recognize during these times.

If your previous retreat was with companions:

- **What aspects of your retreat were improved by the presence of others praying with you?** To answer this question... Through visualization and a consideration of your memories, become aware of these special moments and express your gratitude for them to God.

- **What aspects of your retreat were diminished by the presence of others praying with you?** To answer this question... Again, through visualization and a consideration of your memories, become aware of these moments and ask God to help you understand the emotional and spiritual dynamics that shaped these times.

- **If any, which activities with your companions during your previous retreat brought you joy?** To answer this question... Again, through visualization and a consideration of your memories, become aware of these special moments and express your gratitude for them to God.

- **If any, which activities with your companions during your previous retreat brought you sorrow or sadness?** To answer this question... Again, through visualization and a consideration of your memories, become aware of these special moments and ask God to help you understand the emotional and spiritual dynamics that shaped these times.

Note: *If your previous retreat was with companions and away from home, you should repeat the previous set of questions focusing on the logistical and practical matters you encountered during your time together.*

Finally, after making this review and addressing the issues raised by these questions, take some time to reaffirm your desire to walk with God once again with the confidence that comes from your experiences of God's love, guidance, and protection during your previous retreat. As with your earlier retreat, you may face spiritual and emotional challenges during your upcoming time of prayer, which you now know from direct experience that God is traveling with you and instilling in you holy desires that will transform you into an instrument of divine love.

Remember as you move forward the words of Saint Paul's Letter to the Romans:

> *The Spirit helps us in our weakness; for we do not know how to pray as we ought, but that very Spirit intercedes with sighs too deep for words. And God, who searches the heart, knows what is the mind of the Spirit, because the Spirit intercedes for the saints according to the will of God.*
>
> *We know that all things work together for good for those who love God, who are called according to his purpose for those whom he foreknew he also predestined to be conformed to the image of his Son, in order that he might be the firstborn within a large family. And those whom he predestined he also called; and those whom he called he also justified; and those whom he justified he also glorified.*
> (Romans 8:26-30)

Prelude
Praying with Jesus and Saint Brigid

During the days or weeks of this retreat, you will be accompanied by two companions: Jesus and Saint Brigid. So, it is important for you to have a clear image in your mind of how they look, speak and act.

Note: It is important to remember that these images are not intended to be historically accurate. Instead, they provide you with an image of how you perceive these two individuals and how you think they will act while you are with them.

Begin by calming yourself and putting aside all other concerns.

Then, when you are ready, allow an image of Jesus to come into your mind. He is alone, either standing or sitting. Look at him carefully, noting his physical features and demeanor as he looks back at you. Take your time with this first encounter and become aware of the love and care Jesus radiates toward you. After a short while, watch as a person approaches Jesus and observe how he interacts with that individual. Then, watch and listen as a crowd gathers around Jesus. Observe any nuances of his behavior that seem particularly unexpected and hear the sound of his voice as he speaks to different people.

Take as long as you need to make these observations. Then, remaining in your imagination, listen as Jesus instructs you, "Pray then in this way… Our Father in heaven, hallowed be your name. Your kingdom come. Your will be done, on earth as it is in heaven. Give us this day our daily bread. And forgive us our debts, as we also have forgiven our debtors. And do not bring us to the time of trial, but rescue us from the evil one." (Matthew 6: 9-13)

Take a moment to linger in the sounds and resonances of Jesus' voice, then allow this image to fade from your consciousness before summarizing your impressions, reactions, and observations in your workbook.

Then, read the description of Saint Brigid presented on page 309.

Gradually, guided by the description, allow an image of Saint Brigid to emerge in your mind. She also is alone, either standing or sitting. Note her physical features and demeanor while she looks back at you. Again, take your time with this first encounter and be aware of how you feel in Brigid's presence. Consider power of her personality, how it manifests itself, and her gaze toward you. Then, see other people approach Brigid – first a few and then many. Watch and listen as she engages these different people and speaks with them, noting any nuances in Brigid's behavior that seem unexpected while listening to the sound of her voice as she speaks with these different people.

As with your time with Jesus, take as long as you need to make these observations of Saint Brigid. Then, while remaining in your imagination as much as possible, listen to Brigid's voice as you read "The Things Brigid Wished For" (found on page 314) – also known as "I would wish for a great lake of ale for the King of Kings". Allow the rhythm and pace of your reading to be guided by Brigid's voice.

Linger in the sounds and resonances of Saint Brigid's voice for a moment. Then, allow this image to fade from your consciousness before summarizing your impressions, reactions, and observations in your workbook.

1. The Incarnation

1.1a   Let Thanks Arise On Every Side

a prayer on the Incarnation

Take a moment to quiet your spirit, becoming completely present to this time and place. Allow all other thoughts and concerns to fall away as you come into the presence of God. Then, when you are ready, begin.

Let thanks arise on every side
To Christ my help, my God of Might,
    Who has my body glorified
    And raised it to the throne of light.

Then let my heart with love o'erflow
My word and deeds be all of light,
    That when I leave these walks below,
    My soul shall climb the heavenly height.

A Hymn, sung or heard (optional)

Ancient of days, enthroned on high!
The Father unbegotten He,
    Whom space contains not, nor time,
    Who was and is and shall be:
And one-born Son, and Holy Ghost,
Who co-eternal glory share:
    One only God, of Persons Three,
    We praise, acknowledge, and declare.

Christ the Most High from heaven descends,
The Cross his sign and banner bright.
    The sun in darkness shrouds His face,
    The moon no more pours forth her light:
The stars upon the earth shall fall
As figs drop from the parent tree,
    When earth's broad space is bathed in fire,
    And men to dens and mountains flee.

Zeal of the Lord, consuming fire,
Shall 'whelm the foes, amazed and dumb,

>   Whose stony hearts will not receive
>   That Christ hath from the Father come:
> But I shall soar my Lord to meet,
> And so with him shall ever be,
>   To reap the due rewards amidst
>   The glories of Eternity.

Read or recite Psalm 40.

Holy Lord,
Under my thoughts may I God-thoughts find.
Half of my sins escape my mind.
>   For what I said, or did not say,
>   Pardon me, O Lord, I pray.

Read Luke 1: 26-38, aloud or quietly.

O Lord, Jesus the Christ,
If I were in Heaven my harp I would sound
With apostles and angels and saints all around,
>   Praising and thanking the Son who is crowned,
>   May the poor race of Eve for that heaven be bound!

Holy Lord,
Descending from your throne above,
You sought the sluggish world to win,
>   Moved by the power of mighty love.
>   Lest earth be lost in death and sin.

Brought forth, a sacrifice divine
To expiate our deeds of doom,
>   Your way was through the sacred shrine
>   Of earth's most precious Virgin's womb.

O Holy Lord,
>   God with the Father and the Spirit,
For me is many a snare designed,
To fill my mind with doubts and fears;
>   Far from the land of holy saints,
>   I dwell within my vale of tears.

Let faith, let hope, let love –
Traits far above the cold world's way –
    With patience, humility, and awe,
    Become my guides from day to day.

I acknowledge, the evil I have done.
From the day of my birth till the day of my death,
    Through the sight of my eyes,
Through the hearing of my ears,
    Through the sayings of my mouth,
Through the thoughts of my heart,
    Through the touch of my hands,
Through the course of my way,
    Through all I said and did not,
Through all I promised and fulfilled not,
    Through all the laws and holy commandments I broke.
I ask even now absolution of you,
    For fear I may have never asked it as was right,
    And that I might not live to ask it again,

O Holy Lord, my King in Heaven,
May you not let my soul stray from you,
May you keep me in a good state,
    May you turn me toward what is good to do,
    May you protect me from dangers, small and great.
May you fill my eyes with tears of repentance,
    So I may avoid the sinner's awful sentence.
May the Grace of the God for ever be with me,
    And whatever my needs, may the Triune God give me.

Select one of the following options for the Lord's Prayer.

Option A

O Jesus Christ,
Lord of heaven and earth,
Help me pray as you yourself taught:
    "Our Father in heaven,
    hallowed be your name.
    Your kingdom come.

*Your will be done,
on earth as it is in heaven.
Give us this day our daily bread.
And forgive us our debts,
as we also have forgiven our debtors.
And do not bring us to the time of trial,
but rescue us from the evil one."
(Matthew 6: 9-13)*
From the foes of my land,
from the foes of my faith,
From the foes who would us dissever,
    O Lord, preserve me, in life and in death,
    With the Sign of the Cross for ever.
    *For the kingdom, the power, and the glory
    are yours now and for ever. Amen.*

Please proceed with "I beseech you, O Lord…," found after Option B.

Option B

O Jesus Christ,
Lord of heaven and earth,
Help me pray as you yourself taught:
    *Our Father in heaven,
    hallowed be your name,
    your kingdom come,
    your will be done,
    on earth as in heaven.
    Give us today our daily bread.
    Forgive us our sins
    as we forgive those who sin against us.
    Lead us not into temptation
    but deliver us from evil.*
From the foes of my land,
from the foes of my faith,
From the foes who would us dissever,
    O Lord, preserve me, in life and in death,
    With the Sign of the Cross for ever.
    For the kingdom, the power, and the glory

are yours now and for ever. Amen.

I beseech you, O Lord.
God in Heaven, unsurpassed in power and might;
    Be behind me, Be on my left,
    Be before me, Be on my right!
Against each danger, you are my help;
In distress, upon you I call.
    In dark times, may you sustain me
    And lift me up again when I fall.
Lord over heaven and of earth,
You know my offenses.
    Yet, listening to my pleadings,
    You guide me away from sinful pretenses.
Lord of all creation and the many creatures,
You bestow on me many earthly treasures.
    Revealing love in each life and season,
    You share with me heavenly pleasures.
May you arouse me
In moments both of joy and of strife;
    Most holy Lord, bring me new life!

A Hymn, sung or heard (optional)

O Jesus Christ,
    Lord of heaven and earth,
    You are my riches, my store, my provision,
My star through the years
When troubles rend me,
    Through times of strife and tears,
    Sweet Jesus, defend me.

Your name is power; I call out "Save me!",
And lo, your glory shines aflame,
    While heaven and hell with trembling knee
    Bow down before your holy name.

To you I come, to you I cry,
O ruler of the judgment day;
    Defend me by your grace, lest I

With powers of gloom be cast away.

End this time of prayer by taking some time to bring to mind the various ways God shields you from harm or guides you through the world's tumult. Then, when you are ready, conclude by saying:

O Holy Lord, King in Heaven,
I place myself at the edge of your grace,
    On the floor of your house myself I place,
And to banish the sin of my heart away,
    I lower my knee to you this day.
Through life's torrents of pain may you bring me whole,
    And, O Lord Jesus Christ, preserve also my soul. Amen.

1.1b Preparation for Prayer

Consideration of the Readings

After reciting or prayerfully reading the prayer sequence for this day or week:

- Read the "A Meditation on the Incarnation" from *The Spiritual Exercises of Saint Ignatius* (found on page 300). Allow yourself to linger on any thoughts or phrases that seem particularly meaningful to you or especially relevant to your life. Then, record these highlights in your workbook so you will remember them during your meditation.
- Read about Gabriel's appearance to Mary in Luke 1:26-38. Make a mental note of each person's appearance and actions during the episode as well as the key elements of the story and its setting. Again, consider any aspects of this story that speak strongly to you before recording these observations in your workbook.
- Read about Mary's visit to Elizabeth in Luke 1:39-56. Again, note each person's appearance and actions during the episode as well as the key elements of the story and its setting, including the setting in your workbook. Then, record any aspects of this story that speak strongly to you.

Note: *You also should take a moment to consider any aspect of the prayer sequence from this day or week that seemed particularly significant to you.*

Contemplation of Your Needs:

When you are ready, concentrating on your breath or an object near you, allow any distractions to fade from your consciousness as you become aware of your desire to live in God's goodness. Feel yourself yearning to properly use the many gifts God has given you, to experience God's continuing care, and to be open to the immense love God shows for you, then:

- Read "A Prophecy about the Unborn Brigid" (found on page 309). Allow yourself to linger on any thoughts, phrases or images that seem particularly meaningful or significant to your earlier preparations or prayer.

- Pray for your desires in the coming day or week. Ask that the divine presence all around you may be revealed, offering you inner knowledge of Jesus Christ who became human for you so you may better love and follow him. Also ask that, in this day or week of prayer, you may recognize and welcome into your life the profound love at the heart of the Trinity that leads to the Incarnation.
- Conclude by praying that you might learn from Mary's openness to God's desires and manifest that openness in your own faith journey. Then, take a moment record any significant thoughts, emotions or reactions from these moments in your workbook.

After this, put your notes aside. Without straining your memory, consider in turn each of the readings for the coming day or week and allow them to take shape in your imagination – even if all you remember are small fragments. Prayerfully ponder how each reading affects you emotionally without overtly thinking about their content, asking God to illuminate the spiritual gifts offered in each reading – quieting your mind and creating a receptive space in yourself to see or hear the response.

Finally, conclude by allowing these desires to fade from your consciousness as you offer this traditional Irish prayer collected by Douglas Hyde in *The Religious Songs of Connacht*:

O God, I believe in you; strengthen my belief.
I trust in you; confirm my trust.
I love you; double my love.
I repent that I angered you,
Increase my repentance.
Fill you my heart with awe without despair;
With hope, without over-confidence;
With piety without infatuation;
And with joy without excess.
My God, consent to guide me by your wisdom;
To constrain me by your right;
To comfort me by your mercy;
And to protect me by your power. Amen.

Allow these words to linger on your mind and in your heart for a few moments and then, while they are still fresh in your memory, write the most important thoughts, feelings, and desires from this preparatory time in your retreat journal.

1.2   A Meditation on the Incarnation

In this meditation, you will reflect upon the love at the heart of the Incarnation through your prayerful reflection on the "Meditation concerning the Incarnation of Christ" presented in *The Spiritual Exercises of Saint Ignatius*.

[1]   Begin by reading the "A Meditation on the Incarnation" in *The Spiritual Exercises of Saint Ignatius* (found on page 300) and reviewing your notes on it from your preparations.

[2]   Then, focus on this specific time and place as you allow all other concerns to fall away. As you become still, become aware of your desires during this moment of prayer. Remember your desire to experience the divine presence all around you so you may attain a deep "felt knowledge" of Jesus Christ, who became human for you so you may better love and follow him. Recall your desire that, in this day or week of prayer, you may recognize and welcome into your life the profound love at the heart of the Trinity that leads to the Incarnation. Finally, ask that you might learn from Mary's openness to God's desires and manifest that openness in your own faith journey.

As these desires fill your consciousness, let all other concerns fall aside as you focus on this specific time and place of prayer.

[3]   Then, read the meditation on the Incarnation slowly and deliberately.

- As you read, take time to stop and ponder each point within it as you are asked first to imagine the appearance of the Trinity and then observe their actions as they see the deplorable state of humanity, decide to intervene in human history through the Incarnation, select Mary of Nazareth as an instrument of their divine love. When you pause, allow images shaped by the words and thoughts of the passages to form in your imagination. See and hear the way each statement expresses a need or desire in your life.

- Take more time with passages that seem particularly significant or meaning to you. Become aware of the passages from the "Meditation concerning the Incarnation of Christ" which you accept easily and any of those which cause you difficulty. Clarify these thoughts and feeling as much as possible while remaining focused on each specific statement within the "Meditation concerning the Incarnation of Christ".

- After finishing the reading, as the angel Gabriel appears to Mary, allow the various words and images of your prayer to flow freely in your consciousness without being controlled. Become aware of those aspects of the Principle and Foundation that arouse positive desires in you, toward God and toward others (including nonhuman creatures). Become aware of those aspects of the reading that make you feel shame for being unworthy of this act of divine love.
- When you are ready, allow these thoughts and images to fade from your consciousness and become aware of God's presence – experienced in your imagination either as a single entity or as the Holy Trinity – with you in this moment. Then, have an open and informal conversation about your experience of the "Meditation concerning the Incarnation of Christ". Speak candidly about how it expresses your own desires and fears, giving space for God to respond to your concerns or to explain the divine desires expressed in the meditation.

<u>Note:</u> *Saint Ignatius says this conversational prayer (called a colloquy) should "be made similarly to the language of a friend to a friend, or of a servant to his Lord; now by asking some favour, now by accusing myself of some fault; sometimes by communicating my own affairs of any kind, and asking counsel or help concerning them (Sp.Ex. #54)."*

- Then, gradually allow your thoughts to recede as you focus on God's broader presence in your life and in the world around you.

[4] Finally, conclude by allowing these desires to fade from your consciousness as you offer this traditional Irish prayer collected by Douglas Hyde in *The Religious Songs of Connacht*:

> *Confirm me in your love divine,*
> *Smooth for my feet life's rugged way;*
> *My will with yours entwine,*
> *Lest evil lead my steps astray.*
> *Be with my still as guard and guide,*
> *Keep me in holy sanctity,*
> *Let my firm faith on you abide,*
> *From fraud and error hold me free. Amen.*

[5] Afterward, take 10-15 minutes in a quiet space to reflect on the most significant moments from this time of prayer and record your reflections in your retreat journal.

1.3　A Contemplation of Luke 1:26-38

In this contemplation of Luke 1:26-38, you will see and hear Mary accept God's invitation to become an instrument of divine love.

[1]　　Begin by reading the biblical selection and reviewing your notes on it from your earlier preparations.

[2]　　Then, focus on this specific time and place as you allow all other concerns to fall away. Then, when you are ready, consider the people and place in this moment of prayer.

- Allow an image of Mary to emerge in your imagination, noting her physical characteristics and mannerisms. Look at what she is wearing or carrying, observing her clothing and any objects she is holding. Make a note of what she is doing and whether she is sitting, standing, or walking. Ponder this mental image, allowing any other observations about Mary to form in your mind.

- Then, remember the images of your meditation on the Incarnation. Recall the appearance of the Trinity your earlier prayers and how they communicated with one another. Bring to your mind the images of humanity from your earlier prayers and the feelings they evoked in you. Finally, consider the appearance and demeanor of Gabriel. Take a moment to ponder this mental image. Become familiar with the participants of your upcoming prayer.

- Gradually, allow yourself to become aware of the location of this encounter between Mary and Gabriel. Pay attention to its physical characteristics as you ponder this mental image. Look around the place and notice more details about it – noting if it is indoor or outdoor, if it is in dim or bright light, if it is still and silent or filled with noise, if it has an unusual smell or not, etc. Become familiar with the location of your upcoming prayer.

- Take a moment to remain in this place, then allow these images to fade from your consciousness.

[3]　　After you become still, become aware of your desires during this moment of prayer. Remember your desire to experience the divine presence all around you so you may attain a deep "felt knowledge" of Jesus Christ, who became human for you so you may better love and follow him. Recall your desire that, in this day or week of prayer, you may recognize and welcome into your life the profound love at the heart of the Trinity that leads to the Incarnation. Finally, ask that you might learn from Mary's openness to God's desires and manifest that openness in your own faith journey.

As these desires fill your consciousness, let all other concerns fall aside as you focus on this specific time and place of prayer.

[4] When you are ready, allow the story of Mary and Gabriel to unfold in your imagination.

- Relying on the memories from your earlier prayer, see and hear the Trinity speaking about the condition of humanity and the need for the Son to become human. Become aware of the deep love at the heart of this conversation as an image of Mary appears in your imagination, knowing you are about to witness a momentous event.

- Ask God to help you share in this moment by listening quietly to the conversations within the Trinity as well as during the meeting between Mary and Gabriel.

- Then, watch and listen as Mary speaks with Gabriel. You may want to quietly read the passage while remaining prayerfully aware of your mental image of Mary and Gabriel or you may choose to stay completely within the imagined realm of your prayer. Whichever you choose, know that God will offer you the words from the biblical passage that you need to hear – even if only in fragments.

- As Mary accepts God's invitation, remember she is a young woman struggling to remain faithful to God's desires despite the challenges she will face because of this decision. Remember also that you share in this struggle when trying to respond to God's desires in your life.

- Then, allow the image of Mary and Gabriel to fade from your imagination as you become aware of the phrases and images from this moment of prayer which touched you most deeply. Recall the emotions and memories – including any sounds or smells – evoked during your prayer. Allow these seminal aspects of your meditation to linger on your mind and in your heart, making a mental note of any special feelings evoked by them.

[5] When you are ready, become aware of God's presence – again, experienced in your imagination either as a single entity or as the Holy Trinity – with you in this moment and have an open and informal conversation about this prayer period and how the passage from Luke's gospel expresses your own needs or desires. Remember to give space for God to respond or to highlight different aspects from the biblical selection and your experiences during this meditation. Then, gradually allow your thoughts to recede as you focus on God's broader presence in your life and in the world around you.

[6]   Finally, conclude by allowing these desires to fade from your consciousness as you offer this traditional Irish prayer collected by Douglas Hyde in *The Religious Songs of Connacht*:

> *Confirm me in your love divine,*
> *Smooth for my feet life's rugged way;*
> *My will with yours entwine,*
> *Lest evil lead my steps astray.*
> *Be with my still as guard and guide,*
> *Keep me in holy sanctity,*
> *Let my firm faith on you abide,*
> *From fraud and error hold me free. Amen.*

[7]   Afterward, take 10-15 minutes in a quiet space to reflect on the most significant moments from this time of prayer and record your reflections in your retreat journal.

1.4 A Contemplation of Luke 1:39-56

In this contemplation of Luke 1:39-56, you will see and hear Mary as she visits her cousin Elizabeth.

[1] Begin by reading the biblical selection and reviewing your notes on it from your earlier preparations.

[2] Then, focus on this specific time and place as you allow all other concerns to fall away. Then, when you are ready, consider the people and place in this moment of prayer.

- Allow an image of Mary to emerge in your imagination, noting her physical characteristics and mannerisms. Look at what she is wearing or carrying, observing her clothing and any objects she is holding. Make a note of what she is doing. Ponder this mental image, allowing any other observations about Mary to form in your mind.

- Then, as a mental image of a visibly pregnant Elizabeth emerges, observe what she is doing and whether she is sitting, standing, or walking. See how she behaves toward Mary. Look around to see if there are any other people with or near Elizabeth. If there are, make a note of their appearance and demeanor before pondering this mental image, and allowing other impressions of this moment to form in your imagination. Become familiar with the men and women you will encounter during your prayer as well as their behavior.

- Gradually, allow yourself to become aware of the location of this meeting between Mary and Elizabeth. Pay attention to its physical characteristics and the arrangement of the people in it. As you ponder this mental image, look around the place and notice more details about it – noting if it is in dim or bright light, if it is still and silent or filled with noise, if it has an unusual smell or not, etc. Become familiar with the location of your upcoming prayer.

- Take a moment to remain in this place with these men and women, then allow these images to fade from your consciousness.

[3] After you become still, become aware of your desires during this moment of prayer. Remember your desire to experience the divine presence all around you so you may attain a deep "felt knowledge" of Jesus Christ, who became human for you so you may better love and follow him. Recall your desire that, in this day or week of prayer, you may recognize and welcome into your life the profound love at the heart of the Trinity that leads to the Incarnation. Finally, ask that you might demonstrate Mary's openness to God's desires as well as

Elizabeth's joyful awareness of God's presence in your own faith journey.

As these desires fill your consciousness, let all other concerns fall aside as you focus on this specific time and place of prayer.

[4] Again, when you are ready, allow the image of Mary and Elizabeth to reemerge in your imagination.

- As Elizabeth sees Mary approaching, observe her reaction and ask God to help you share in this moment by listening quietly to the conversation between Mary and Elizabeth. You may feel drawn to imagine yourself standing among Elizabeth's other relatives (if you see them participating in this contemplation) or you may observe the meeting between Mary and Elizabeth without participating in it.

- Then, watch and listen as the women speak. You may want to quietly read the passage while remaining prayerfully aware of your mental image of Mary and Gabriel or you may choose to stay completely within the imagined realm of your prayer. Whichever you choose, know that God will offer you the words from the biblical passage that you need to hear – even if only in fragments.

- Afterward, allow these images to fade from your imagination as you become aware of the phrases and images from this moment of prayer which touched you most deeply. Recall the emotions and memories – including any sounds or smells – evoked during your prayer. Allow these seminal aspects of your meditation to linger on your mind and in your heart, making a mental note of any special feelings evoked by them.

[5] When you are ready, become aware of God's presence – again, experienced either as a single entity or as the Holy Trinity – with you in this moment and have an open and informal conversation about this prayer period and how the passage from Luke's gospel expresses your own needs or desires. Remember to give space for God to respond or to highlight different aspects from the biblical selection and your experiences during this meditation. Then, gradually allow your thoughts to recede as you focus on God's broader presence in your life and in the world around you.

[6] Finally, conclude by allowing these desires to fade from your consciousness as you offer this traditional Irish prayer collected by Douglas Hyde in *The Religious Songs of Connacht*:

> *Confirm me in your love divine,*
> *Smooth for my feet life's rugged way;*
> *My will with yours entwine,*

Lest evil lead my steps astray.
Be with my still as guard and guide,
Keep me in holy sanctity,
Let my firm faith on you abide,
From fraud and error hold me free. Amen.

[7]   Afterward, take 10-15 minutes in a quiet space to reflect on the most significant moments from this time of prayer and record your reflections in your retreat journal.

1.5 A Meditation on Luke 1:26-38

In this meditation on Luke 1:26-38, you will see and hear Saint Brigid instruct her disciples on remaining open to God's most challenging desires.

[1] Begin by reading the biblical selection and reviewing your notes on it from your earlier preparations.

[2] Then, focus on this specific time and place as you allow all other concerns to fall away. Then, when you are ready, consider the people and place in this moment of prayer.

- Allow an image of Brigid to emerge in your imagination, noting her physical characteristics and mannerisms. Look at what she is wearing or carrying, observing her clothing and any objects she is holding. Make a note of whether she is sitting, standing, or walking. Ponder this mental image, allowing any other observations about Brigid to form in your mind.

- Then, observe the disciples around Saint Brigid. Note how many disciples are with Brigid, making a mental note of their appearance and demeanor. Observe whether they are sitting, standing, or walking. Take a moment to ponder this mental image, allowing other impressions of these people to form. Become familiar with the men and women you will encounter during your prayer as well as their behavior.

- Gradually, allow yourself to become aware of the location of this moment with Saint Brigid. Observe whether it is inside or outside, paying attention to its physical characteristics and the arrangement of the people in it. As you ponder this mental image, look around the place and notice more details about it – noting if it is in dim or bright light, if it is still and silent or filled with noise, if it has an unusual smell or not, etc. Become familiar with the location of your upcoming prayer.

- Take a moment to remain in this place with these men and women, then allow these images to fade from your consciousness.

[3] After you become still, become aware of your desires during this moment of prayer. Remember your desire to experience the divine presence all around you so you may attain a deep "felt knowledge" of Jesus Christ, who became human for you so you may better love and follow him. Recall your desire that, in this day or week of prayer, you may recognize and welcome into your life the profound love at the heart of the Trinity that leads to the Incarnation. Finally, ask that you

might learn from Mary's openness to God's desires and manifest that openness in your own faith journey.

As these desires fill your consciousness, let all other concerns fall aside as you focus on this specific time and place of prayer.

[4] Again, when you are ready, allow the image of Saint Brigid and her disciples to reemerge in your imagination.

- Watch as the group assembles around Brigid. Listen to the sounds of this moment and become comfortable as you prepare to hear Brigid speak. Feel the anticipation of the people around you and share in that enthusiasm.

- As you hear Brigid invite her companions to listen, ask God to help you share in this experience – either by joining these events or by listening quietly to them. Focus your attention on Saint Brigid, noting her physical appearance and her emotional demeanor.

- Then, relying on the memories from your earlier prayer, watch and listen as Brigid tells the story of Mary's encounter with Gabriel. You may want to quietly read the passage while remaining prayerfully aware of your mental image of Brigid or you may choose to stay completely within the imagined realm of your prayer. Whichever you choose, know that God will offer you the words from the biblical passage that you need to hear – even if only in fragments.

- Afterward, hear Brigid explain the passage. Listen to her as she explains the meaning and significance of God's promise expressed in Mary's acceptance go God's desire that she bear the savior of humanity and creation.

– Again, look around as Brigid speaks and see the reactions of her disciples. Become aware of their feelings and how they behave toward Brigid and one another.

– Remember that Brigid is speaking to men and women struggling to remain faithful to God's desires and promises while living difficult lives which challenge their faith. Remember that she also is speaking to you.

- After Saint Brigid finishes speaking, allow her image and this place to fade from your imagination as you become aware of the phrases and images from this moment of prayer which touched you most deeply. Recall the emotions and memories – including any sounds or smells – evoked during your prayer. Allow these seminal aspects of your meditation to linger on your mind and in your heart, making a mental note of any special feelings evoked by them.

[5]   When you are ready, become aware of God's presence – either as a single entity or as the Holy Trinity – with you in this moment and have an open and informal conversation about this prayer period and how the passage from Luke's gospel expresses your own needs or desires. Remember to give space for God to respond or to highlight different aspects from the biblical selection and your experiences during this meditation. Then, gradually allow your thoughts to recede as you focus on God's broader presence in your life and in the world around you.

[6]   Finally, conclude by allowing these desires to fade from your consciousness as you offer this traditional Irish prayer collected by Douglas Hyde in *The Religious Songs of Connacht*:

> *Confirm me in your love divine,*
> *Smooth for my feet life's rugged way;*
> *My will with yours entwine,*
> *Lest evil lead my steps astray.*
> *Be with my still as guard and guide,*
> *Keep me in holy sanctity,*
> *Let my firm faith on you abide,*
> *From fraud and error hold me free. Amen.*

[7]   Afterward, take 10-15 minutes in a quiet space to reflect on the most significant moments from this time of prayer and record your reflections in your retreat journal.

1.6 An Application of the Senses

[1] Become aware of your prayerful desires during this day or week. Bring to mind your desire to experience an inner knowledge of Jesus Christ who became human for you so you may better love and follow him. Also ask that, in this day or week of prayer, God may help you recognize and welcome into your life the profound love at the heart of the Trinity that leads to the Incarnation.

[2] When you are ready, in your imagination, call to mind the various prayers of the preceding day or days. Allow the images and words of these prayers to linger and then slowly fade from your consciousness.

- Remember your meditation on the Incarnation from *The Spiritual Exercises of Saint Ignatius*. Consider the images and feelings evoked in you during your prayer, feeling God's presence in these memories and becoming aware of the specific sensations associated with each image.
- Recall your imaginative contemplations of Luke 1:26-38, considering them in the same way as your memories of your meditation on the Incarnation.
- Review your imaginative contemplation of Luke 1:39-56 in the same manner as the previous prayers.

As these prayers enter your memory, make a mental note of which senses are most active. You may see an image or a color, hear a sound or a phrase, or smell a scent or a fragrance. You may even taste a flavor or feel a sensation on your skin.

[3] Then, relax and allow these various memories and experiences to quietly enter and leave your consciousness without being controlled – whether they are clear or diffuse, whether they come quickly or slowly. Linger on the sensory images and memories being evoked in you – noticing any images or colors, any sounds or phrases, any scents or fragrances, any flavors or physical sensations associated with each prayer.

[4] When you are ready, become completely still and clear your mind of all thoughts and concerns. Allow an image of a special personal space to form in your imagination, a place where you are completely comfortable and alone. Then, watch as God enters that place and forms a small image or object for you that expresses the thought or awareness that you most need to carry with you into your life.

Reverently pick up the object or image, a reflection of the most important gift you have been given during this time of prayer. Look at it carefully and become aware of the divine presence contained within it. Take a moment to register what it looks like and how it feels in your hand. Then, feel the joy and confidence that comes from touching the presence of God as you accept this gift, offering a short prayer of gratitude while you relax into the pleasure of this moment.

[5] Then, conclude by allowing these images to fade from your consciousness as you offer this traditional Irish prayer collected by Douglas Hyde in *The Religious Songs of Connacht*:

Confirm me in your love divine,
Smooth for my feet life's rugged way;
My will with yours entwine,
Lest evil lead my steps astray.
Be with my still as guard and guide,
Keep me in holy sanctity,
Let my firm faith on you abide,
From fraud and error hold me free. Amen.

[6] While your experiences are still fresh in your mind, record the most significant impressions or sensations from this time of prayer in your retreat journal.

1.7 Review of Prayer

[1] Remember your desires during the preceding day or week of prayer. Become aware of the divine presence all around you, offering you inner knowledge of Jesus Christ who became human for you so you may better love and follow him. Recall your desire to recognize and welcome into your life the profound love at the heart of the Trinity that leads to the Incarnation.

After bringing these thoughts and desires into your consciousness, ask God once again to fulfill these desires in your own life and in your interactions with others.

[2] Then, take a moment to allow the words, thoughts, and feelings from your prayers during the last day or week to linger – on your mind and in your heart – before asking God to reveal the fulfillment of your deepest desires in these various memories.

• Think about the prayer sequence at the beginning of this day or week. Make a mental note of any words, insights or images that remain particularly significant or meaningful to you.

• Ponder the story, "A Prophecy about the Unborn Brigid". Note any words, insights, or images from it that remain particularly significant or meaningful to you.

• Remember your meditation on the Incarnation from *The Spiritual Exercises of Saint Ignatius*.

– Consider the most powerful images, phrases, or feelings from your prayer. Ask yourself what gifts God gave to you through these moments, perhaps offering you new insights or perhaps affirming an important aspect of your faith. Ask yourself how God may be calling you to change through these moments, being as specific as possible.

– Examine your disposition as you prayed, noting whether prayer came easily or with resistance. Recall the easiest moments in your prayer and any moments of joy you may have experienced. Remember also if you encountered any difficulty opening yourself to God or if you felt any sadness as you prayed. Ask God to help you understand why these feelings surfaced.

– Bring to mind any moments when you added personal elements (e.g., familiar places or people from your life) or connected your prayers to other scriptures or spiritual writings. Ask yourself how these additions helped or hindered you as you prayed. Again, if you do not know why this happened, ask God to help you understand.

- Recall your imaginative contemplations of Luke 1:26-38. Then, review your prayer in the same way as your earlier reflection on the meditation on the Incarnation.
- Review your imaginative contemplation of Luke 1:39-56 in the same manner as the previous prayers.
- Reflect on the ebb and flow of sensory impressions and feelings that marked your application of the senses. Isolate the most memorable moments and sensory impressions from your prayer and reflect on how God used these moments to give you a particular gift, perhaps offering you new insights or changing you in some way.

[3] Finally, ponder the times when images or feelings from the readings of this day or week surfaced outside these prayer periods. Consider those moments or events in which God's presence or guidance was especially strong as well as any moments when you were struggling. Think about the most memorable aspects of these experiences, asking God to explain their significance.

[4] Take a moment to allow the words, thoughts, and feelings of these prayers to linger on your mind and in your heart. Finally, conclude by allowing these desires to fade from your consciousness as you offer this traditional Irish prayer collected by Douglas Hyde in *The Religious Songs of Connacht*:

> *O God, I believe in you; strengthen my belief.*
> *I trust in you; confirm my trust.*
> *I love you; double my love.*
> *I repent that I angered you,*
> *Increase my repentance.*
> *Fill you my heart with awe without despair;*
> *With hope, without over-confidence;*
> *With piety without infatuation;*
> *And with joy without excess.*
> *My God, consent to guide me by your wisdom;*
> *To constrain me by your right;*
> *To comfort me by your mercy;*
> *And to protect me by your power. Amen.*

[5] After finishing these prayers, summarize your reflections on the gifts or graces you received during the prayers of this last day or week and record these thoughts in your retreat journal.

2. The Nativity and Childhood of Jesus

2.1a Behold The Lamb! He Comes.
a prayer on Jesus' nativity

Take a moment to quiet your spirit, becoming completely present to this time and place. Allow all other thoughts and concerns to fall away as you come into the presence of God. Then, when you are ready, begin.

Behold the Lamb! he comes to bear
From all the world its load of sin;
    O let me in haste, in humble prayer,
    Strive his loving grace to win.

Shine out, O wondrous star, on high,
Enclose the world in flaming light,
    Let me not fall in guilt and die;
    Lord, guard and guide my steps aright.

A Hymn, sung or heard (optional)

On lowly bed of hay he lies,
His palace but a stable poor;
    The God that rules the earth and skies
    Does all our wants and woes endure.

The angel choirs rejoice on high,
Through radiant skies their voices ring,
    The shepherds see the blazing sky,
    And bow before the Infant King.

The Magi follow through the night
The mystic star that goes before;
    By light, they seek the Lord of Light,
    The King and God whom they adore.

All praise and power and glory be
To Jesus whom the Virgin bore;
    To you, Father, equal is he
    And to the Spirit, evermore.

Read or recite Psalm 72.

Holy Lord,
Under my thoughts may I God-thoughts find.
Half of my sins escape my mind.
    For what I said, or did not say,
    Pardon me, O Lord, I pray.

Read Luke 2: 2-20, aloud or quietly.

O Lord, Jesus the Christ,
If I were in Heaven my harp I would sound
With apostles and angels and saints all around,
    Praising and thanking the Son who is crowned,
    May the poor race of Eve for that heaven be bound!

Remember, O Creator Lord,
That from the stainless Virgin's womb
    The flesh of man you did assume
    To save man's flesh from guilt abhorred.

And lo, this day that gave you birth
Shall glorify your holy name,
    Who from the Father's bosom came,
    Sole Son and Saviour of the earth.

The heavens, the earth, the rolling seas,
And all that live beneath the skies
    Uplift to you adoring eyes
    And hail you with new harmonies.

O Holy Lord,
    God with the Father and the Spirit,
For me is many a snare designed,
To fill my mind with doubts and fears;
    Far from the land of holy saints,
    I dwell within my vale of tears.
Let faith, let hope, let love –
Traits far above the cold world's way –
    With patience, humility, and awe,

Become my guides from day to day.

I acknowledge, the evil I have done.
From the day of my birth till the day of my death,
    Through the sight of my eyes,
Through the hearing of my ears,
    Through the sayings of my mouth,
Through the thoughts of my heart,
    Through the touch of my hands,
Through the course of my way,
    Through all I said and did not,
Through all I promised and fulfilled not,
    Through all the laws and holy commandments I broke.
I ask even now absolution of you,
    For fear I may have never asked it as was right,
    And that I might not live to ask it again,

O Holy Lord, my King in Heaven,
May you not let my soul stray from you,
May you keep me in a good state,
    May you turn me toward what is good to do,
    May you protect me from dangers, small and great.
May you fill my eyes with tears of repentance,
    So I may avoid the sinner's awful sentence.
May the Grace of the God for ever be with me,
    And whatever my needs, may the Triune God give me.

Select one of the following options for the Lord's Prayer.

Option A

O Jesus Christ,
Lord of heaven and earth,
Help me pray as you yourself taught:
    "Our Father in heaven,
    hallowed be your name.
    Your kingdom come.
    Your will be done,
    on earth as it is in heaven.
    Give us this day our daily bread.

And forgive us our debts,
as we also have forgiven our debtors.
And do not bring us to the time of trial,
but rescue us from the evil one."
(Matthew 6: 9-13)
From the foes of my land,
from the foes of my faith,
From the foes who would us dissever,
    O Lord, preserve me, in life and in death,
    With the Sign of the Cross for ever.
    For the kingdom, the power, and the glory
    are yours now and for ever. Amen.

Please proceed with "I beseech you, O Lord...," found after Option B.

Option B

O Jesus Christ,
Lord of heaven and earth,
Help me pray as you yourself taught:
    Our Father in heaven,
    hallowed be your name,
    your kingdom come,
    your will be done,
    on earth as in heaven.
    Give us today our daily bread.
    Forgive us our sins
    as we forgive those who sin against us.
    Lead us not into temptation
    but deliver us from evil.
From the foes of my land,
from the foes of my faith,
From the foes who would us dissever,
    O Lord, preserve me, in life and in death,
    With the Sign of the Cross for ever.
    For the kingdom, the power, and the glory
    are yours now and for ever. Amen.

I beseech you, O Lord.

God in Heaven, unsurpassed in power and might;
    Be behind me, Be on my left,
    Be before me, Be on my right!
Against each danger, you are my help;
In distress, upon you I call.
    In dark times, may you sustain me
    And lift me up again when I fall.
Lord over heaven and of earth,
You know my offenses.
    Yet, listening to my pleadings,
    You guide me away from sinful pretenses.
Lord of all creation and the many creatures,
You bestow on me many earthly treasures.
    Revealing love in each life and season,
    You share with me heavenly pleasures.
May you arouse me
In moments both of joy and of strife;
    Most holy Lord, bring me new life!

A Hymn, sung or heard (optional)

O Jesus Christ,
    Lord of heaven and earth,
    You are my riches, my store, my provision,
My star through the years
When troubles rend me,
    Through times of strife and tears,
    Sweet Jesus, defend me.

Jesus, Reedemer of the earth,
Begotten by the God of light,
    Equal in majesty and might,
    Before the day-star had its birth;

The splendour of the Father on high,
Of humankind the living hope,
    Aid all that under heaven's cope
    To embrace the joys you supply!

End this time of prayer by taking some time to bring to mind the various ways God shields you from harm or guides you through the world's tumult. Then, when you are ready, conclude by saying:

O Holy Lord, King in Heaven,
I place myself at the edge of your grace,
    On the floor of your house myself I place,
And to banish the sin of my heart away,
    I lower my knee to you this day.
Through life's torrents of pain may you bring me whole,
    And, O Lord Jesus Christ, preserve also my soul. Amen.

2.1b   Preparation for Prayer

Consideration of the Readings

After reciting or prayerfully reading the prayer sequence for this day or week:
- Read about the birth of Jesus in Luke 2:2-20. Make a mental note of each person's appearance and actions during the episode as well as the key elements of the story and its setting. Then, consider any aspects of this story that speak strongly to you before recording these observations in your workbook.
- Read about the visit of the Magi in Matthew 2:2-15. Again, note each person's appearance and actions during the episode as well as the key elements of the story and its setting, including the setting. Then, record in your workbook any aspects of this story that speak strongly to you.
- Read about the infant Jesus' presentation in the temple in Luke 2:22-40. Again, note each person's appearance and actions during the episode as well as the key elements of the story and its setting before recording any aspects of this story that speak strongly to you.

Note: You also should take a moment to consider any aspect of the prayer sequence from this day or week that seemed particularly significant to you.

Contemplation of Your Needs

When you are ready, concentrating on your breath or an object near you, allow any distractions to fade from your consciousness as you become aware of your desire to live in God's goodness. Feel yourself yearning to properly use the many gifts God has given you, to experience God's continuing care, and to be open to the immense love God shows for you, then:
- Read "The Birth of Brigid" (found on page 310). Allow yourself to linger on any thoughts, phrases or images that seem particularly meaningful or significant to your earlier preparations or prayer.
- Pray for your desires in the coming day or week. Ask that the divine presence all around you may be revealed, offering you inner

knowledge of Jesus Christ who became human for you so you may better love and follow him. Also ask that, in this day or week of prayer, you may feel deep joy at the birth of Jesus and the redemptive significance of his birth.

• Conclude by praying that you may share in the joy expressed by each group encountering the newborn Jesus: the shepherds, the Magi, and Simeon and Anna at the temple.

Then, take a moment record any significant thoughts, emotions, or reactions from these moments in your workbook.

After this, put your notes aside. Without straining your memory, consider in turn each of the readings for the coming day or week and allow them to take shape in your imagination – even if all you remember are small fragments. Prayerfully ponder how each reading affects you emotionally without overtly thinking about their content, asking God to illuminate the spiritual gifts offered in each reading – quieting your mind and creating a receptive space in yourself to see or hear the response.

Finally, conclude by allowing these desires to fade from your consciousness as you offer this traditional Irish prayer collected by Douglas Hyde in *The Religious Songs of Connacht*:

> O God, I believe in you; strengthen my belief.
> I trust in you; confirm my trust.
> I love you; double my love.
> I repent that I angered you,
> Increase my repentance.
> Fill you my heart with awe without despair;
> With hope, without over-confidence;
> With piety without infatuation;
> And with joy without excess.
> My God, consent to guide me by your wisdom;
> To constrain me by your right;
> To comfort me by your mercy;
> And to protect me by your power. Amen.

Allow these words to linger on your mind and in your heart for a few moments and then, while they are still fresh in your memory, write the most important thoughts, feelings and desires from this preparatory time in your retreat journal.

2.2 A Contemplation of Luke 2: 2-20

In this contemplation of Luke 2:2-20, you will see and hear the events surrounding Jesus' birth.

[1]   Begin by reading the biblical selection and reviewing your notes on it from your earlier preparations.

[2]   Then, focus on this specific time and place as you allow all other concerns to fall away. Then, when you are ready, consider the people and place in this moment of prayer.

- Allow an image of the Joseph and Mary to emerge in your imagination, first alone and then with the infant Jesus, noting their physical characteristics and mannerisms. Look at what they are wearing or carrying, observing their clothing and any objects they are is holding. Make a note of what they are doing in each moment. Ponder these mental images, allowing any other observations about Mary and Joseph to form in your mind.

- Then, observe the shepherds in the field at night and make a mental note of their appearance and demeanor. Observe whether they are sitting, standing, or walking while caring for their sheep. Take a moment to ponder this mental image, allowing other impressions of these people to form. Become familiar with the men and women you will encounter during your prayer as well as their behavior. Afterward, see the angel's appearance and demeanor.

- Then, gradually allow yourself to become aware of the location of Jesus' birth and the fields where the shepherds are in. Pay attention to the physical characteristics of these places as you ponder this mental image. Look around these places and notice more details about them – if they are still and silent or filled with noise, if they have an unusual smell or not, etc. Become familiar with the locations of your upcoming prayer.

- Take a moment to remain in this place, then allow these images to fade from your consciousness.

[3]   After you become still, become aware of your desires during this moment of prayer. Remember your desire to experience the divine presence all around you so you may attain a deep "felt knowledge" of Jesus Christ, who became human for you so you may better love and follow him. Recall your desire that, in this day or week of prayer, you may feel deep joy at the birth of Jesus and the redemptive significance

of his birth. Finally, ask that you may share in the joy expressed by the shepherds as they encounter the newborn Jesus.

As these desires fill your consciousness, let all other concerns fall aside as you focus on this specific time and place of prayer.

[4] When you are ready, allow the story of Jesus' birth to unfold in your imagination.

- As you watch and listen as Mary and Joseph approach Bethlehem – seeing Mary's discomfort in the last moments of her pregnancy and watching Joseph's growing concern for his wife – ask God to help you share in this moment, either by listening quietly to the events surrounding Jesus' birth or by participating in these events in some way.

- Then, see and hear the events of Joseph and Mary finding a place to stay, Mary giving birth to Jesus and the story told by the shepherds when they come to see the infant Jesus. You may want to quietly read the passage while remaining prayerfully aware of your mental image of Mary and Joseph or you may choose to stay completely within the imagined realm of your prayer. Whichever you choose, know that God will offer you the words from the biblical passage that you need to hear – even if only in fragments.

- Afterward, watch and listen as the angel delivers a message of "good news" to the shepherds and how it led them to come to Jesus with optimism and hope. Remember also that you need hope and optimism as you make your journey to Christ.

- Then, allow these images of Mary to fade from your imagination as you become aware of the phrases and images from this moment of prayer which touched you most deeply. Recall the emotions and memories – including any sounds or smells – evoked during your prayer. Allow these seminal aspects of your meditation to linger on your mind and in your heart, making a mental note of any special feelings evoked by them.

[5] When you are ready, become aware of God's presence with you in this moment and have an open and informal conversation about this prayer period and how the passage from Luke's gospel expresses your own needs or desires – giving space for God to respond or to highlight different aspects from the biblical selection and your experiences during this meditation. Then, gradually allow your thoughts to recede as you focus on God's broader presence in your life and in the world around you.

[6]   Finally, conclude by allowing these desires to fade from your consciousness as you offer this traditional Irish prayer collected by Douglas Hyde in *The Religious Songs of Connacht*:

> *Confirm me in your love divine,*
> *Smooth for my feet life's rugged way;*
> *My will with yours entwine,*
> *Lest evil lead my steps astray.*
> *Be with my still as guard and guide,*
> *Keep me in holy sanctity,*
> *Let my firm faith on you abide,*
> *From fraud and error hold me free. Amen.*

[7]   Afterward, take 10-15 minutes in a quiet space to reflect on the most significant moments from this time of prayer and record your reflections in your retreat journal.

2.3 A Contemplation of Matthew 2:2-15

In this contemplation of Matthew 2:2-15, you will see and hear the visit of the Magi to the infant Jesus.

[1]   Begin by reading the biblical selection and reviewing your notes on it from your earlier preparations.

[2]   Then, focus on this specific time and place as you allow all other concerns to fall away. Then, when you are ready, consider the people and place in this moment of prayer.

- Allow an image of the Joseph and Mary with the infant Jesus to emerge in your imagination, noting their physical characteristics and mannerisms. Look at what they are wearing or carrying, observing their clothing and any objects they are is holding. Make a note of what they are doing, making a note of whether they are sitting, standing, or walking. Ponder these mental images, allowing any other observations about Mary and Joseph to form in your mind.
- Then, observe the Magi and make a mental note of their appearance and demeanor. Take a moment to ponder this mental image, allowing other impressions of these people to form. Become familiar with the men and women you will encounter during your prayer as well as their behavior.
- Then, gradually allow yourself to become aware of the location where the Magi come to see Jesus. Pay attention to the physical characteristics of this place as you ponder this mental image. Look around this place and notice more details about it – if it is still and silent or filled with noise, if it has an unusual smell or not, etc. Become familiar with the location of your upcoming prayer.
- Take a moment to remain in this place, then allow these images to fade from your consciousness.

[3]   After you become still, become aware of your desires during this moment of prayer. Remember your desire to experience the divine presence all around you so you may attain a deep "felt knowledge" of Jesus Christ, who became human for you so you may better love and follow him. Recall your desire that, in this day or week of prayer, you may feel deep joy at the birth of Jesus and the redemptive significance of his birth. Finally, ask that you may share in the joyful wonder expressed by the Magi as they encounter the newborn Jesus.

As these desires fill your consciousness, let all other concerns fall aside as you focus on this specific time and place of prayer.

[4]   When you are ready, allow the visit of the Magi to unfold in your imagination.

- As you watch and listen as the Magi approach the Holy Family, ask God to help you share in this moment – either by listening quietly to the events surrounding Jesus' birth or by participating in these events in some way.
- Then, see and hear the events of the Magi's visit. You may want to quietly read the passage while remaining prayerfully aware of your mental image of Mary and Gabriel or you may choose to stay completely within the imagined realm of your prayer. Whichever you choose, know that God will offer you the words from the biblical passage that you need to hear – even if only in fragments.
- Afterward, remember the sense of expectancy they feel when meeting Jesus. Also remember your own sense of expectancy as you approach Jesus in prayer.
- Then, allow the image of the Magi to fade from your imagination as you become aware of the phrases and images from this moment of prayer which touched you most deeply. Recall the emotions and memories – including any sounds or smells – evoked during your prayer. Allow these seminal aspects of your meditation to linger on your mind and in your heart, making a mental note of any special feelings evoked by them.

[5]   When you are ready, become aware of God's presence with you in this moment and have an open and informal conversation about this prayer period and how the passage from Matthew's gospel expresses your own needs or desires – giving space for God to respond or to highlight different aspects from the biblical selection and your experiences during this meditation. Then, gradually allow your thoughts to recede as you focus on God's broader presence in your life and in the world around you.

[6]   Finally, conclude by allowing these desires to fade from your consciousness as you offer this traditional Irish prayer collected by Douglas Hyde in *The Religious Songs of Connacht*:

>   *Confirm me in your love divine,*
>   *Smooth for my feet life's rugged way;*
>   *My will with yours entwine,*
>   *Lest evil lead my steps astray.*
>   *Be with my still as guard and guide,*
>   *Keep me in holy sanctity,*
>   *Let my firm faith on you abide,*

From fraud and error hold me free. Amen.

[7]　Afterward, take 10-15 minutes in a quiet space to reflect on the most significant moments from this time of prayer and record your reflections in your retreat journal.

2.4 A Contemplation of Luke 2:22-40

In this contemplation of Luke 2:22-40, you will see and hear the reactions of Simeon and Anna to the infant Jesus when he is presented at the temple.

[1]   Begin by reading the biblical selection and reviewing your notes on it from your earlier preparations.

[2]   Then, focus on this specific time and place as you allow all other concerns to fall away. Then, when you are ready, consider the people and place in this moment of prayer.

- Allow an image of the Joseph and Mary carrying the infant Jesus into the temple to emerge in your imagination, noting their physical characteristics and mannerisms. Look at what they are wearing, observing their clothing and any other objects they are is holding. Make a note of what they are doing. As you ponder these mental images, allow any other observations about Mary, Joseph, and Jesus to form in your mind.

- Then, observe the Simeon and Anna and make a mental note of their appearance and demeanor. Observe whether they are sitting, standing, or walking when Joseph and Mary bring the infant Jesus to the temple. Take a moment to ponder this mental image, allowing other impressions of these Simeon and Anna to form. Take a moment to see the other people at the temple (e.g., the priests, other worshippers, etc.), noting their appearance and demeanor. Become familiar with the men and women you will encounter during your prayer as well as their behavior.

- Then, gradually allow yourself to become aware of the temple. Pay attention to the physical characteristics of this place as you ponder this mental image. Look around this place and notice more details about it – if it is still and silent or filled with noise, if it has an unusual smell or not, etc. Become familiar with the location of your upcoming prayer.

- Take a moment to remain in this place, then allow these images to fade from your consciousness.

[3]   After you become still, become aware of your desires during this moment of prayer. Remember your desire to experience the divine presence all around you so you may attain a deep "felt knowledge" of Jesus Christ, who became human for you so you may better love and follow him. Recall your desire that, in this day or week of prayer, you

may feel deep joy at the birth of Jesus and the redemptive significance of his birth. Finally, ask that you may share in the joyful exaltation demonstrated by Simeon and Anna as they encounter the infant Jesus at the temple.

As these desires fill your consciousness, let all other concerns fall aside as you focus on this specific time and place of prayer.

[4] When you are ready, allow the events of Jesus' presentation at the temple to unfold in your imagination.

- As you focus on Joseph and Mary with their newborn infant, ask God to help you share in this moment – either by listening quietly to the events surrounding Jesus' presentation or by participating in these events in some way.

- Then, see and hear the events at the temple. You may want to quietly read the passage while remaining prayerfully aware of your mental image of Mary and Gabriel or you may choose to stay completely within the imagined realm of your prayer. Whichever you choose, know that God will offer you the words from the biblical passage that you need to hear – even if only in fragments.

- Afterward, remember the sense of expectancy they feel when meeting Jesus. Also remember your own sense of expectancy as you approach Jesus in prayer.

- Then, allow these images to fade from your imagination as you become aware of the phrases and images from this moment of prayer which touched you most deeply. Recall the emotions and memories – including any sounds or smells – evoked during your prayer. Allow these seminal aspects of your meditation to linger on your mind and in your heart, making a mental note of any special feelings evoked by them.

[5] When you are ready, become aware of God's presence with you in this moment and have an open and informal conversation about this prayer period and how the passage from Luke's gospel expresses your own needs or desires – giving space for God to respond or to highlight different aspects from the biblical selection and your experiences during this meditation. Then, gradually allow your thoughts to recede as you focus on God's broader presence in your life and in the world around you.

[6] Finally, conclude by allowing these desires to fade from your consciousness as you offer this traditional Irish prayer collected by Douglas Hyde in *The Religious Songs of Connacht*:

Confirm me in your love divine,

Smooth for my feet life's rugged way;
My will with yours entwine,
Lest evil lead my steps astray.
Be with my still as guard and guide,
Keep me in holy sanctity,
Let my firm faith on you abide,
From fraud and error hold me free. Amen.

[7] Afterward, take 10-15 minutes in a quiet space to reflect on the most significant moments from this time of prayer and record your reflections in your retreat journal.

2.5 A Meditation on Luke 2:2-20

In this meditation on Luke 2:2-20, you will see and hear Saint Brigid preach to a crowd about the divine love demonstrated through Jesus' humble birth.

[1]   Begin by reading the biblical selection and reviewing your notes on it from your earlier preparations.

[2]   Then, focus on this specific time and place as you allow all other concerns to fall away. Then, when you are ready, consider the people and place in this moment of prayer.

• Allow an image of Brigid to emerge in your imagination, noting her physical characteristics and mannerisms. Look at what she is wearing or carrying, observing her clothing and any objects she is holding. Make a note of whether she is sitting, standing, or walking. Ponder this mental image, allowing any other observations about Jesus to form in your mind.

• Then, observe the men and women around Saint Brigid. Note how many people are with Brigid, making a mental note of their appearance and demeanor. Look at Brigid's disciples, observing where they are standing and how they behave toward Brigid. Look at the crowd, noting their attitude and behavior toward Saint Brigid. Observe whether the people are sitting, standing, or walking. Take a moment to ponder this mental image, allowing other impressions of these men and women to form. Become familiar with the men and women you will encounter during your prayer as well as their behavior.

• Gradually, allow yourself to become aware of the location of this encounter with Brigid. Pay attention to its physical characteristics and the arrangement of the people in it. As you ponder this mental image, look around the place and notice more details about it – noting if it is in dim or bright light, if it is still and silent or filled with noise, if it has an unusual smell or not, etc. Become familiar with the location of your upcoming prayer.

• Take a moment to remain in this place with these men and women, then allow these images to fade from your consciousness.

[3]   After you become still, become aware of your desires during this moment of prayer. Remember your desire to experience the divine presence all around you so you may attain a deep "felt knowledge" of Jesus Christ, who became human for you so you may better love and follow him. Recall your desire that, in this day or week of prayer, you

may feel deep joy at the birth of Jesus and the redemptive significance of his birth. Finally, ask that you may share in the joy expressed by each group encountering the newborn Jesus: the shepherds, the Magi, and Simeon and Anna at the temple.

As these desires fill your consciousness, let all other concerns fall aside as you focus on this specific time and place of prayer.

[4]   Again, when you are ready, allow the image of Saint Brigid and her disciples to reemerge in your imagination.

• Watch as the group assembles around Brigid. Listen to the sounds of this moment and become comfortable as you prepare to hear Brigid speak. Feel the anticipation of the people around you and share in that enthusiasm.

• As you hear Saint Brigid quieting the crowd, ask God to help you share in their experience – either by joining them or by listening quietly to them. Focus your attention on Brigid, noting her physical appearance and her emotional demeanor.

• Then, relying on the memories from your earlier prayer, watch and listen as Brigid tells the story of Jesus' birth. You may want to quietly read the passage while remaining prayerfully aware of your mental image of Brigid or you may choose to stay completely within the imagined realm of your prayer. Whichever you choose, know that God will offer you the words from the biblical passage that you need to hear – even if only in fragments.

• Afterward, hear Saint Brigid the divine love and humility displayed in Jesus' birth. Listen to her as she explains the meaning and significance of God's desire become human in a lowly form as well as how the divine majesty could not be completely hidden.

– Again, look around as Brigid speaks and see the reactions of her disciples and the men and women in the crowd. Become aware of their feelings and how they behave toward Brigid and one another.

– Remember that Brigid is speaking to men and women struggling to remain faithful to God's desires and promises while living difficult lives which challenge their faith. Remember that she also is speaking to you.

• After Brigid finishes speaking, allow her image and this place to fade from your imagination as you become aware of the phrases and images from this moment of prayer which touched you most deeply. Recall the emotions and memories – including any sounds or smells – evoked during your prayer. Allow these seminal aspects of your meditation to linger on your mind and in your heart, making a mental note of any special feelings evoked by them.

[5]   When you are ready, become aware of God's presence with you in this moment and have an open and informal conversation about this prayer period and how the passage from Luke's gospel expresses your own needs or desires – giving space for God to respond or to highlight different aspects from the biblical selection and your experiences during this meditation. Then, gradually allow your thoughts to recede as you focus on God's broader presence in your life and in the world around you.

[6]   Finally, conclude by allowing these desires to fade from your consciousness as you offer this traditional Irish prayer collected by Douglas Hyde in *The Religious Songs of Connacht*:

> *Confirm me in your love divine,*
> *Smooth for my feet life's rugged way;*
> *My will with yours entwine,*
> *Lest evil lead my steps astray.*
> *Be with my still as guard and guide,*
> *Keep me in holy sanctity,*
> *Let my firm faith on you abide,*
> *From fraud and error hold me free. Amen.*

[7]   Afterward, take 10-15 minutes in a quiet space to reflect on the most significant moments from this time of prayer and record your reflections in your retreat journal.

2.6 An Application of the Senses

[1] Become aware of your prayerful desires during this day or week. Bring to mind your desire to experience an inner knowledge of Jesus Christ who became human for you so you may better love and follow him. Also ask that, in this day or week of prayer, you may feel deep joy at the birth of Jesus and the redemptive significance of that birth.

[2] When you are ready, in your imagination, call to mind the various prayers of the preceding day or days. Allow the images and words of these prayers to linger and then slowly fade from your consciousness.

- Remember your imaginative contemplation and meditation concerning Luke 2:2-20. Consider the images and feelings evoked in you during your prayer, feeling God's presence in these memories and becoming aware of the specific sensations associated with each image.
- Recall your imaginative contemplation of Matthew 2:2-15, considering them in the same way as your memories of Luke 2.
- Review your imaginative contemplation of Luke 2:22-40 in the same manner as the previous prayers.

As these prayers enter your memory, make a mental note of which senses are most active. You may see an image or a color, hear a sound or a phrase, or smell a scent or a fragrance. You may even taste a flavor or feel a sensation on your skin.

[3] Then, relax and allow these various memories and experiences to quietly enter and leave your consciousness without being controlled – whether they are clear or diffuse, whether they come quickly or slowly. Linger on the sensory images and memories being evoked in you – noticing any images or colors, any sounds or phrases, any scents or fragrances, any flavors or physical sensations associated with each prayer.

[4] When you are ready, become completely still and clear your mind of all thoughts and concerns. Allow an image of a special personal space to form in your imagination, a place where you are completely comfortable and alone. Then, watch as God enters that place and forms a small image or object for you that expresses the thought or awareness that you most need to carry with you into your life.

Reverently pick up the object or image, a reflection of the most important gift you have been given during this time of prayer. Look at it carefully and become aware of the divine presence contained within it. Take a moment to register what it looks like and how it feels in your hand. Then, feel the joy and confidence that comes from touching the presence of God as you accept this gift, offering a short prayer of gratitude while you relax into the pleasure of this moment.

[5]   Then, conclude by allowing these images to fade from your consciousness as you offer this traditional Irish prayer collected by Douglas Hyde in *The Religious Songs of Connacht*:

>*Confirm me in your love divine,*
>*Smooth for my feet life's rugged way;*
>*My will with yours entwine,*
>*Lest evil lead my steps astray.*
>*Be with my still as guard and guide,*
>*Keep me in holy sanctity,*
>*Let my firm faith on you abide,*
>*From fraud and error hold me free. Amen.*

[6]   While your experiences are still fresh in your mind, record the most significant impressions or sensations from this time of prayer in your retreat journal.

2.7   Review of Prayer

[1]   Remember your desires during the preceding day or week of prayer. Become aware of the divine presence all around you, offering you inner knowledge of Jesus Christ who became human for you so you may better love and follow him. Recall your desire to feel deep joy at the birth of Jesus and the redemptive significance of that birth.

After bringing these thoughts and desires into your consciousness, ask God once again to fulfill these desires in your own life and in your interactions with others.

[2]   Then, take a moment to allow the words, thoughts, and feelings from your prayers during the last day or week to linger – on your mind and in your heart – before asking God to reveal the fulfillment of your deepest desires in these various memories.

• Think about the prayer sequence at the beginning of this day or week. Make a mental note of any words, insights or images that remain particularly significant or meaningful to you.

• Ponder the story, "The Birth of Brigid". Note any words, insights, or images from it that remain particularly significant or meaningful to you.

• Remember your imaginative contemplation and meditation concerning of Luke 2:2-20.

– Consider the most powerful images, phrases, or feelings from your prayer. Ask yourself what gifts God gave to you through these moments, perhaps offering you new insights or perhaps affirming an important aspect of your faith. Ask yourself how God may be calling you to change through these moments, being as specific as possible.

– Examine your disposition as you prayed, noting whether prayer came easily or with resistance. Recall the easiest moments in your prayer and any moments of joy you may have experienced. Remember also if you encountered any difficulty opening yourself to God or if you felt any sadness as you prayed. Ask God to help you understand why these feelings surfaced.

– Bring to mind any moments when you added personal elements (e.g., familiar places or people from your life) or connected your prayers to other scriptures or spiritual writings. Ask yourself how these additions helped or hindered you as you prayed. Again, if you do not know why this happened, ask God to help you understand.

- Recall your imaginative contemplation of Matthew 2:2-15. Then, review your prayer in the same way as your earlier reflection on Luke 2.
- Review your imaginative contemplation of Luke 2:22-40 in the same manner as the previous prayers.
- Reflect on the ebb and flow of sensory impressions and feelings that marked your application of the senses. Isolate the most memorable moments and sensory impressions from your prayer and reflect on how God used these moments to give you a particular gift, perhaps offering you new insights or changing you in some way.

[3] Finally, ponder the times when images or feelings from the readings of this day or week surfaced outside these prayer periods. Consider those moments or events in which God's presence or guidance was especially strong as well as any moments when you were struggling. Think about the most memorable aspects of these experiences, asking God to explain their significance.

[4] Take a moment to allow the words, thoughts, and feelings of these prayers to linger on your mind and in your heart. Finally, conclude by allowing these desires to fade from your consciousness as you offer this traditional Irish prayer collected by Douglas Hyde in *The Religious Songs of Connacht*:

> *O God, I believe in you; strengthen my belief.*
> *I trust in you; confirm my trust.*
> *I love you; double my love.*
> *I repent that I angered you,*
> *Increase my repentance.*
> *Fill you my heart with awe without despair;*
> *With hope, without over-confidence;*
> *With piety without infatuation;*
> *And with joy without excess.*
> *My God, consent to guide me by your wisdom;*
> *To constrain me by your right;*
> *To comfort me by your mercy;*
> *And to protect me by your power. Amen.*

[5] After finishing these prayers, summarize your reflections on the gifts or graces you received during the prayers of this last day or week and record these thoughts in your retreat journal.

3. The Hidden Life of Jesus

3.1a   Gentle Jesus, Fount Of Healing
a prayer for spiritual guidance and renewal

Take a moment to quiet your spirit, becoming completely present to this time and place. Allow all other thoughts and concerns to fall away as you come into the presence of God. Then, when you are ready, begin.

Gentle Jesus, fount of healing,
Solace unto souls appealing
By the mildness of your grace,
      Calm my restless mind, and render
      Soothing thoughts therein and tender;
      Pride and bitterness efface.

By your fostering care provided
All my life shall thus be guided,
Safe in faith, from evil free;
      Kindled by your kindness, never
      From your love my soul shall sever,
      All my desires in you shall be.

A Hymn, sung or heard (optional)

My God, my life, my love, my light,
My strength, my joy, my treasure,
      Let it be my thought both day and night
      In you to take my pleasure.
Increase my love, as I sigh and groan
      My careless lips to move it,
      And let my thoughts be fixed alone
On right living, with all sins abhorred.

Blot out my crimes and me forgive,
O Lord do not deny me,
      And grant my thoughts for ever be
      On Jesus Crucified.
In honour of your passion's sake,
      This new year's gift bestow me,
      That I into protection take

Sweet Jesus, my King and Lord.

To God the Father glory be,
For his mercy still I crave,
    And to His Son who died for me
    Who spilt his blood to me save.
And to the Holy Ghost all three.
They on us bestow gifts and grace,
    And should our thoughts for ever be
    That the Godhead's love we embrace.

Read or recite Psalm 127.

Holy Lord,
Under my thoughts may I God-thoughts find.
Half of my sins escape my mind.
    For what I said, or did not say,
    Pardon me, O Lord, I pray.

Read Luke 2: 41-52, aloud or quietly.

O Lord, Jesus the Christ,
If I were in Heaven my harp I would sound
With apostles and angels and saints all around,
    Praising and thanking the Son who is crowned,
    May the poor race of Eve for that heaven be bound!

Holy Lord,
Now since I am come to the brink of death
And my latest breath must soon be drawn,
    May heaven, though late, be my aim and mark
    From day till dark, and from dark till dawn.

O Jesus Christ, who has died for men,
And has risen again without stain or spot,
    Unto those who have sought it, you show the way,
    Oh why, in my days, have I sought it not!

O Holy Lord,
    God with the Father and the Spirit,

For me is many a snare designed,
To fill my mind with doubts and fears;
    Far from the land of holy saints,
    I dwell within my vale of tears.
Let faith, let hope, let love –
Traits far above the cold world's way –
    With patience, humility, and awe,
    Become my guides from day to day.

I acknowledge, the evil I have done.
From the day of my birth till the day of my death,
    Through the sight of my eyes,
Through the hearing of my ears,
    Through the sayings of my mouth,
Through the thoughts of my heart,
    Through the touch of my hands,
Through the course of my way,
    Through all I said and did not,
Through all I promised and fulfilled not,
    Through all the laws and holy commandments I broke.
I ask even now absolution of you,
    For fear I may have never asked it as was right,
    And that I might not live to ask it again,

O Holy Lord, my King in Heaven,
May you not let my soul stray from you,
May you keep me in a good state,
    May you turn me toward what is good to do,
    May you protect me from dangers, small and great.
May you fill my eyes with tears of repentance,
    So I may avoid the sinner's awful sentence.
May the Grace of the God for ever be with me,
    And whatever my needs, may the Triune God give me.

Select one of the following options for the Lord's Prayer.

Option A

O Jesus Christ,
Lord of heaven and earth,

Help me pray as you yourself taught:
> "Our Father in heaven,
> hallowed be your name.
> Your kingdom come.
> Your will be done,
> on earth as it is in heaven.
> Give us this day our daily bread.
> And forgive us our debts,
> as we also have forgiven our debtors.
> And do not bring us to the time of trial,
> but rescue us from the evil one."
> (Matthew 6: 9-13)

From the foes of my land,
from the foes of my faith,
From the foes who would us dissever,
> O Lord, preserve me, in life and in death,
> With the Sign of the Cross for ever.
> *For the kingdom, the power, and the glory*
> *are yours now and for ever. Amen.*

Please proceed with "I beseech you, O Lord…," found after Option B.

Option B

O Jesus Christ,
Lord of heaven and earth,
Help me pray as you yourself taught:
> *Our Father in heaven,*
> *hallowed be your name,*
> *your kingdom come,*
> *your will be done,*
> *on earth as in heaven.*
> *Give us today our daily bread.*
> *Forgive us our sins*
> *as we forgive those who sin against us.*
> *Lead us not into temptation*
> *but deliver us from evil.*

From the foes of my land,
from the foes of my faith,

From the foes who would us dissever,
>   O Lord, preserve me, in life and in death,
>   With the Sign of the Cross for ever.
>   *For the kingdom, the power, and the glory
>   are yours now and for ever. Amen.*

I beseech you, O Lord.
God in Heaven, unsurpassed in power and might;
>   Be behind me, Be on my left,
>   Be before me, Be on my right!

Against each danger, you are my help;
In distress, upon you I call.
>   In dark times, may you sustain me
>   And lift me up again when I fall.

Lord over heaven and of earth,
You know my offenses.
>   Yet, listening to my pleadings,
>   You guide me away from sinful pretenses.

Lord of all creation and the many creatures,
You bestow on me many earthly treasures.
>   Revealing love in each life and season,
>   You share with me heavenly pleasures.

May you arouse me
In moments both of joy and of strife;
>   Most holy Lord, bring me new life!

A Hymn, sung or heard (optional)

O Jesus Christ,
>   Lord of heaven and earth,
>   You are my riches, my store, my provision,

My star through the years
When troubles rend me,
>   Through times of strife and tears,
>   Sweet Jesus, defend me.

Gentle Jesus, Fount of pleasure,
Be your love my dearest treasure,
Let my soul your passion feel;
>   Be that passion faith's foundation,

> Love's desire and recreation,
> And of hope the sign and seal.

Cleanse my heart from evil yearning,
Fire therein a holy burning,
For the blessed life above;
> In the end to me be given,
> Lord, eternal joy in heaven
> As a comrade in your love.

> ***End this time of prayer by taking some time to bring to mind the various ways God shields you from harm or guides you through the world's tumult. Then, when you are ready, conclude by saying:***

O Holy Lord, King in Heaven,
I place myself at the edge of your grace,
> On the floor of your house myself I place,
And to banish the sin of my heart away,
> I lower my knee to you this day.
Through life's torrents of pain may you bring me whole,
> And, O Lord Jesus Christ, preserve also my soul. Amen.

3.1b Preparation for Prayer

Consideration of the Readings

After reciting or prayerfully reading the prayer sequence for this day or week:
- Read about the adolescent Jesus at the temple in Luke 2:41-52. Again, make a mental note of each person's appearance and actions during the episode as well as the key elements of the story and its setting. Then, consider any aspects of this story that speak strongly to you before recording these observations in your workbook.
- Read Romans 12:9-21. Again, pay careful attention to any phrases or images that seem particularly meaningful to you. Then, record these highlights in your workbook.
- Read Romans 14:13-23. Again, note any phrases or images that seem particularly meaningful to you and record these highlights in your workbook.
- Read the brief observation about Jesus in Luke 2:52. Allow your imagination to expand on this remark and record these ruminations in your workbook.

Note: *You also should take a moment to consider any aspect of the prayer sequence from this day or week that seemed particularly significant to you.*

Contemplation of Your Needs

When you are ready, concentrating on your breath or an object near you, allow any distractions to fade from your consciousness as you become aware of your desire to live in God's goodness. Feel yourself yearning to properly use the many gifts God has given you, to experience God's continuing care, and to be open to the immense love God shows for you, then:
- Read "Brigid Returns to Her Father" (found on page 311). Allow yourself to linger on any thoughts, phrases or images that seem particularly meaningful or significant to your earlier preparations or prayer.
- Pray for your desires in the coming day or week. Ask that the divine presence all around you may be revealed, offering you inner

knowledge of Jesus Christ who became human for you so you may better love and follow him. Also ask that, in this day or week of prayer, you may experience the growth of Jesus as he becomes aware of his mission – allowing these insights into his development to illumine your own sense of growing purpose.

• Conclude by praying for a deep "felt knowledge" of how your development as a Christian means growing in Christ or allowing Christ to grow in you. Then, take a moment record any significant thoughts, emotions, or reactions from these moments in your workbook.

After this, put your notes aside. Without straining your memory, consider in turn each of the readings for the coming day or week and allow them to take shape in your imagination – even if all you remember are small fragments. Prayerfully ponder how each reading affects you emotionally without overtly thinking about their content, asking God to illuminate the spiritual gifts offered in each reading – quieting your mind and creating a receptive space in yourself to see or hear the response.

Finally, conclude by allowing these desires to fade from your consciousness as you offer this traditional Irish prayer collected by Douglas Hyde in *The Religious Songs of Connacht*:

> O God, I believe in you; strengthen my belief.
> I trust in you; confirm my trust.
> I love you; double my love.
> I repent that I angered you,
> Increase my repentance.
> Fill you my heart with awe without despair;
> With hope, without over-confidence;
> With piety without infatuation;
> And with joy without excess.
> My God, consent to guide me by your wisdom;
> To constrain me by your right;
> To comfort me by your mercy;
> And to protect me by your power. Amen.

Allow these words to linger on your mind and in your heart for a few moments and then, while they are still fresh in your memory, write the most important thoughts, feelings, and desires from this preparatory time in your retreat journal.

3.2   A Contemplation of Luke 2:41-52

In this contemplation of Luke 2:41-52, you will see and hear the adolescent Jesus speaking with the scholars in the temple.

[1]   Begin by reading the biblical selection and reviewing your notes on it from your earlier preparations.

[2]   Then, focus on this specific time and place as you allow all other concerns to fall away. Then, when you are ready, consider the people and place in this moment of prayer.

- Allow an image of the adolescent Jesus to emerge in your imagination, noting his physical characteristics and mannerisms. Look at what he is wearing or carrying, observing his clothing and any objects he is holding. Ponder this mental image, allowing any other observations about Jesus to form in your mind.

- Observe the people around Jesus. Note how many people are with Jesus, making a mental note of their appearance and demeanor. Look at the scholars, observing whether they are sitting or standing as well as how they behave toward Jesus. Look at the crowd, noting their attitude and behavior toward the young Jesus. Observe whether the people are sitting, standing, or walking. Take a moment to ponder this mental image, allowing other impressions of these men and women to form. Become familiar with the men and women you will encounter during your prayer as well as their behavior.

- Then, see Joseph and Mary. Make a mental note of their appearance and demeanor as they find Jesus after days of searching for him.

- Gradually, allow yourself to become aware of the appearance of the temple. Pay attention to its physical characteristics and the arrangement of the people in it. As you ponder this mental image, look around the place and notice more details about it – noting if it is in dim or bright light, if it is still and silent or filled with noise, if it has an unusual smell or not, etc. Become familiar with the location of your upcoming prayer.

- Take a moment to remain in this place with these men and women, then allow these images to fade from your consciousness.

[3]   After you become still, become aware of your desires during this moment of prayer. Remember your desire to experience the divine presence all around you so you may attain a deep "felt knowledge" of Jesus Christ, who became human for you so you may better love and

follow him. Recall your desire that, in this day or week of prayer, you may experience the growth of Jesus as he becomes aware of his mission – allowing these insights into his development to illumine your own sense of growing purpose. Finally, ask for a deep "felt knowledge" of how your development as a Christian means allowing Christ to grow in you.

As these desires fill your consciousness, let all other concerns fall aside as you focus on this specific time and place of prayer.

[4] Again, when you are ready, allow the image of Jesus and the scholars to reemerge in your imagination.

• As you see the group assembled around Jesus, ask God to help you enter this moment – either by joining these events or by listening quietly to them. Focus your attention on Jesus, noting his physical appearance and his emotional demeanor.

• Then, watch and listen as Jesus speaks with scholars. You may want to quietly read the passage while remaining prayerfully aware of your mental image of Jesus or you may choose to stay completely within the imagined realm of your prayer. Whichever you choose, know that God will offer you the words from the biblical passage that you need to hear – even if only in fragments.

• After Jesus finishes speaking, allow his image and this place to fade from your imagination as you become aware of the phrases and images from this moment of prayer which touched you most deeply. Recall the emotions and memories – including any sounds or smells – evoked during your prayer. Allow these seminal aspects of your meditation to linger on your mind and in your heart, making a mental note of any special feelings evoked by them.

[5] When you are ready, become aware of God's presence with you in this moment and have an open and informal conversation about this prayer period and how the passage from Luke's gospel expresses your own needs or desires – giving space for God to respond or to highlight different aspects from the biblical selection and your experiences during this meditation. Then, gradually allow your thoughts to recede as you focus on God's broader presence in your life and in the world around you.

[6] Finally, conclude by allowing these desires to fade from your consciousness as you offer this traditional Irish prayer collected by Douglas Hyde in *The Religious Songs of Connacht*:

Confirm me in your love divine,
Smooth for my feet life's rugged way;

My will with yours entwine,
Lest evil lead my steps astray.
Be with my still as guard and guide,
Keep me in holy sanctity,
Let my firm faith on you abide,
From fraud and error hold me free. Amen.

[7] Afterward, take 10-15 minutes in a quiet space to reflect on the most significant moments from this time of prayer and record your reflections in your retreat journal.

3.3 A Meditation on Romans 12:9-21

In this meditation on Romans 12:9-21 (using Luke 2:52), you will see and hear Saint Brigid teaching her disciples about the attributes of a Christian as she imagines Jesus' life during his "hidden years".

[1]   Begin by reading the biblical selection and reviewing your notes on it from your earlier preparations.

[2]   Then, focus on this specific time and place as you allow all other concerns to fall away. Then, when you are ready, consider the people and place in this moment of prayer.

• Allow an image of Brigid to emerge in your imagination, noting her physical characteristics and mannerisms. Look at what she is wearing or carrying, observing her clothing and any objects she is holding. Make a note of whether she is sitting, standing, or walking. Ponder this mental image, allowing any other observations about Brigid to form in your mind.

• Then, observe the disciples around Saint Brigid. Note how many disciples are with Brigid, making a mental note of their appearance and demeanor. Observe whether they are sitting, standing, or walking. Take a moment to ponder this mental image, allowing other impressions of these people to form. Become familiar with the men and women you will encounter during your prayer as well as their behavior.

• Gradually, allow yourself to become aware of the location of this moment with Saint Brigid. Observe whether it is inside or outside, paying attention to its physical characteristics and the arrangement of the people in it. As you ponder this mental image, look around the place and notice more details about it – noting if it is in dim or bright light, if it is still and silent or filled with noise, if it has an unusual smell or not, etc. Become familiar with the location of your upcoming prayer.

• Take a moment to remain in this place with these men and women, then allow these images to fade from your consciousness.

[3]   After you become still, become aware of your desires during this moment of prayer. Remember your desire to experience the divine presence all around you so you may attain a deep "felt knowledge" of Jesus Christ, who became human for you so you may better love and follow him. Recall your desire that, in this day or week of prayer, you may experience the growth of Jesus as he becomes aware of his mission – allowing these insights into his development to illumine your own

sense of growing purpose. Finally, ask for a deep "felt knowledge" of how your development as a Christian means allowing Christ to grow in you.

As these desires fill your consciousness, let all other concerns fall aside as you focus on this specific time and place of prayer.

[4] Again, when you are ready, allow the image of Saint Brigid and her disciples to reemerge in your imagination.

- Watch as the group assembles around Brigid. Listen to the sounds of this moment and become comfortable as you prepare to hear Brigid speak. Feel the anticipation of the people around you and share in that enthusiasm.

- As you hear Brigid invite her companions to listen, ask God to help you enter this moment – either by joining these events or by listening quietly to them. Focus your attention on Saint Brigid, noting her physical appearance and her emotional demeanor.

- Then, watch and listen as Brigid recites Romans 12:9-21. You may want to quietly read the passage while remaining prayerfully aware of your mental image of Brigid or you may choose to stay completely within the imagined realm of your prayer. Whichever you choose, know that God will offer you the words from the biblical passage that you need to hear – even if only in fragments.

- Afterward, hear Brigid quote Luke 2:52, saying, "Jesus increased in wisdom and in years, and in divine and human favor" before explaining the ways Jesus reflected the values in Paul's epistle during his childhood, adolescence, and early adulthood.

– Look around as Brigid speaks and see the reactions of her disciples. Become aware of their feelings and how they behave toward Brigid and one another.

– Remember that Brigid is speaking to men and women striving to remain faithful to their Christian vocations. Remember that she also is speaking to you.

- After Saint Brigid finishes speaking, allow her image and this place to fade from your imagination as you become aware of the phrases and images from this moment of prayer which touched you most deeply. Recall the emotions and memories – including any sounds or smells – evoked during your prayer. Allow these seminal aspects of your meditation to linger on your mind and in your heart, making a mental note of any special feelings evoked by them.

[5] When you are ready, become aware of God's presence with you in this moment and have an open and informal conversation about

this prayer period and how the passage from Paul's epistle expresses your own needs or desires – giving space for God to respond or to highlight different aspects from the biblical selection and your experiences during this meditation. Then, gradually allow your thoughts to recede as you focus on God's broader presence in your life and in the world around you.

[6]   Finally, conclude by allowing these desires to fade from your consciousness as you offer this traditional Irish prayer collected by Douglas Hyde in *The Religious Songs of Connacht*:

> *Confirm me in your love divine,*
> *Smooth for my feet life's rugged way;*
> *My will with yours entwine,*
> *Lest evil lead my steps astray.*
> *Be with my still as guard and guide,*
> *Keep me in holy sanctity,*
> *Let my firm faith on you abide,*
> *From fraud and error hold me free. Amen.*

[7]   Afterward, take 10-15 minutes in a quiet space to reflect on the most significant moments from this time of prayer and record your reflections in your retreat journal.

3.4 A Meditation on Romans 14:13-23

In this meditation on Romans 14:13-23 (using Luke 2:52), you again will see and hear Saint Brigid teaching her disciples about the attributes of a Christian as she imagines the life of Jesus during his "hidden years".

[1] Begin by reading the biblical selection and reviewing your notes on it from your earlier preparations.

[2] Then, focus on this specific time and place as you allow all other concerns to fall away. Then, when you are ready, consider the people and place in this moment of prayer.

• Again, allow an image of Brigid to emerge in your imagination, as you note her physical characteristics and mannerisms. Look at what she is wearing or carrying, observing her clothing and any objects she is holding. Make a note of whether she is sitting, standing, or walking. Ponder this mental image, allowing any other observations about Brigid to form in your mind.

• Then, observe the disciples around Saint Brigid. Note how many disciples are with Brigid, making a mental note of their appearance and demeanor. Observe whether they are sitting, standing, or walking. Take a moment to ponder this mental image, allowing other impressions of these people to form. Become familiar with the men and women you will encounter during your prayer as well as their behavior.

• Gradually, allow yourself to become aware of the location of this moment with Saint Brigid. Observe whether it is inside or outside, paying attention to its physical characteristics and the arrangement of the people in it. As you ponder this mental image, look around the place and notice more details about it – noting if it is in dim or bright light, if it is still and silent or filled with noise, if it has an unusual smell or not, etc. Become familiar with the location of your upcoming prayer.

• Take a moment to remain in this place with these men and women, then allow these images to fade from your consciousness.

[3] After you become still, become aware of your desires during this moment of prayer. Remember your desire to experience the divine presence all around you so you may attain a deep "felt knowledge" of Jesus Christ, who became human for you so you may better love and follow him. Recall your desire that, in this day or week of prayer, you may experience the growth of Jesus as he becomes aware of his mission – allowing these insights into his development to illumine your own

sense of growing purpose. Finally, ask for a deep "felt knowledge" of how your development as a Christian allowing Christ to grow in you.

As these desires fill your consciousness, let all other concerns fall aside as you focus on this specific time and place of prayer.

[4]   Again, when you are ready, allow the image of Saint Brigid and her disciples to reemerge in your imagination.

- Watch as the group assembles around Brigid. Listen to the sounds of this moment and become comfortable as you prepare to hear Brigid speak. Feel the anticipation of the people around you and share in that enthusiasm.

- As you hear Brigid invite her companions to listen, ask God to help you share in this experience – either by joining these events or by listening quietly to them. Focus your attention on Saint Brigid, noting her physical appearance and her emotional demeanor.

- Then, watch and listen as Brigid recites Romans 14:13-23. You may want to quietly read the passage while remaining prayerfully aware of your mental image of Brigid or you may choose to stay completely within the imagined realm of your prayer. Whichever you choose, know that God will offer you the words from the biblical passage that you need to hear – even if only in fragments.

- Afterward, again hear Brigid quote Luke 2:52, saying, "Jesus increased in wisdom and in years, and in divine and human favor" before explaining the ways Jesus reflected the values in Paul's epistle during his childhood, adolescence, and early adulthood.

– Look around as Brigid speaks and see the reactions of her disciples. Become aware of their feelings and how they behave toward Brigid and one another.

– Remember that Brigid is speaking to men and women striving to remain faithful to their Christian vocations. Remember that she also is speaking to you.

- After Saint Brigid finishes speaking, allow her image and this place to fade from your imagination as you become aware of the phrases and images from this moment of prayer which touched you most deeply. Recall the emotions and memories – including any sounds or smells – evoked during your prayer. Allow these seminal aspects of your meditation to linger on your mind and in your heart, making a mental note of any special feelings evoked by them.

[5]   When you are ready, become aware of God's presence with you in this moment and have an open and informal conversation about this prayer period and how the passage from Paul's epistle expresses

your own needs or desires – giving space for God to respond or to highlight different aspects from the biblical selection and your experiences during this meditation. Then, gradually allow your thoughts to recede as you focus on God's broader presence in your life and in the world around you.

[6]   Finally, conclude by allowing these desires to fade from your consciousness as you offer this traditional Irish prayer collected by Douglas Hyde in *The Religious Songs of Connacht*:

>   *Confirm me in your love divine,*
>   *Smooth for my feet life's rugged way;*
>   *My will with yours entwine,*
>   *Lest evil lead my steps astray.*
>   *Be with my still as guard and guide,*
>   *Keep me in holy sanctity,*
>   *Let my firm faith on you abide,*
>   *From fraud and error hold me free. Amen.*

[7]   Afterward, take 10-15 minutes in a quiet space to reflect on the most significant moments from this time of prayer and record your reflections in your retreat journal.

3.5 A Consideration of Jesus' "Hidden Years"

In this consideration of Luke 2:52, you will contemplate your own perceptions of Jesus' "hidden years" as well as your own need for Christ's continuing guidance and support.

[1]   Begin by re-reading Luke 2:41-52, Romans 12:9-21 and Romans 14:13-23. Then, review your notes on these readings from your earlier preparations.

[2]   Then, focus on this specific time and place as you allow all other concerns to fall away.

[3]   After you become still, become aware of your desires during this moment of prayer. Remember your desire to experience the divine presence all around you so you may attain a deep "felt knowledge" of Jesus Christ, who became human for you so you may better love and follow him. Recall your desire that, in this day or week of prayer, you may experience the growth of Jesus as he becomes aware of his mission – allowing these insights into his development to illumine your own sense of growing purpose. Finally, ask for a deep "felt knowledge" of how your development as a Christian means growing in Christ or allowing Christ to grow in you.

As these desires fill your consciousness, let all other concerns fall aside as you focus on this specific time and place of prayer.

[4]   When you are ready, remember Luke 2:52: "Jesus increased in wisdom and in years, and in divine and human favor."

• Then, recall the most memorable words and images from your prayers on Jesus at the temple and his "hidden years". Allow the various words and images of your earlier prayers to flow freely in your consciousness without being controlled.

• Become aware of the phrases and images from these earlier moments of prayer which touched you most deeply. Recall the emotions and memories – including any sounds or smells – evoked during your prayer. Allow these seminal aspects of your meditation to linger on your mind and in your heart, making a mental note of any special feelings evoked by them.

• Finally, let these words and images fade from your consciousness. Remember that Jesus shared completely in our humanity and shared our journey from childhood to adulthood. So, ask God to help you see and hear the ways that Jesus shared in your own experiences of childhood, adolescence, and adulthood. As the moment emerge in your imagination, ask that you may either remain aware of God's sustaining presence in your life – both when nurturing personal growth and healing any trauma you encountered. Allow yourself to linger in these memories and feel the consolation of Jesus' loving presence in the events of your own early life.

[5]   When you are ready, become aware of Jesus' presence with you in this moment and have an open and informal conversation about your own needs or desires as you consider your own "hidden life" – giving space for Jesus to respond or to highlight different moments in your prayer. Then, gradually allow your thoughts to recede as you focus on God's broader presence in your life and in the world around you.

[5]   When you are ready, become aware of God's presence with you in this moment and have open and informal conversation.

[6]   Finally, conclude by allowing these desires to fade from your consciousness as you offer this traditional Irish prayer collected by Douglas Hyde in *The Religious Songs of Connacht*:

> *Confirm me in your love divine,*
> *Smooth for my feet life's rugged way;*
> *My will with yours entwine,*
> *Lest evil lead my steps astray.*
> *Be with my still as guard and guide,*
> *Keep me in holy sanctity,*
> *Let my firm faith on you abide,*
> *From fraud and error hold me free. Amen.*

[7]   Afterward, take 10-15 minutes in a quiet space to reflect on the most significant moments from this time of prayer and record your reflections in your retreat journal.

3.6 An Application of the Senses

[1]   Become aware of your prayerful desires during this day or week. Bring to mind your desire to experience an inner knowledge of Jesus Christ who became human for you so you may better love and follow him. Also ask that, in this day or week of prayer, you may experience the growth of Jesus as he becomes aware of his mission – allowing these insights into his development to illumine your own sense of growing purpose.

[2]   When you are ready, in your imagination, call to mind the various prayers of the preceding day or days. Allow the images and words of these prayers to linger and then slowly fade from your consciousness.

- Remember your imaginative contemplation of Luke 2:41-52. Consider the images and feelings evoked in you during your prayer, feeling God's presence in these memories and becoming aware of the specific sensations associated with each image.
- Recall your meditations on Romans 12:9-21 (with Luke 2:52), considering them in the same way as your memories of Luke 2.
- Review your meditation on Romans 14:13-23 (with Luke 2:52) in the same manner as the previous prayers.
- Reminisce on your personal consideration of Luke 2:52 in the same manner as the previous prayers.

As these prayers enter your memory, make a mental note of which senses are most active. You may see an image or a color, hear a sound or a phrase, or smell a scent or a fragrance. You may even taste a flavor or feel a sensation on your skin.

[3]   Then, relax and allow these various memories and experiences to quietly enter and leave your consciousness without being controlled – whether they are clear or diffuse, whether they come quickly or slowly. Linger on the sensory images and memories being evoked in you – noticing any images or colors, any sounds or phrases, any scents or fragrances, any flavors or physical sensations associated with each prayer.

[4]   When you are ready, become completely still and clear your mind of all thoughts and concerns. Allow an image of a special personal space to form in your imagination, a place where you are completely comfortable and alone. Then, watch as God enters that place and forms a small image or object for you that expresses the

thought or awareness that you most need to carry with you into your life.

Reverently pick up the object or image, a reflection of the most important gift you have been given during this time of prayer. Look at it carefully and become aware of the divine presence contained within it. Take a moment to register what it looks like and how it feels in your hand. Then, feel the joy and confidence that comes from touching the presence of God as you accept this gift, offering a short prayer of gratitude while you relax into the pleasure of this moment.

[5]   Then, conclude by allowing these images to fade from your consciousness as you offer this traditional Irish prayer collected by Douglas Hyde in *The Religious Songs of Connacht*:

Confirm me in your love divine,
Smooth for my feet life's rugged way;
My will with yours entwine,
Lest evil lead my steps astray.
Be with my still as guard and guide,
Keep me in holy sanctity,
Let my firm faith on you abide,
From fraud and error hold me free. Amen.

[6]   While your experiences are still fresh in your mind, record the most significant impressions or sensations from this time of prayer in your retreat journal.

3.7 Review of Prayer

[1] Remember your desires during the preceding day or week of prayer. Become aware of the divine presence all around you, offering you inner knowledge of Jesus Christ who became human for you so you may better love and follow him. Recall your desire to experience the growth of Jesus as he becomes aware of his mission – allowing these insights into his development to illumine your own sense of growing purpose.

After bringing these thoughts and desires into your consciousness, ask God once again to fulfill these desires in your own life and in your interactions with others.

[2] Then, take a moment to allow the words, thoughts, and feelings from your prayers during the last day or week to linger – on your mind and in your heart – before asking God to reveal the fulfillment of your deepest desires in these various memories.

• Think about the prayer sequence at the beginning of this day or week. Make a mental note of any words, insights or images that remain particularly significant or meaningful to you.

• Ponder the story, "Brigid Returns to Her Father". Note any words, insights, or images from it that remain particularly significant or meaningful to you.

• Remember your imaginative contemplation of Luke 2:41-52.

– Consider the most powerful images, phrases, or feelings from your prayer. Ask yourself what gifts God gave to you through these moments, perhaps offering you new insights or perhaps affirming an important aspect of your faith. Ask yourself how God may be calling you to change through these moments, being as specific as possible.

– Examine your disposition as you prayed, noting whether prayer came easily or with resistance. Recall the easiest moments in your prayer and any moments of joy you may have experienced. Remember also if you encountered any difficulty opening yourself to God or if you felt any sadness as you prayed. Ask God to help you understand why these feelings surfaced.

– Bring to mind any moments when you added personal elements (e.g., familiar places or people from your life) or connected your prayers to other scriptures or spiritual writings. Ask yourself how these additions helped or hindered you as you prayed. Again, if you do not know why this happened, ask God to help you understand.

- Recall your meditations on Romans 12:9-21 (with Luke 2:52). Then, review your prayer in the same way as your earlier reflection on Luke 2.
- Review your meditation on Romans 14:13-23 (with Luke 2:52) in the same manner as the previous prayers.
- Reminisce on your personal consideration of Luke 2:52 in the same manner as the previous prayers.
- Reflect on the ebb and flow of sensory impressions and feelings that marked your application of the senses. Isolate the most memorable moments and sensory impressions from your prayer and reflect on how God used these moments to give you a particular gift, perhaps offering you new insights or changing you in some way.

[3] Finally, ponder the times when images or feelings from the readings of this day or week surfaced outside these prayer periods. Consider those moments or events in which God's presence or guidance was especially strong as well as any moments when you were struggling. Think about the most memorable aspects of these experiences, asking God to explain their significance.

[4] Take a moment to allow the words, thoughts, and feelings of these prayers to linger on your mind and in your heart. Finally, conclude by allowing these desires to fade from your consciousness as you offer this traditional Irish prayer collected by Douglas Hyde in *The Religious Songs of Connacht*:

> O God, I believe in you; strengthen my belief.
> I trust in you; confirm my trust.
> I love you; double my love.
> I repent that I angered you,
> Increase my repentance.
> Fill you my heart with awe without despair;
> With hope, without over-confidence;
> With piety without infatuation;
> And with joy without excess.
> My God, consent to guide me by your wisdom;
> To constrain me by your right;
> To comfort me by your mercy;
> And to protect me by your power. Amen.

[5] After finishing these prayers, summarize your reflections on the gifts or graces you received during the prayers of this last day or week and record these thoughts in your retreat journal.

4. Jesus' Baptism and the Temptation in the Desert

4.1a Dear Redeemer, Loved And Loving
a prayer of praise for Jesus' redemptive mission

Take a moment to quiet your spirit, becoming completely present to this time and place. Allow all other thoughts and concerns to fall away as you come into the presence of God. Then, when you are ready, begin.

Dear Redeemer, loved and loving,
All my faith I place in you;
your undying truths you teach,
    With unfailing force to me,
    Come in tender love, my Saviour;
    Fill with faith the fragile breast;
Lift my spirit to your comfort,
    Let me find in you sweet rest.

O my loving Lord, I love you
More than all things here below;
    I renounce whate'er offends you,
    Fling it from me as a foe.
Heaven and earth bow down before you,
And in all, your love I see;
    Let me cleave to you forever
    And, dear Lord, cleave you to me.

A Hymn, sung or heard (optional)

Jesus, our heavenly Lord and King,
You did the world's salvation bring,
    And by your death upon the tree,
    Did out of bondage make us free.

Hear now our prayers, O Son of God,
Preserve the gifts your hand bestowed,
    Unto your love all nations draw,
    And bring mankind to know your law.

The tongues of all creation call
And hail your name as Lord of all:

       Their life arose from God's command,
       Their living hope, from your right hand.

The Father's luminous thrones above,
With beating wings and words of love,
       The cherubim and seraphim,
       Sing out to you their ceaseless hymn.

They sing to you in sweet accord,
Their, "Holy, holy, holy Lord";
       Great God of hosts and victories,
       your glory fills the earth and skies.

Read or recite Psalm 42.

Holy Lord,
Under my thoughts may I God-thoughts find.
Half of my sins escape my mind.
       For what I said, or did not say,
       Pardon me, O Lord, I pray.

Read Luke 4: 14-22, aloud or quietly.

O Lord, Jesus the Christ,
If I were in Heaven my harp I would sound
With apostles and angels and saints all around,
       Praising and thanking the Son who is crowned,
       May the poor race of Eve for that heaven be bound!

Holy Lord,
Amid heavenly splendors ranged on high,
To you angelic choirs outcry;
       And bands of bright archangels praise
       Your name in never-ending lays.

Lord, guide me by your blessed light,
And bring me to your heavenly height,
       Enroll me with your blessed throng
       To sing your praise in deathless song.

O Holy Lord,
    God with the Father and the Spirit,
For me is many a snare designed,
To fill my mind with doubts and fears;
    Far from the land of holy saints,
    I dwell within my vale of tears.
Let faith, let hope, let love –
Traits far above the cold world's way –
    With patience, humility, and awe,
    Become my guides from day to day.

I acknowledge, the evil I have done.
From the day of my birth till the day of my death,
    Through the sight of my eyes,
Through the hearing of my ears,
    Through the sayings of my mouth,
Through the thoughts of my heart,
    Through the touch of my hands,
Through the course of my way,
    Through all I said and did not,
Through all I promised and fulfilled not,
    Through all the laws and holy commandments I broke.
I ask even now absolution of you,
    For fear I may have never asked it as was right,
    And that I might not live to ask it again,

O Holy Lord, my King in Heaven,
May you not let my soul stray from you,
May you keep me in a good state,
    May you turn me toward what is good to do,
    May you protect me from dangers, small and great.
May you fill my eyes with tears of repentance,
    So I may avoid the sinner's awful sentence.
May the Grace of the God for ever be with me,
    And whatever my needs, may the Triune God give me.

Select one of the following options for the Lord's Prayer.

Option A

O Jesus Christ,
Lord of heaven and earth,
Help me pray as you yourself taught:
> *"Our Father in heaven,*
> *hallowed be your name.*
> *Your kingdom come.*
> *Your will be done,*
> *on earth as it is in heaven.*
> *Give us this day our daily bread.*
> *And forgive us our debts,*
> *as we also have forgiven our debtors.*
> *And do not bring us to the time of trial,*
> *but rescue us from the evil one."*
> *(Matthew 6: 9-13)*

From the foes of my land,
from the foes of my faith,
From the foes who would us dissever,
> O Lord, preserve me, in life and in death,
> With the Sign of the Cross for ever.
> *For the kingdom, the power, and the glory*
> *are yours now and for ever. Amen.*

Please proceed with "I beseech you, O Lord…," found after Option B.

Option B

O Jesus Christ,
Lord of heaven and earth,
Help me pray as you yourself taught:
> *Our Father in heaven,*
> *hallowed be your name,*
> *your kingdom come,*
> *your will be done,*
> *on earth as in heaven.*
> *Give us today our daily bread.*
> *Forgive us our sins*
> *as we forgive those who sin against us.*
> *Lead us not into temptation*
> *but deliver us from evil.*

From the foes of my land,
from the foes of my faith,
From the foes who would us dissever,
> O Lord, preserve me, in life and in death,
> With the Sign of the Cross for ever.
> *For the kingdom, the power, and the glory*
> *are yours now and for ever. Amen.*

I beseech you, O Lord.
God in Heaven, unsurpassed in power and might;
> Be behind me, Be on my left,
> Be before me, Be on my right!

Against each danger, you are my help;
In distress, upon you I call.
> In dark times, may you sustain me
> And lift me up again when I fall.

Lord over heaven and of earth,
You know my offenses.
> Yet, listening to my pleadings,
> You guide me away from sinful pretenses.

Lord of all creation and the many creatures,
You bestow on me many earthly treasures.
> Revealing love in each life and season,
> You share with me heavenly pleasures.

May you arouse me
In moments both of joy and of strife;
> Most holy Lord, bring me new life!

A Hymn, sung or heard (optional)

O Jesus Christ,
> Lord of heaven and earth,
> You are my riches, my store, my provision,

My star through the years
When troubles rend me,
> Through times of strife and tears,
> Sweet Jesus, defend me.

Behold, the shadows fly the dawn,
Night yields unto the star of day;

So may the shades of vice be gone,
And every stain be washed away.

Hear me, dear Lord, while day is young,
Banish, I pray, all guilt and crime,
And let your love by every tongue
Be sung unto the end of time.

End this time of prayer by taking some time to bring to mind the various ways God shields you from harm or guides you through the world's tumult. Then, when you are ready, conclude by saying:

O Holy Lord, King in Heaven,
I place myself at the edge of your grace,
On the floor of your house myself I place,
And to banish the sin of my heart away,
I lower my knee to you this day.
Through life's torrents of pain may you bring me whole,
And, O Lord Jesus Christ, preserve also my soul. Amen.

4.1b   Preparation for Prayer

Consideration of the Readings

After reciting or prayerfully reading the prayer sequence for this day or week:
- Read about John the Baptist and Jesus in Matthew 3:1-17. Again, make a mental note of each person's appearance and actions during the episode as well as the key elements of the story and its setting. Then, consider any aspects of this story that speak strongly to you before recording these observations in your workbook.
- Read about the temptation of Jesus in Luke 4:1-13, noting the appearance of Jesus and the tempter while observing their actions during the episode as well as the key elements of the story. Then, record any aspects of this story that speak strongly to you.
- Read about the beginning of Jesus' ministry in Luke 4:14-22. Again, note each person's appearance and actions during the episode as well as the key elements of the story and its setting before recording any aspects of this story that speak strongly to you.

Note: You also should consider any aspect of the prayer sequence from this day or week that seemed particularly significant to you.

Contemplation of Your Needs

When you are ready, allow any distractions to fade from your consciousness as you become aware of your desire to live in God's goodness. Feel yourself yearning to properly use the many gifts God has given you, to experience God's continuing care, and to be open to the immense love God shows for you, then:
- Read "Brigid's Father Attempts to Sell Her" (found on page 311). Allow yourself to linger on any thoughts, phrases or images that seem particularly meaningful or significant to your earlier preparations or prayer.
- Pray for your desires in the coming day or week. Ask that the divine presence all around you may be revealed, offering you inner knowledge of Jesus Christ who became human for you so you may better love and follow him. Also ask that, in this day or week of prayer,

you may walk with Jesus as he opens himself to his mission in life – seeing his humility as he approaches John the Baptist as well as his temptations in the wilderness before speaking in the synagogue in Nazareth.
• Conclude by praying that you might experience the same sense of conviction and humility in your own life.
Then, record any significant thoughts, emotions, or reactions from these moments in your workbook.

After this, put your notes aside. Without straining your memory, consider in turn each of the readings for the coming day or week and allow them to take shape in your imagination. Prayerfully ponder how each reading affects you emotionally without overtly thinking about their content, asking God to illuminate the spiritual gifts offered in each reading – quieting your mind and creating a receptive space in yourself to see or hear the response.

Finally, conclude by allowing these desires to fade from your consciousness as you offer this traditional Irish prayer:
> *O God, I believe in you; strengthen my belief.*
> *I trust in you; confirm my trust.*
> *I love you; double my love.*
> *I repent that I angered you,*
> *Increase my repentance.*
> *Fill you my heart with awe without despair;*
> *With hope, without over-confidence;*
> *With piety without infatuation;*
> *And with joy without excess.*
> *My God, consent to guide me by your wisdom;*
> *To constrain me by your right;*
> *To comfort me by your mercy;*
> *And to protect me by your power. Amen.*

Allow these words to linger on your mind and in your heart for a few moments and then, while they are still fresh in your memory, write the most important thoughts, feelings, and desires from this preparatory time in your journal.

4.2 A Contemplation of Matthew 3:1-17

In this contemplation of Matthew 3:1-17, you will see and hear the events surrounding Jesus' baptism by John the Baptist.

[1]　Begin by reading the biblical selection and reviewing your notes on it from your earlier preparations.

[2]　Focus on this specific time and place as you allow all other concerns to fall away. Then, when you are ready, consider the people and place in this moment of prayer.

- Allow an image of Jesus to emerge in your imagination, noting his physical characteristics and mannerisms. Look at what he is wearing or carrying. Ponder this mental image, allowing any other observations about Jesus to form in your mind.

- Observe the people around Jesus, making a mental note of their appearance and demeanor. Look at John the Baptist and his disciples, observing where they are standing. Look at the crowd, noting their various appearances and demeanors. Observe whether people are sitting, standing, or walking. Take a moment to ponder this mental image, allowing other impressions of these men and women to form. Become familiar with the men and women you will encounter during your prayer as well as their behavior.

- Allow yourself to become aware of the location of this moment of prayer, paying attention to its physical characteristics and the arrangement of the people in it. Look around the place and notice more details about it – if it is still and silent or filled with noise, if it has an unusual smell or not, etc. Become familiar with the location of your upcoming prayer.

- Take a moment to remain in this place with these men and women before allowing these images to fade from your consciousness.

[3]　Become aware of your desires during this moment of prayer. Remember your desire to experience the divine presence all around you so you may attain a deep "felt knowledge" of Jesus Christ, who became human for you so you may better love and follow him. Recall your desire that you may walk with Jesus as he opens himself to his mission in life – seeing his humility as he approaches John the Baptist. Also, ask that you might express the same sense of conviction and humility in your own life.

As these desires fill your consciousness, let all other concerns fall aside as you focus on this time and place of prayer.

[4]   Allow the image of Jesus and the crowd to reemerge in your imagination.

- Watch as men and women of all sorts come to John the Baptist and confess their sins. Listen to the sounds of this moment and become comfortable in it. Feel the anticipation of the people around you and share in that enthusiasm.
- Ask God to help you share in these events – either by joining them or by listening quietly to them.
- Watch and listen as John confronts the Pharisees and Sadducees before observing Jesus' baptism and the events around it. You may want to quietly read the passage while remaining prayerfully aware of your mental image of Jesus or you may choose to stay completely within the imagined realm of your prayer. Whichever you choose, know that God will offer you the words from the biblical passage that you need to hear – even if only in fragments.
- Then, allow this image and place to fade from your imagination as you become aware of the phrases and images from this moment which touched you most deeply. Recall the emotions and memories – including any sounds or smells – evoked during your prayer. Allow these seminal aspects of your meditation to linger on your mind and in your heart, noting any special feelings evoked by them.

[5]   When you are ready, become aware of Jesus' presence with you in this moment and have an open and informal conversation about this prayer period and how the passage from Matthew's gospel expresses your own needs or desires – giving space for Jesus to respond or to highlight different aspects from the biblical account and your experiences during this contemplation. Then, gradually allow your thoughts to recede as you focus on God's broader presence in your life and in the world around you.

[6]   Conclude by allowing these desires to fade from your consciousness as you offer this traditional Irish prayer:

> *Confirm me in your love divine,*
> *Smooth for my feet life's rugged way;*
> *My will with yours entwine,*
> *Lest evil lead my steps astray.*
> *Be with my still as guard and guide,*
> *Keep me in holy sanctity,*
> *Let my firm faith on you abide,*
> *From fraud and error hold me free. Amen.*

[7]   Afterward, take 10-15 minutes in a quiet space to reflect on the most significant moments from this time of prayer and record your reflections in your retreat journal.

4.3 A Contemplation of Luke 4:1-13

In this contemplation of Luke 4:1-13, you will see and hear the temptations encountered by Jesus in the desert after his baptism.

[1] Begin by reading the biblical selection and reviewing your notes on it from your earlier preparations.

[2] Focus on this specific time and place as you allow all other concerns to fall away. Then, when you are ready, consider the people and place in this moment of prayer.

- Allow an image of Jesus to emerge in your imagination, noting his physical characteristics and mannerisms. Look at what he is wearing or carrying. Make a note of whether he is sitting, standing, or walking. Ponder this mental image, allowing any other observations about Jesus to form in your mind.

- Watch as an image of the Tempter emerges in your imagination. Take a moment to ponder this mental image, allowing other impressions to form in your mind. Become familiar with the mannerisms and attitudes of this evil being you will encounter during your prayer.

- Allow yourself to become aware of the location of this moment of prayer. Look around the place and notice more details about it – if it is in dim or bright light, if it is still and silent or filled with noise, if it has an unusual smell or not, etc. Become familiar with the location of your upcoming prayer.

- Take a moment to remain in this place before allowing these images to fade from your consciousness.

[3] Become aware of your desires during this moment of prayer. Remember your desire to experience the divine presence all around you so you may attain a deep "felt knowledge" of Jesus Christ, who became human for you so you may better love and follow him. Recall your desire that you may walk with Jesus as he opens himself to his mission in life – seeing his humility as he faces temptations in the wilderness. Also, ask that you might express the same sense of conviction and humility in your own life.

As these desires fill your consciousness, let all other concerns fall aside as you focus on this time and place of prayer.

[4] Allow the image of Jesus to reemerge in your imagination.

- Watch and listen as Jesus prays while alone in the wilderness. Focus your attention on Jesus, noting his physical appearance and his

demeanor. Listen to the sounds of this moment and become comfortable with them.
- Ask God to help you share in Jesus' prayers and experiences – either by joining him or by listening quietly to him.
- See and hear the appearance of the Tempter, observing its physical appearance and attitude toward Jesus. Become aware of how this appearance affects Jesus and his demeanor.
- Then, watch and listen as Jesus confronts the Tempter. You may want to quietly read the passage while remaining prayerfully aware of your mental image of Jesus and the Tempter or you may choose to stay completely within the imagined realm of your prayer. Whichever you choose, know that God will offer you the words from the biblical passage that you need to hear – even if only in fragments.
- Afterward, allow this image and place to fade from your imagination as you become aware of the phrases and images from this moment which touched you most deeply. Recall the emotions and memories – including any sounds or smells – evoked during your prayer. Allow these seminal aspects of your meditation to linger on your mind and in your heart, noting any special feelings evoked by them.

[5] When you are ready, become aware of Jesus' presence with you in this moment and have an open and informal conversation about this prayer period and how the passage from Luke's gospel expresses your own needs or desires – giving space for Jesus to respond or to highlight different aspects from the biblical account and your experiences during this contemplation. Then, gradually allow your thoughts to recede as you focus on God's broader presence in your life and in the world around you.

[6] Conclude by allowing these desires to fade from your consciousness as you offer this traditional Irish prayer:

> *Confirm me in your love divine,*
> *Smooth for my feet life's rugged way;*
> *My will with yours entwine,*
> *Lest evil lead my steps astray.*
> *Be with my still as guard and guide,*
> *Keep me in holy sanctity,*
> *Let my firm faith on you abide,*
> *From fraud and error hold me free. Amen.*

[7]   Afterward, take 10-15 minutes in a quiet space to reflect on the most significant moments from this time of prayer and record your reflections in your retreat journal.

4.4 A Contemplation of Luke 4:14-22

In this contemplation of Luke 4:14-22, you will see and hear Jesus begin his ministry in Galilee.

[1] Begin by reading the biblical selection and reviewing your notes on it from your earlier preparations.

[2] Focus on this specific time and place as you allow all other concerns to fall away. Then, when you are ready, consider the people and place in this moment of prayer.

• Allow an image of Jesus to emerge in your imagination, noting his physical characteristics and mannerisms. Look at what he is wearing or carrying. Make a note of whether he is sitting, standing, or walking. Ponder this mental image, allowing any other observations about Jesus to form in your mind.

• Note how many people are with Jesus, making a mental note of their appearance and demeanor. Look at Jesus' disciples, observing where they are standing and how they behave toward Jesus. Look at the crowd, noting their attitude and behavior toward Jesus. Observe whether the people are sitting, standing, or walking. Take a moment to ponder this mental image, allowing other impressions of these men and women to form. Become familiar with the men and women you will encounter during your prayer as well as their behavior.

• Allow yourself to become aware of the location of this moment of prayer. Observe the synagogue in Nazareth, paying attention to its physical characteristics and the arrangement of the people in it. Look around the place and notice more details about it – if it is in dim or bright light, if it is still and silent or filled with noise, if it has an unusual smell or not, etc. Become familiar with the location of your upcoming prayer.

• Take a moment to remain in this place with these men and women before allowing these images to fade from your consciousness.

[3] Become aware of your desires during this moment of prayer. Remember your desire to experience the divine presence all around you so you may attain a deep "felt knowledge" of Jesus Christ, who became human for you so you may better love and follow him. Recall your desire that you may walk with Jesus as he opens himself to his mission in life – seeing his humility as he speaks in the synagogue in Nazareth. Also, ask that you might express the same sense of conviction and humility in your own life.

As these desires fill your consciousness, let all other concerns fall aside as you focus on this time and place of prayer.

[4] Allow the image of Jesus to reemerge in your imagination as he enters the synagogue.

- As you hear Jesus begin to calm the crowd, ask God to help you share in this experience – either by joining these events or by listening quietly to them. Focus your attention on Jesus, noting his physical appearance and his demeanor.

- Watch as the group assembles around Jesus. Listen to the sounds of this moment and become comfortable as you prepare to hear Jesus speak. Feel the anticipation of the people around you and share in that enthusiasm.

- Then, watch and listen as Jesus preaches in Nazareth and observe the reactions of those around him. At this point you may want to quietly read the passage while remaining prayerfully aware of your mental image of Jesus or you may choose to stay completely within the imagined realm of your prayer. Whichever you choose, know that God will offer you the words from the biblical passage that you need to hear – even if only in fragments.

- After Jesus finishes speaking, allow his image and this place to fade from your imagination as you become aware of the phrases and images from this moment which touched you most deeply. Recall the emotions and memories – including any sounds or smells – evoked during your prayer. Allow these seminal aspects of your meditation to linger on your mind and in your heart, noting any special feelings evoked by them.

[5] When you are ready, become aware of Jesus' presence with you in this moment and have an open and informal conversation about this prayer period and how the passage from Luke's gospel expresses your own needs or desires – giving space for Jesus to respond or to highlight different aspects from the biblical account and your experiences during this contemplation. Then, gradually allow your thoughts to recede as you focus on God's broader presence in your life and in the world around you.

[6] Conclude by allowing these desires to fade from your consciousness as you offer this traditional Irish prayer:

> *Confirm me in your love divine,*
> *Smooth for my feet life's rugged way;*
> *My will with yours entwine,*
> *Lest evil lead my steps astray.*

> *Be with my still as guard and guide,*
> *Keep me in holy sanctity,*
> *Let my firm faith on you abide,*
> *From fraud and error hold me free. Amen.*

[7] Afterward, take 10-15 minutes in a quiet space to reflect on the most significant moments from this time of prayer and record your reflections in your retreat journal.

4.5   A Meditation on Luke 4:14-22

In this meditation on Luke 4:14-22, you will see and hear Saint Brigid teaching her disciples about the redeemed world promised by Christ.

[1]   Begin by reading the biblical selection and reviewing your notes on it from your earlier preparations.

[2]   Focus on this specific time and place as you allow all other concerns to fall away. Then, when you are ready, consider the people and place in this moment of prayer.

• Allow an image of Brigid to emerge in your imagination, noting her physical characteristics and mannerisms. Look at what she is wearing or carrying. Make a note of whether she is sitting, standing, or walking. Ponder this mental image, allowing any other observations about Brigid to form in your mind.

• Observe the people around Saint Brigid, becoming aware of their appearance and demeanor. Observe whether they are sitting, standing, or walking. Take a moment to ponder this mental image, allowing other impressions of these men and women to form.

• Allow yourself to become aware of the location of this moment of prayer. Observe its physical characteristics and the arrangement of the people in it. Look around the place and notice more details about it – if it is in dim or bright light, if it is still and silent or filled with noise, if it has an unusual smell or not, etc.

• Take a moment to remain in this place with these men and women before allowing these images to fade from your consciousness.

[3]   Become aware of your desires during this moment of prayer. Remember your desire to experience the divine presence all around you so you may attain a deep "felt knowledge" of Jesus Christ, who became human for you so you may better love and follow him. Recall your desire that you may walk with Jesus as he opened himself to his mission in life so that you might express the same sense of conviction and humility in your own life.

As these desires fill your consciousness, let all other concerns fall aside as you focus on this time and place of prayer.

[4]   Allow the image of Saint Brigid and her disciples to reemerge in your imagination.

• Watch as the group assembles around Brigid. Listen to the sounds of this moment and become comfortable as you prepare to hear

Brigid speak. Feel the anticipation of the people around you and share in that enthusiasm.

- As you hear Brigid invite her companions to listen, ask God to help you share in their conversation – either by joining them or by listening quietly to them. Focus your attention on Saint Brigid, noting her physical appearance and her demeanor.

- Then, relying on the memories from your earlier prayer, watch and listen as Brigid tells the story of Jesus preaching in Nazareth at the beginning of his public ministry while also discussing the divine promise expressed in the passage from Isaiah read by Jesus. You may want to quietly read the passage while remaining prayerfully aware of your mental image or you may choose to stay completely within the imagined realm of your prayer. Whichever you choose, know that God will offer you the words from the biblical passage that you need to hear – even if only in fragments.

- Remember that Brigid is speaking to men and women anxiously expecting God to transform their lives. Remember she also is speaking to you.

- After Brigid finishes speaking, allow her image and this place to fade from your imagination as you become aware of the phrases and images from this moment which touched you most deeply. Recall the emotions and memories – including any sounds or smells – evoked during your prayer. Allow these seminal aspects of your meditation to linger on your mind and in your heart, noting any special feelings evoked by them.

[5] When you are ready, become aware of Jesus' presence with you in this moment and have an open and informal conversation about this prayer period and how the passage from Luke's gospel expresses your own needs or desires – giving space for Jesus to respond or to highlight different aspects from the biblical account and your experiences during this contemplation. Then, gradually allow your thoughts to recede as you focus on God's broader presence in your life and in the world around you.

[6] Conclude by allowing these desires to fade from your consciousness as you offer this traditional Irish prayer:

Confirm me in your love divine,
Smooth for my feet life's rugged way;
My will with yours entwine,
Lest evil lead my steps astray.
Be with my still as guard and guide,

Keep me in holy sanctity,
Let my firm faith on you abide,
From fraud and error hold me free. Amen.

[7]   Afterward, take 10-15 minutes in a quiet space to reflect on the most significant moments from your prayer and record your reflections in your retreat journal.

4.6 An Application of the Senses

[1] Become aware of your prayerful desires during this day or week. Bring to mind your desire to experience an inner knowledge of Jesus Christ who became human for you so you may better love and follow him. Also ask that, in this day or week of prayer, you may walk with Jesus as he opens himself to his mission in life – seeing his humility as he approaches John the Baptist as well as his temptations in the desert before speaking in the synagogue in Nazareth.

[2] When you are ready, call to mind the various prayers of the preceding day or days. Allow the images and words of these prayers to linger and then slowly fade from your consciousness.

- Remember your imaginative contemplation of Matthew 3:1-17. Consider the images and feelings evoked in you during your prayer, feeling God's presence in these memories and becoming aware of the specific sensations associated with each image.

- Recall your imaginative contemplation of Luke 4:1-13, considering it in the same way as the memories of your meditation on Matthew 3.

- Review your imaginative contemplations of Luke 4:14-22 in the same manner as the previous prayers.

Make a mental note of which senses are most active. You may see an image or a color, hear a sound or a phrase, or smell a scent or a fragrance. You may even taste a flavor or feel a sensation on your skin.

[3] Then, relax and allow these various memories and experiences to quietly enter and leave your consciousness without being controlled. Linger on the sensory images and memories being evoked in you – noticing any images or colors, any sounds or phrases, any scents or fragrances, any flavors or physical sensations associated with each prayer.

[4] When you are ready, become completely still and clear your mind of all thoughts and concerns. Allow an image of a special personal space to form in your imagination. Then, watch as God enters that place and forms a small image or object for you that expresses the thought or awareness that you most need to carry with you into your life.

Reverently pick up the object or image, a reflection of the most important gift you have been given during this time of prayer. Look at it carefully and become aware of the divine presence contained within it. Take a moment to register what it looks like and how it feels in your hand. Then, feel the joy and confidence that comes from touching the presence of God as you accept this gift, offering a short prayer of gratitude while you relax into the pleasure of this moment.

[5]   Then, conclude by allowing these images to fade from your consciousness as you offer this traditional Irish prayer:

> *Confirm me in your love divine,*
> *Smooth for my feet life's rugged way;*
> *My will with yours entwine,*
> *Lest evil lead my steps astray.*
> *Be with my still as guard and guide,*
> *Keep me in holy sanctity,*
> *Let my firm faith on you abide,*
> *From fraud and error hold me free. Amen.*

[6]   While your experiences are still fresh in your mind, record the most significant impressions or sensations from this time of prayer in your retreat journal.

4.7 Review of Prayer

[1] Remember your desires during the preceding day or week of prayer. Become aware of the divine presence all around you, offering you inner knowledge of Jesus Christ who became human for you so you may better love and follow him. Recall your desire to walk with Jesus as he opens himself to his mission in life – seeing his humility as he approaches John the Baptist as well as his temptations in the desert before speaking in the synagogue in Nazareth.

Ask God once again to fulfill these desires in your own life and in your interactions with others.

[2] Then, take a moment to allow the words, thoughts, and feelings from your prayers during the last day or week to linger before asking God to reveal the fulfillment of your deepest desires in these various memories.

• Think about the prayer sequence at the beginning of this day or week. Make a mental note of any words, insights or images that remain particularly significant or meaningful to you.

• Ponder the story, "Brigid's Father Attempts to Sell Her". Note any words, insights, or images from it that remain particularly significant or meaningful to you.

• Remember your imaginative contemplation of Matthew 3:1-17.

– Consider the most powerful images, phrases, or feelings from your prayer. Ask yourself what gifts God gave to you through these moments, perhaps offering you new insights or perhaps affirming an important aspect of your faith. Ask yourself how God may be calling you to change through these moments, being as specific as possible.

– Examine your disposition as you prayed, noting whether prayer came easily or with resistance. Recall the easiest moments in your prayer and any moments of joy you may have experienced. Remember also if you encountered any difficulty opening yourself to God or if you felt any sadness as you prayed. Ask God to help you understand why these feelings surfaced.

– Bring to mind any moments when you added personal elements (e.g., familiar places or people from your life) or connected your prayers to other scriptures or spiritual writings. Ask yourself how these additions helped or hindered you as you prayed. Again, if you do not know why this happened, ask God to help you understand.

- Recall imaginative contemplation of your imaginative contemplation of Luke 4:1-13. Then, review your prayer in the same way as your earlier reflection on Matthew 3.
- Review your imaginative contemplations of Luke 4:14-22 in the same manner as the previous prayers.
- Reflect on the ebb and flow of sensory impressions and feelings that marked your application of the senses. Isolate the most memorable moments and sensory impressions from your prayer and reflect on how God used these moments to give you a particular gift.

[3] Finally, ponder the times when images or feelings from the readings of this day or week surfaced outside these prayer periods. Consider those moments or events in which God's presence or guidance was especially strong as well as any moments when you were struggling. Think about the most memorable aspects of these experiences, asking God to explain their significance.

[4] Take a moment to allow the words, thoughts, and feelings of these prayers to linger on your mind and in your heart. Finally, conclude by allowing these desires to fade from your consciousness as you offer this traditional Irish prayer:

> *O God, I believe in you; strengthen my belief.*
> *I trust in you; confirm my trust.*
> *I love you; double my love.*
> *I repent that I angered you,*
> *Increase my repentance.*
> *Fill you my heart with awe without despair;*
> *With hope, without over-confidence;*
> *With piety without infatuation;*
> *And with joy without excess.*
> *My God, consent to guide me by your wisdom;*
> *To constrain me by your right;*
> *To comfort me by your mercy;*
> *And to protect me by your power. Amen.*

[5] After finishing these prayers, summarize your reflections on the gifts or graces you received during the prayers of this last day or week and record these thoughts in your retreat journal.

5. The Call of Christ

5.1a   Hear Me, Christ, My King
a humble petition to enter God's Kingdom

Take a moment to quiet your spirit, becoming completely present to this time and place. Allow all other thoughts and concerns to fall away as you come into the presence of God. Then, when you are ready, begin.

Hear me, Christ, my King,
      Hear you the praise I bring,
      And lead me on;
In tender mercy bend,
My soul from harm defend,
      And let my hopes ascend
      Unto your throne.

Upon the road of life
Keep me from stain and strife
In your sweet care;
      Extend your right hand, Lord,
      Your gracious aid afford,
Be you my watch and ward;
      Lord, hear my prayer.

A Hymn, sung or heard (optional)

'Til the Trinity thought, and thinking pitied
The race that was lying beneath the rod,
      And the Son of Grace came down through space
      To the womb of Mary Mother of God.

If your neighbour offend you, O passion's slave,
You will not forgive him, through spite and pride,
      Yet see how the Son of Grace forgave
      The person who pierced God's holy side.

The heart that abhors its earthly neighbour
As a brimstone lump in the breast shall lie,
      And the perjured tongue, that is loosely hung,
      Like a salted flame in the mouth shall fry.

At the hour of doom, on the awful Mount
We all must gather beneath God's eye,
    And the priest for his flock give a sharp account,
    And account for the tares in his wheat and rye.

Is it not little we think about the grace of the Son,
And how he was tortured in our place
    And so forgiveness of the sin of Adam won –
    Ending humankind's sorrowful disgrace.

Read or recite Psalm 63.

Holy Lord,
Under my thoughts may I God-thoughts find.
Half of my sins escape my mind.
    For what I said, or did not say,
    Pardon me, O Lord, I pray.

Read John 1: 35-51, aloud or quietly.

O Lord, Jesus the Christ,
If I were in Heaven my harp I would sound
With apostles and angels and saints all around,
    Praising and thanking the Son who is crowned,
    May the poor race of Eve for that heaven be bound!

Holy Lord,
Glory and honour and lasting praise,
Through endless days to the Son of God,
    You have bought your glory, dear Lord,
    With sweat of brow and fume of blood.

Through toilsome years thrice ten and three,
Each day to you was the poor man's day,
    Teaching and learning all his needs,
    On the road that leads the heavenly way.

O Holy Lord,
    God with the Father and the Spirit,

For me is many a snare designed,
To fill my mind with doubts and fears;
> Far from the land of holy saints,
> I dwell within my vale of tears.
Let faith, let hope, let love –
Traits far above the cold world's way –
> With patience, humility, and awe,
> Become my guides from day to day.

I acknowledge, the evil I have done.
From the day of my birth till the day of my death,
> Through the sight of my eyes,
Through the hearing of my ears,
> Through the sayings of my mouth,
Through the thoughts of my heart,
> Through the touch of my hands,
Through the course of my way,
> Through all I said and did not,
Through all I promised and fulfilled not,
> Through all the laws and holy commandments I broke.
I ask even now absolution of you,
> For fear I may have never asked it as was right,
> And that I might not live to ask it again,

O Holy Lord, my King in Heaven,
May you not let my soul stray from you,
May you keep me in a good state,
> May you turn me toward what is good to do,
> May you protect me from dangers, small and great.
May you fill my eyes with tears of repentance,
> So I may avoid the sinner's awful sentence.
May the Grace of the God for ever be with me,
> And whatever my needs, may the Triune God give me.

Select one of the following options for the Lord's Prayer.

Option A

O Jesus Christ,
Lord of heaven and earth,

Help me pray as you yourself taught:
> "Our Father in heaven,
> hallowed be your name.
> Your kingdom come.
> Your will be done,
> on earth as it is in heaven.
> Give us this day our daily bread.
> And forgive us our debts,
> as we also have forgiven our debtors.
> And do not bring us to the time of trial,
> but rescue us from the evil one."
> (Matthew 6: 9-13)

From the foes of my land,
from the foes of my faith,
From the foes who would us dissever,
> O Lord, preserve me, in life and in death,
> With the Sign of the Cross for ever.
> *For the kingdom, the power, and the glory*
> *are yours now and for ever. Amen.*

Please proceed with "I beseech you, O Lord…," found after Option B.

Option B

O Jesus Christ,
Lord of heaven and earth,
Help me pray as you yourself taught:
> *Our Father in heaven,*
> *hallowed be your name,*
> *your kingdom come,*
> *your will be done,*
> *on earth as in heaven.*
> *Give us today our daily bread.*
> *Forgive us our sins*
> *as we forgive those who sin against us.*
> *Lead us not into temptation*
> *but deliver us from evil.*

From the foes of my land,
from the foes of my faith,

From the foes who would us dissever,
> O Lord, preserve me, in life and in death,
> With the Sign of the Cross for ever.
> *For the kingdom, the power, and the glory*
> *are yours now and for ever. Amen.*

I beseech you, O Lord.
God in Heaven, unsurpassed in power and might;
> Be behind me, Be on my left,
> Be before me, Be on my right!
Against each danger, you are my help;
In distress, upon you I call.
> In dark times, may you sustain me
> And lift me up again when I fall.
Lord over heaven and of earth,
You know my offenses.
> Yet, listening to my pleadings,
> You guide me away from sinful pretenses.
Lord of all creation and the many creatures,
You bestow on me many earthly treasures.
> Revealing love in each life and season,
> You share with me heavenly pleasures.
May you arouse me
In moments both of joy and of strife;
> Most holy Lord, bring me new life!

A Hymn, sung or heard (optional)

O Jesus Christ,
> Lord of heaven and earth,
> You are my riches, my store, my provision,
My star through the years
When troubles rend me,
> Through times of strife and tears,
> Sweet Jesus, defend me.

All lingering shadows from my mind expel,
With dreams and motions that in darkness dwell,
> My bosom purge of all that brings stain,
> And bathe my spirit in your crystal well.

Within my soul let saving faith find place,
Let hope draw radiance from your tender face.
> And let my heart in brotherhood expand
> The love of God and neighbour; grant this grace.

> ***End this time of prayer by taking some time to bring to mind the various ways God shields you from harm or guides you through the world's tumult. Then, when you are ready, conclude by saying:***

O Holy Lord, King in Heaven,
I place myself at the edge of your grace,
> On the floor of your house myself I place,
And to banish the sin of my heart away,
> I lower my knee to you this day.
Through life's torrents of pain may you bring me whole,
> And, O Lord Jesus Christ, preserve also my soul. Amen.

5.1b Preparation for Prayer

Consideration of the Readings

After reciting or prayerfully reading the prayer sequence for this day or week:

- Read about the call of Jesus' first disciples in John 1:35-51 and Luke 5:5-11. Again, make a mental note of each person's appearance and actions during the episode as well as the key elements of the story and its setting. Then, consider any aspects of this story that speak strongly to you before recording these observations in your workbook.
- Read about Jesus' call to Levi in Luke 5:27-38. Again, note each person's appearance and actions during the episode as well as the key elements of the story and its setting before recording any aspects of this story that speak strongly to you.

Note: You also should consider any aspect of the prayer sequence from this day or week that seemed particularly significant to you.

Contemplation of Your Needs

When you are ready, allow any distractions to fade from your consciousness as you become aware of your desire to live in God's goodness. Feel yourself yearning to properly use the many gifts God has given you, to experience God's continuing care, and to be open to the immense love God shows for you, then:

- Read "Brigid and the Religious Scholar" (found on page 312). Allow yourself to linger on any thoughts, phrases or images that seem particularly meaningful or significant to your earlier preparations or prayer.
- Pray for your desires in the coming day or week. Ask that the divine presence all around you may be revealed, offering you inner knowledge of Jesus Christ who became human for you so you may better love and follow him. Also ask that, in this day or week of prayer, you may witness the many different men and women called to follow as Jesus' disciples and the unique ways in which each of them is called.

- Conclude by praying for a greater awareness of Christ's call in your life and the specific ways in which you have been asked to follow him.

Then, record any significant thoughts, emotions, or reactions from these moments in your workbook.

After this, put your notes aside. Without straining your memory, consider in turn each of the readings for the coming day or week and allow them to take shape in your imagination. Prayerfully ponder how each reading affects you emotionally without overtly thinking about their content, asking God to illuminate the spiritual gifts offered in each reading – quieting your mind and creating a receptive space in yourself to see or hear the response.

Finally, conclude by allowing these desires to fade from your consciousness as you offer this traditional Irish prayer:

O God, I believe in you; strengthen my belief.
I trust in you; confirm my trust.
I love you; double my love.
I repent that I angered you,
Increase my repentance.
Fill you my heart with awe without despair;
With hope, without over-confidence;
With piety without infatuation;
And with joy without excess.
My God, consent to guide me by your wisdom;
To constrain me by your right;
To comfort me by your mercy;
And to protect me by your power. Amen.

Allow these words to linger on your mind and in your heart for a few moments and then, while they are still fresh in your memory, write the most important thoughts, feelings, and desires from this preparatory time in your journal.

5.2   A Contemplation of John 1:35-51

In this contemplation of John 1:35-51, you will see and hear Jesus invite his first disciples to join him in his ministry.

[1]   Begin by reading the biblical selection and reviewing your notes on it.

[2]   Then, focus on this specific time and place as you allow all other concerns to fall away before considering the people and place in this moment of prayer.

• Allow an image of Jesus to emerge in your imagination, noting his physical characteristics and mannerisms. Look at what he is wearing or carrying. Make a note of whether he is sitting, standing, or walking. Ponder this mental image, allowing any other observations about Jesus to form in your mind.

• Observe the men and women around Jesus, especially John the Baptist and his disciples. Make a mental note of their appearance and demeanor, noting where they are standing and how they behave toward Jesus. Make a mental note of whether the people are sitting, standing, or walking. Take a moment to ponder this mental image, allowing other impressions of these men and women to form. Become familiar with the men and women you will encounter during your prayer as well as their behavior.

• Allow yourself to become aware of the location of this moment of prayer, paying attention to its physical characteristics and the arrangement of the people in it. Look around the place and notice more details about it – if it is still and silent or filled with noise, if it has an unusual smell or not, etc. Become familiar with the location of your upcoming prayer.

• Take a moment to remain in this place with these people before allowing these images to fade from your consciousness.

[3]   Become aware of your desires during this moment of prayer. Remember your desire to experience the divine presence all around you so you may attain a deep "felt knowledge" of Jesus Christ, who became human for you so you may better love and follow him. Recall your desire that, in this day or week of prayer, you may witness the many different men and women called to follow as Jesus' disciples and the unique ways in which each of them is called. Also, ask for a greater awareness of Christ's call in your life and the specific ways in which you have been asked to follow him.

As these desires fill your consciousness, let all other concerns fall aside as you focus on this time and place of prayer.

[4]　　Allow the image of Jesus and the crowd to reemerge in your imagination.

• Watch as John the Baptist becomes aware of Jesus and speaks about him as the "Lamb of God". Listen to the sounds of this moment and become comfortable in it. Feel John's anticipation in this moment and share in his enthusiasm.

• Ask God to help you share in this moment – either by joining in it or by listening quietly to it. Focus your attention on Jesus, noting his physical appearance and his demeanor.

• Then, watch and listen as Jesus meets and calls his first disciples. You may want to quietly read the passage while remaining prayerfully aware of your mental image of Jesus or you may choose to stay completely within the imagined realm of your prayer. Whichever you choose, know that God will offer you the words from the biblical passage that you need to hear – even if only in fragments.

• Afterward, allow this image and this place to fade from your imagination as you become aware of the phrases and images from this moment which touched you most deeply. Recall the emotions and memories – including any sounds or smells – evoked during your prayer. Allow these seminal aspects of your meditation to linger on your mind and in your heart, noting any special feelings evoked by them.

[5]　　When you are ready, become aware of Jesus' presence with you in this moment and have an open and informal conversation about this prayer period and how the passage from John's gospel expresses your own needs or desires as he calls you to follow him – giving space for Jesus to respond or to highlight different aspects from the biblical account and your experiences during this contemplation. Then, gradually allow your thoughts to recede as you focus on God's broader presence in your life and in the world around you.

[6]　　Conclude by allowing these desires to fade from your consciousness as you offer this traditional Irish prayer:

Confirm me in your love divine,
Smooth for my feet life's rugged way;
My will with yours entwine,
Lest evil lead my steps astray.
Be with my still as guard and guide,
Keep me in holy sanctity,

Let my firm faith on you abide,
From fraud and error hold me free. Amen.

[7]   Afterward, take 10-15 minutes in a quiet space to reflect on the most significant moments from this time of prayer and record your reflections in your journal.

5.3 A Contemplation of Luke 5:5-11

In this contemplation of Luke 5:5-11, you again will see and hear Jesus invite his first disciples to join him in his ministry.

[1] Begin by reading the biblical selection and reviewing your notes on it.

[2] Then, focus on this specific time and place as you allow all other concerns to fall away before considering the people and place in this moment of prayer.

- Allow an image of Jesus to emerge in your imagination, noting his physical characteristics and mannerisms. Look at what he is wearing or carrying. Make a note of whether he is sitting, standing, or walking. Ponder this mental image, allowing any other observations about Jesus to form in your mind.

- Observe the people around Jesus, especially Simon the fisherman. Make a mental note of their appearance and demeanor, noting where they are standing and how they behave toward Jesus. Make a mental note of whether the people are sitting, standing, or walking. Take a moment to ponder this mental image, allowing other impressions of these men and women to form. Become familiar with the men and women you will encounter during your prayer as well as their behavior.

- Allow yourself to become aware of the location of this moment of prayer, paying attention to its physical characteristics and the arrangement of the people in it. Look around the place and notice more details about it – if it is still and silent or filled with noise, if it has an unusual smell or not, etc. Become familiar with the location of your upcoming prayer.

- Take a moment to remain in this place with these men and women before allowing these images to fade from your consciousness.

[3] Become aware of your desires during this moment of prayer. Remember your desire to experience the divine presence all around you so you may attain a deep "felt knowledge" of Jesus Christ, who became human for you so you may better love and follow him. Recall your desire that, in this day or week of prayer, you may witness the many different men and women called to follow as Jesus' disciples and the unique ways in which each of them is called. Also, ask for a greater awareness of Christ's call in your life and the specific ways in which you have been asked to follow him.

As these desires fill your consciousness, let all other concerns fall aside as you focus on this time and place of prayer.

[4] Allow the image of Jesus and the crowd to reemerge in your imagination.

- Watch as a crowd gathers around Jesus on the shore of Lake Gennesaret. Feel their anticipation as they wait to hear Jesus speak and share in their enthusiasm.

- Ask God to help you share in this moment – either by joining in it or by listening quietly to it. Focus your attention on Jesus, noting his physical appearance and his demeanor.

- Then, watch and listen as Jesus preaches to the crowd from a boat before calling Simon, James, and John to be his disciples. You may want to quietly read the passage while remaining prayerfully aware of your mental image of Jesus or you may choose to stay completely within the imagined realm of your prayer. Whichever you choose, know that God will offer you the words from the biblical passage that you need to hear – even if only in fragments.

- Afterward, allow this image and this place to fade from your imagination as you become aware of the phrases and images from this moment which touched you most deeply. Recall the emotions and memories – including any sounds or smells – evoked during your prayer. Allow these seminal aspects of your meditation to linger on your mind and in your heart, noting any special feelings evoked by them.

[5] When you are ready, become aware of Jesus' presence with you in this moment and have an open and informal conversation about this prayer period and how the passage from Luke's gospel expresses your own needs or desires as he calls you to follow him – giving space for Jesus to respond or to highlight different aspects from the biblical account and your experiences during this contemplation. Then, gradually allow your thoughts to recede as you focus on God's broader presence in your life and in the world around you.

[6] Conclude by allowing these desires to fade from your consciousness as you offer this traditional Irish prayer:

Confirm me in your love divine,
Smooth for my feet life's rugged way;
My will with yours entwine,
Lest evil lead my steps astray.
Be with my still as guard and guide,
Keep me in holy sanctity,

Let my firm faith on you abide,
From fraud and error hold me free. Amen.

[7] Afterward, take 10-15 minutes in a quiet space to reflect on the most significant moments from this time of prayer and record your reflections in your journal.

5.4 A Contemplation of Luke 5:27-38

In this contemplation of Luke 5:27-38, you will see and hear Jesus invite Levi to join him in his ministry as well as encounter the Pharisees' hostility toward Jesus.

[1] Begin by reading the biblical selection and reviewing your notes on it.

[2] Then, focus on this specific time and place as you allow all other concerns to fall away before considering the people and place in this moment of prayer.

- Allow an image of Jesus to emerge in your imagination, noting his physical characteristics and mannerisms. Look at what he is wearing or carrying. Make a note of whether he is sitting, standing, or walking. Ponder this mental image, allowing any other observations about Jesus to form in your mind.

- Observe the people around Jesus, especially Levi the tax collector and the Pharisees. Make a mental note of their appearance and demeanor, noting where they are standing and how they behave toward Jesus. Make a mental note of whether the people are sitting, standing, or walking. Take a moment to ponder this mental image, allowing other impressions of these men and women to form. Become familiar with the men and women you will encounter during your prayer as well as their behavior.

- Allow yourself to become aware of the location of this moment of prayer, paying attention to its physical characteristics and the arrangement of the people in it. Look around the place and notice more details about it – if it is still and silent or filled with noise, if it has an unusual smell or not, etc. Become familiar with the location of your upcoming prayer.

- Take a moment to remain in this place with these men and women before allowing these images to fade from your consciousness.

[3] Become aware of your desires during this moment of prayer. Remember your desire to experience the divine presence all around you so you may attain a deep "felt knowledge" of Jesus Christ, who became human for you so you may better love and follow him. Recall your desire that, in this day or week of prayer, you may witness the many different people called to follow as Jesus' disciples and the unique ways in which each of them is called. Also, ask for a greater

awareness of Christ's call in your life and the specific ways in which you have been asked to follow him.

As these desires fill your consciousness, let all other concerns fall aside as you focus on this time and place of prayer.

[4] Allow the image of Jesus and the crowd to reemerge in your imagination.

- Watch as Jesus instructs Levi to follow him. Feel the joy Levi felt as he left everything to follow Jesus and share in his enthusiasm.

- Ask God to help you share in this experience – either by joining these events or by listening quietly to them. Focus your attention on Jesus, noting his physical appearance and his demeanor.

- Then, watch and listen as Jesus calls Levi to be his disciple, much to the chagrin of the Pharisees. You may want to quietly read the passage while remaining prayerfully aware of your mental image of Jesus or you may choose to stay completely within the imagined realm of your prayer. Whichever you choose, know that God will offer you the words from the biblical passage that you need to hear – even if only in fragments.

- Look around as Jesus speaks to Levi and the Pharisees. See the different reactions to Jesus, becoming aware of feelings both Levi and the Pharisees as well as how they behave toward Jesus and one another.

- Remember that Jesus also is speaking to you as he invites these his first disciples to follow a new and unknown path of love and service, a journey that will require faith and perseverance.

- Afterward, allow this image and this place to fade from your imagination as you become aware of the phrases and images from this moment which touched you most deeply. Recall the emotions and memories – including any sounds or smells – evoked during your prayer. Allow these seminal aspects of your meditation to linger on your mind and in your heart, noting any special feelings evoked by them.

[5] When you are ready, become aware of Jesus' presence with you in this moment and have an open and informal conversation about this prayer period and how the passage from Luke's gospel expresses your own needs or desires as he calls you to follow him – giving space for Jesus to respond or to highlight different aspects from the biblical account and your experiences during this contemplation. Then, gradually allow your thoughts to recede as you focus on God's broader presence in your life and in the world around you.

[6]   Conclude by allowing these desires to fade from your consciousness as you offer this traditional Irish prayer:
> *Confirm me in your love divine,*
> *Smooth for my feet life's rugged way;*
> *My will with yours entwine,*
> *Lest evil lead my steps astray.*
> *Be with my still as guard and guide,*
> *Keep me in holy sanctity,*
> *Let my firm faith on you abide,*
> *From fraud and error hold me free. Amen.*

[7]   Afterward, take 10-15 minutes in a quiet space to reflect on the most significant moments from this time of prayer and record your reflections in your journal.

5.5 A Meditation on Luke 5:27-38

In this meditation on Luke 5:27-38, you will see and hear Saint Brigid teach her disciples about the liberating effect of Christ's call follow him and the resistance they might encounter from others.

[1] Begin by reading the biblical selection and reviewing your notes on it.

[2] Then, focus on this specific time and place as you allow all other concerns to fall away before considering the people and place in this moment of prayer.

- Allow an image of Brigid to emerge in your imagination, noting her physical characteristics and mannerisms. Look at what she is wearing or carrying. Make a note of whether she is sitting, standing, or walking. Ponder this mental image, allowing any other observations about Brigid to form in your mind.

- Observe the people around Saint Brigid, becoming aware of their appearance and demeanor. Observe whether they are sitting, standing, or walking. Take a moment to ponder this mental image, allowing other impressions of these men and women to form.

- Allow yourself to become aware of the location of this moment of prayer. Observe its physical characteristics and the arrangement of the people in it. Look around the place and notice more details about it – if it is in dim or bright light, if it is still and silent or filled with noise, if it has an unusual smell or not, etc.

- Take a moment to remain in this place with these people before allowing these images to fade from your consciousness.

[3] Become aware of your desires during this moment of prayer. Remember your desire to experience the divine presence all around you so you may attain a deep "felt knowledge" of Jesus Christ, who became human for you so you may better love and follow him. Recall your desire that, in this day or week of prayer, you may witness the many different men and women called to follow as Jesus' disciples and the unique ways in which each of them is called. Also, ask for a greater awareness of Christ's call in your life and the specific ways in which you have been asked to follow him.

As these desires fill your consciousness, let all other concerns fall aside as you focus on this time and place of prayer.

[4] Allow the image of Saint Brigid and her disciples to reemerge in your imagination.

- Watch as the group assembles around Brigid. Listen to the sounds of this moment and become comfortable as you prepare to hear Brigid speak. Feel the anticipation of the people around you and share in that enthusiasm.
- As you hear Brigid invite her companions to listen, ask God to help you share in their conversation – either by joining them or by listening quietly to them. Focus your attention on Saint Brigid, noting her physical appearance and her demeanor.
- Then, relying on the memories from your earlier prayer, watch and listen as Brigid tells the story of Jesus calling Levi to follow him while also discussing the hostility of the Pharisees toward Jesus. You may want to quietly read the passage while remaining prayerfully aware of your mental image or you may choose to stay completely within the imagined realm of your prayer. Whichever you choose, know that God will offer you the words from the biblical passage that you need to hear – even if only in fragments.
- After Brigid finishes speaking, allow her image and this place to fade from your imagination as you become aware of the phrases and images from this moment which touched you most deeply. Recall the emotions and memories – including any sounds or smells – evoked during your prayer. Allow these seminal aspects of your meditation to linger on your mind and in your heart, noting any special feelings evoked by them.

[5] When you are ready, become aware of Jesus' presence with you in this moment and have an open and informal conversation about this prayer period and how the passage from Luke's gospel expresses your own needs or desires as he calls you to follow him – giving space for Jesus to respond or to highlight different aspects from the biblical account and your experiences during this contemplation. Then, gradually allow your thoughts to recede as you focus on God's broader presence in your life and in the world around you.

[6] Conclude by allowing these desires to fade from your consciousness as you offer this traditional Irish prayer:

> *Confirm me in your love divine,*
> *Smooth for my feet life's rugged way;*
> *My will with yours entwine,*
> *Lest evil lead my steps astray.*
> *Be with my still as guard and guide,*
> *Keep me in holy sanctity,*
> *Let my firm faith on you abide,*

From fraud and error hold me free. Amen.
[7]   Afterward, take 10-15 minutes in a quiet space to reflect on the most significant moments from your prayer and record your reflections in your journal.

5.6 An Application of the Senses

[1]   Become aware of your prayerful desires during this day or week. Bring to mind your desire to experience an inner knowledge of Jesus Christ who became human for you so you may better love and follow him. Also ask that, in this day or week of prayer, you may witness the many different people called to follow as Jesus' disciples and the unique ways in which each of them is called.

[2]   When you are ready, call to mind the various prayers of the preceding day or days. Allow the images and words of these prayers to linger and then slowly fade from your consciousness.

- Remember your imaginative contemplations of John 1:35-51 and Luke 5:5-11. Consider the images and feelings evoked in you during your prayer, feeling God's presence in these memories and becoming aware of the specific sensations associated with each image.
- Recall your imaginative contemplation and meditation concerning Luke 5:27-38, considering them in the same way as the memories of your meditation on your earlier prayers.

Make a mental note of which senses are most active. You may see an image or a color, hear a sound or a phrase, or smell a scent or a fragrance. You may even taste a flavor or feel a sensation on your skin.

[3]   Then, relax and allow these various memories and experiences to quietly enter and leave your consciousness without being controlled. Linger on the sensory images and memories being evoked in you – noticing any images or colors, any sounds or phrases, any scents or fragrances, any flavors or physical sensations associated with each prayer.

[4]   When you are ready, become completely still and clear your mind of all thoughts and concerns. Allow an image of a special personal space to form in your imagination. Then, watch as God enters that place and forms a small image or object for you that expresses the thought or awareness that you most need to carry with you into your life.

Reverently pick up the object or image, a reflection of the most important gift you have been given during this time of prayer. Look at it carefully and become aware of the divine presence contained within it. Take a moment to register what it looks like and how it feels in your hand. Then, feel the joy and confidence that comes from touching the presence of God as you accept this gift, offering a short prayer of gratitude while you relax into the pleasure of this moment.

[5]   Then, conclude by allowing these images to fade from your consciousness as you offer this traditional Irish prayer:

> *Confirm me in your love divine,*
> *Smooth for my feet life's rugged way;*
> *My will with yours entwine,*
> *Lest evil lead my steps astray.*
> *Be with my still as guard and guide,*
> *Keep me in holy sanctity,*
> *Let my firm faith on you abide,*
> *From fraud and error hold me free. Amen.*

[6]   While your experiences are still fresh in your mind, record the most significant impressions or sensations from this time of prayer in your retreat journal.

5.7 Review of Prayer

[1] Remember your desires during the preceding day or week of prayer. Become aware of the divine presence all around you, offering you inner knowledge of Jesus Christ who became human for you so you may better love and follow him. Recall your desire to witness the many different men and women called to follow as Jesus' disciples and the unique ways in which each of them is called.

Ask God once again to fulfill these desires in your own life and in your interactions with others.

[2] Then, take a moment to allow the words, thoughts, and feelings from your prayers during the last day or week to linger before asking God to reveal the fulfillment of your deepest desires in these various memories.

• Think about the prayer sequence at the beginning of this day or week. Make a mental note of any words, insights or images that remain particularly significant or meaningful to you.

• Ponder the story, "Brigid and the Religious Scholar". Note any words, insights, or images from it that remain particularly significant or meaningful to you.

• Remember your imaginative contemplations of John 1:35-51 and Luke 5:5-11.

– Consider the most powerful images, phrases, or feelings from your prayer. Ask yourself what gifts God gave to you through these moments, perhaps offering you new insights or perhaps affirming an important aspect of your faith. Ask yourself how God may be calling you to change through these moments, being as specific as possible.

– Examine your disposition as you prayed, noting whether prayer came easily or with resistance. Recall the easiest moments in your prayer and any moments of joy you may have experienced. Remember also if you encountered any difficulty opening yourself to God or if you felt any sadness as you prayed. Ask God to help you understand why these feelings surfaced.

– Bring to mind any moments when you added personal elements (e.g., familiar places or people from your life) or connected your prayers to other scriptures or spiritual writings. Ask yourself how these additions helped or hindered you as you prayed. Again, if you do not know why this happened, ask God to help you understand.

- Recall your imaginative contemplation and meditation concerning Luke 5:27-38. Then, review your prayer in the same way as your memories of your earlier prayer.
- Reflect on the ebb and flow of sensory impressions and feelings that marked your application of the senses. Isolate the most memorable moments and sensory impressions from your prayer and reflect on how God used these moments to give you a particular gift.

[3] Finally, ponder the times when images or feelings from the readings of this day or week surfaced outside these prayer periods. Consider those moments or events in which God's presence or guidance was especially strong as well as any moments when you were struggling. Think about the most memorable aspects of these experiences, asking God to explain their significance.

[4] Take a moment to allow the words, thoughts, and feelings of these prayers to linger on your mind and in your heart. Finally, conclude by allowing these desires to fade from your consciousness as you offer this traditional Irish prayer:

> *O God, I believe in you; strengthen my belief.*
> *I trust in you; confirm my trust.*
> *I love you; double my love.*
> *I repent that I angered you,*
> *Increase my repentance.*
> *Fill you my heart with awe without despair;*
> *With hope, without over-confidence;*
> *With piety without infatuation;*
> *And with joy without excess.*
> *My God, consent to guide me by your wisdom;*
> *To constrain me by your right;*
> *To comfort me by your mercy;*
> *And to protect me by your power. Amen.*

[5] After finishing these prayers, summarize your reflections on the gifts or graces you received during the prayers of this last day or week and record these thoughts in your retreat journal.

6. Committing Oneself to Christ

6.1a   The Victor, Christ, With Flag Unfurled
a prayer on the demands of following Jesus

Take a moment to quiet your spirit, becoming completely present to this time and place. Allow all other thoughts and concerns to fall away as you come into the presence of God. Then, when you are ready, begin.

The Victor, Christ, with flag unfurled
Brings triumph o'er the sinful world,
> The king of darkness quells, and opes
> The gates of heaven to human hopes.

Dear Jesus, bring us purity,
That you our paschal joy may be;
> Be with us always; let your love
> Illume our spirits from above.

A Hymn, sung or heard (optional)

Remember, O friend, your end of sorrow,
Spend not your time with lies and folly,
> Forsake the world troubled and hollow,
> Sweet at the first but worse shall follow.

Though strong you are and smart and smiling,
Full of wealth and health, most lively,
> Make no boast, the whole are lying
> Unsubstantial shadows flying.

Though plenty of gold you hold and jewels,
Silver white, brass bright, and pewter,
> Sheep and kind, with swine ground-rooting,
> Castles and holds of untold-of beauty.

Take no heed of the creed or the wealth of the world,
Do not boast of its host or its banners unfurled,
> you art made out of clay, into clay to be turned,
> And into the room of the tomb to be hurled.

Read or recite Psalm 23.

Holy Lord,
Under my thoughts may I God-thoughts find.
Half of my sins escape my mind.
    For what I said, or did not say,
    Pardon me, O Lord, I pray.

Read Galatians 5: 16-25, aloud or quietly.

O Lord, Jesus the Christ,
If I were in Heaven my harp I would sound
With apostles and angels and saints all around,
    Praising and thanking the Son who is crowned,
    May the poor race of Eve for that heaven be bound!

Holy Lord,
To the Trinity's presence the soul must mount,
To the judgments it comes, and its sins it bears,
    And nought that it pleads for itself shall count
    Save fastings, and givings of alms, and prayers.

If you gave but a glass of the water cold,
(The simplest drink on the green earth's sod)
    Your reward is before you, a thousand-fold,
    If the thing has been done for the sake of God.

Three things there be, the reward of man
For offending God – 'tis a risk to run –
    Misfortune's fall, and a shortened span,
    And the pains of hell when all is done.

O Holy Lord,
    God with the Father and the Spirit,
For me is many a snare designed,
To fill my mind with doubts and fears;
    Far from the land of holy saints,
    I dwell within my vale of tears.
Let faith, let hope, let love –
Traits far above the cold world's way –

      With patience, humility, and awe,
      Become my guides from day to day.

I acknowledge, the evil I have done.
From the day of my birth till the day of my death,
      Through the sight of my eyes,
Through the hearing of my ears,
      Through the sayings of my mouth,
Through the thoughts of my heart,
      Through the touch of my hands,
Through the course of my way,
      Through all I said and did not,
Through all I promised and fulfilled not,
      Through all the laws and holy commandments I broke.
I ask even now absolution of you,
      For fear I may have never asked it as was right,
      And that I might not live to ask it again,

O Holy Lord, my King in Heaven,
May you not let my soul stray from you,
May you keep me in a good state,
      May you turn me toward what is good to do,
      May you protect me from dangers, small and great.
May you fill my eyes with tears of repentance,
      So I may avoid the sinner's awful sentence.
May the Grace of the God for ever be with me,
      And whatever my needs, may the Triune God give me.

Select one of the following options for the Lord's Prayer.

Option A

O Jesus Christ,
Lord of heaven and earth,
Help me pray as you yourself taught:
      "Our Father in heaven,
      hallowed be your name.
      Your kingdom come.
      Your will be done,
      on earth as it is in heaven.

*Give us this day our daily bread.
And forgive us our debts,
as we also have forgiven our debtors.
And do not bring us to the time of trial,
but rescue us from the evil one."
(Matthew 6: 9-13)*
From the foes of my land,
from the foes of my faith,
From the foes who would us dissever,
    O Lord, preserve me, in life and in death,
    With the Sign of the Cross for ever.
    *For the kingdom, the power, and the glory
    are yours now and for ever. Amen.*

Please proceed with "I beseech you, O Lord...," found after Option B.

Option B

O Jesus Christ,
Lord of heaven and earth,
Help me pray as you yourself taught:
    *Our Father in heaven,
    hallowed be your name,
    your kingdom come,
    your will be done,
    on earth as in heaven.
    Give us today our daily bread.
    Forgive us our sins
    as we forgive those who sin against us.
    Lead us not into temptation
    but deliver us from evil.*
From the foes of my land,
from the foes of my faith,
From the foes who would us dissever,
    O Lord, preserve me, in life and in death,
    With the Sign of the Cross for ever.
    *For the kingdom, the power, and the glory
    are yours now and for ever. Amen.*

I beseech you, O Lord.
God in Heaven, unsurpassed in power and might;
> Be behind me, Be on my left,
> Be before me, Be on my right!
Against each danger, you are my help;
In distress, upon you I call.
> In dark times, may you sustain me
> And lift me up again when I fall.
Lord over heaven and of earth,
You know my offenses.
> Yet, listening to my pleadings,
> You guide me away from sinful pretenses.
Lord of all creation and the many creatures,
You bestow on me many earthly treasures.
> Revealing love in each life and season,
> You share with me heavenly pleasures.
May you arouse me
In moments both of joy and of strife;
> Most holy Lord, bring me new life!

A Hymn, sung or heard (optional)

O Jesus Christ,
> Lord of heaven and earth,
> You are my riches, my store, my provision,
My star through the years
When troubles rend me,
> Through times of strife and tears,
> Sweet Jesus, defend me.

Be you my lasting joy, O Lord,
My love on earth, my high reward;
> Kind Ruler of the world, inspire
> My longing soul with holy fire.
To you I bow my heart in prayer,
Lord, keep me from the tempter's snare;
> Lift up my soul with heavenly grace,
> And fit me for your dwelling-place.

End this time of prayer by taking some time to bring to mind the various ways God shields you from harm or guides you through the world's tumult. Then, when you are ready, conclude by saying:

O Holy Lord, King in Heaven,
I place myself at the edge of your grace,
    On the floor of your house myself I place,
And to banish the sin of my heart away,
    I lower my knee to you this day.
Through life's torrents of pain may you bring me whole,
    And, O Lord Jesus Christ, preserve also my soul. Amen.

6.1b   Preparation for Prayer

Consideration of the Readings

After reciting or prayerfully reading the prayer sequence for this day or week:

• Read the Meditation on the Two Standards as well as the considerations of the Three Classes of Persons and the Three Modes of Humility from *The Spiritual Exercises of Saint Ignatius* (found on pages 302, 304, and 305). Allow yourself to linger on any thoughts or phrases that seem particularly meaningful to you or especially relevant to your life. Then, record these highlights in your workbook so you will remember them during your meditation.

• Read Galatians 5:16-25. Again, pay careful attention to any phrases or images that seem particularly meaningful to you. Then, record these highlights in your workbook so you will remember them during this day or week of prayer.

Note: *You also should consider any aspect of the prayer sequence from this day or week that seemed particularly significant to you.*

Contemplation of Your Needs

When you are ready, allow any distractions to fade from your consciousness as you become aware of your desire to live in God's goodness. Feel yourself yearning to properly use the many gifts God has given you, to experience God's continuing care, and to be open to the immense love God shows for you, then:

• Read "Brigid and the Two Lepers" (found on page 312). Allow yourself to linger on any thoughts, phrases or images that seem particularly meaningful or significant to your earlier preparations or prayer.

• Pray for your desires in the coming day or week. Ask that the divine presence all around you may be revealed, offering you inner knowledge of Jesus Christ who became human for you so you may better love and follow him. Ask also that you may understand the precious invitation at the heart of meditations on the Two Standards, the Three Classes of Persons and the Three Modes of Humility.

- Conclude by praying for guidance and awareness of God's desires in you during these meditations.

Then, record any significant thoughts, emotions, or reactions from these moments in your workbook.

After this, put your notes aside. Without straining your memory, consider in turn each of the readings for the coming day or week and allow them to take shape in your imagination. Prayerfully ponder how each reading affects you emotionally without overtly thinking about their content, asking God to illuminate the spiritual gifts offered in each reading – quieting your mind and creating a receptive space in yourself to see or hear the response.

Finally, conclude by allowing these desires to fade from your consciousness as you offer this traditional Irish prayer:

> *O God, I believe in you; strengthen my belief.*
> *I trust in you; confirm my trust.*
> *I love you; double my love.*
> *I repent that I angered you,*
> *Increase my repentance.*
> *Fill you my heart with awe without despair;*
> *With hope, without over-confidence;*
> *With piety without infatuation;*
> *And with joy without excess.*
> *My God, consent to guide me by your wisdom;*
> *To constrain me by your right;*
> *To comfort me by your mercy;*
> *And to protect me by your power. Amen.*

Allow these words to linger on your mind and in your heart for a few moments and then, while they are still fresh in your memory, write the most important thoughts, feelings and desires from this preparatory time in your journal.

6.2 The "Meditation concerning Two Standards"

In this consideration, you will reflect upon the images and spiritual vision of the "Meditation concerning Two Standards" presented in *The Spiritual Exercises of Saint Ignatius*.

[1]   Begin by reading the "Meditation concerning Two Standards" in *The Spiritual Exercises of Saint Ignatius* (Sp.Ex. #136-147, found on page 302) and reviewing your notes on it from your preparations.

[2]   Then, focus on this specific time and place as you allow all other concerns to fall away. As you become still, become aware of your desires during this moment of prayer. Remember your desire to experience the divine presence all around you so you may attain a deep "felt knowledge" of Jesus Christ, who became human for you so you may better love and follow him. Recall your desire that you may understand the precious invitation at the heart of meditation on the Two Standards. Also, ask that you may receive knowledge of the deceits of the evil leader and the true life offered by Christ during this meditation.

As these desires fill your consciousness, let all other concerns fall aside as you focus on this specific time and place of prayer.

[3]   Then, slowly and deliberately, re-read the "Meditation concerning Two Standards".

- As you read, take time to stop and ponder each statement within it as you read. When you pause, allow images shaped by the words and thoughts of the passages to form in your imagination. See and hear the way each statement expresses a need or desire in your life.

- Take more time with passages that seem particularly significant or meaning to you. Become aware of the passages from the "Meditation concerning Two Standards" which you accept easily and any of those which cause you difficulty. Clarify these thoughts and feeling as much as possible while remaining focused on each specific statement within this meditation.

- After finishing the reading, allow the various words and images of your prayer to flow freely in your consciousness without being controlled. Become aware of those aspects of the "Meditation concerning Two Standards" that arouse holy desires in you, toward God and toward others (including nonhuman creatures). Become aware of those aspects of the reading that make you feel shame for those times you fall short of these ideals.

- When you are ready, allow these thoughts and images to fade from your consciousness and become aware of Jesus' presence with you in this moment. Then, have an open and informal conversation about your experience of the Meditation concerning Two Standards. Speak about how it expresses your own desires and fears, giving space for Jesus to respond to your concerns or to explain the divine desires expressed in this meditation.
- Then, gradually allow your thoughts to recede as you focus on God's broader presence in your life and in the world around you.

[4] Finally, conclude by offering the triple colloquy described by Ignatius in his *Spiritual Exercises* (*Sp.Ex.* #147, see page 303).

- Approach Mary and ask her help in approaching her son and in embracing his standard – even if it means facing poverty and humiliation. Ask also that you may reflect the love of Jesus in all your choices and actions in life. Conclude by praying the Hail Mary before walking together to Jesus.

<u>Note:</u> *If your religious tradition is uncomfortable approaching Mary in prayer, you should ignore this prayer and proceed to the next step in the colloquy.*

- Approach Jesus and ask to embrace his standard – even if it means facing poverty and humiliation. Ask also that you may reflect his loving behavior in all your choices and actions in life. Conclude by praying the "Anima Christi" ("Soul of Christ", see page 303) before walking together with Jesus to God the Father.
- Approach God the Father and ask help in remaining faithful to the standard of Christ. Ask also that you may reflect love and generosity in all your choices and actions in life. Then, conclude by praying the Lord's Prayer and allowing these images to o fade from your consciousness.

[5] Afterward, take 10-15 minutes in a quiet space to reflect on the most significant moments from this time of prayer and record your reflections in your journal.

6.3 The "Meditation concerning Three Classes of Persons"

In this consideration, you will reflect upon the words and spiritual vision of the "Meditation concerning Three Classes of Persons" presented in *The Spiritual Exercises of Saint Ignatius*.

[1]   Begin by reading the "Meditation concerning Three Classes of Persons" in *The Spiritual Exercises of Saint Ignatius* (*Sp.Ex.* #149-156, found on page 304) and reviewing your notes on it from your preparations.

[2]   Then, focus on this specific time and place as you allow all other concerns to fall away. As you become still, become aware of your desires during this moment of prayer. Remember your desire to experience the divine presence all around you so you may attain a deep "felt knowledge" of Jesus Christ, who became human for you so you may better love and follow him. Recall your desire that you may understand the precious invitation at the heart of the meditation on the three classes of men and women. Also, ask for an intimate awareness of God's desires in you during this meditation.

As these desires fill your consciousness, let all other concerns fall aside as you focus on this specific time and place of prayer.

[3]   Then, slowly and deliberately, re-read the "Meditation concerning Three Classes of Persons".

- As you read, take time to stop and ponder each statement within it as you read. When you pause, allow images shaped by the words and thoughts of the passages to form in your imagination. See and hear the way each statement expresses a need or desire in your life.

- Take more time with passages that seem particularly significant or meaning to you. Become aware of the passages from the meditation which you accept easily and any of those which cause you difficulty. Clarify these thoughts and feeling as much as possible while remaining focused on each specific statement within this meditation.

- After finishing the reading, allow the various words and images of your prayer to flow freely in your consciousness without being controlled. Become aware of those aspects of the "Meditation concerning Three Classes of Persons" that arouse holy desires in you, toward God and toward others (including nonhuman creatures). Become aware of those aspects of the reading that make you feel shame for those times you fall short of these ideals.

• When you are ready, allow these thoughts and images to fade from your consciousness and become aware of Jesus' presence with you in this moment. Then, have an open and informal conversation about your experience of the meditation. Speak about how it expresses your own desires and fears, giving space for Jesus to respond to your concerns or to explain the divine desires expressed in this meditation.

• Then, gradually allow your thoughts to recede as you focus on God's broader presence in your life and in the world around you.

[4]   Finally, conclude by offering the triple colloquy described by Ignatius in his *Spiritual Exercises* (*Sp.Ex.* #147, see page 303).

• Approach Mary and ask her help in approaching her son and in demonstrating generosity in all my and actions in life. Conclude by praying the Hail Mary before walking together to Jesus.

Note: Again, if your religious tradition is uncomfortable approaching Mary in prayer, you should ignore this prayer and proceed to the next step in the colloquy.

• Approach Jesus and ask to reflect his loving behavior in all your choices and actions in life. Conclude by praying the "Anima Christi" ("Soul of Christ", see page 303) before walking together with Jesus to God the Father.

• Approach God the Father and ask help in reflecting divine love and generosity in all your choices and actions in life. Then, conclude by praying the Lord's Prayer and allowing these images to o fade from your consciousness.

[5]   Afterward, take 10-15 minutes in a quiet space to reflect on the most significant moments from this time of prayer and record your reflections in your journal.

6.4 The "Three Modes of Humility"

In this consideration, you will reflect upon the words and spiritual vision of the "Three Modes of Humility" presented in *The Spiritual Exercises of Saint Ignatius*.

[1] Begin by reading the "Three Modes of Humility" in *The Spiritual Exercises of Saint Ignatius* (Sp.Ex. #165-168, found on page 305) and reviewing your notes on it from your preparations.

[2] Then, focus on this specific time and place as you allow all other concerns to fall away. As you become still, become aware of your desires during this moment of prayer. Remember your desire to experience the divine presence all around you so you may attain a deep "felt knowledge" of Jesus Christ, who became human for you so you may better love and follow him. Recall your desire that you may understand the precious invitation at the heart of the meditation on the three modes of humility. Also, ask for an intimate awareness of God's desires in you during this meditation.

As these desires fill your consciousness, let all other concerns fall aside as you focus on this specific time and place of prayer.

[3] Then, slowly and deliberately, re-read the "Three Modes of Humility".

- As you read, take time to stop and ponder each statement within it as you read. When you pause, allow images shaped by the words and thoughts of the passages to form in your imagination. See and hear the way each statement expresses a need or desire in your life.

- Take more time with passages that seem particularly significant or meaning to you. Become aware of the passages from the "Three Modes of Humility" which you accept easily and any of those which cause you difficulty. Clarify these thoughts and feeling as much as possible while remaining focused on each specific statement within this meditation.

- After finishing the reading, allow the various words and images of your prayer to flow freely in your consciousness without being controlled. Become aware of those aspects of the "Three Modes of Humility" that arouse holy desires in you, toward God and toward others (including nonhuman creatures). Become aware of those aspects of the reading that make you feel shame for those times you fall short of these ideals.

- When you are ready, allow these thoughts and images to fade from your consciousness and become aware of Jesus' presence with you in this moment. Then, have an open and informal conversation about your experience of the Three Modes of Humility. Speak about how it expresses your own desires and fears, giving space for Jesus to respond to your concerns or to explain the divine desires expressed in this meditation.
- Then, gradually allow your thoughts to recede as you focus on God's broader presence in your life and in the world around you.

[4]   Finally, conclude by offering the triple colloquy described by Ignatius in his *Spiritual Exercises* (*Sp.Ex.* #147, see page 303).

- Approach Mary and ask her help in approaching her son and demonstrating humility when responding to all holy desires and leadings in your life. Conclude by praying the Hail Mary before walking together to Jesus.

Note: Again, if your religious tradition is uncomfortable approaching Mary in prayer, you should ignore this prayer and proceed to the next step in the colloquy.

- Approach Jesus and ask his help in demonstrating humility when responding to all holy desires and leadings in your life. Conclude by praying the "Anima Christi" ("Soul of Christ", see page 303) before walking together with Jesus to God the Father.
- Approach God the Father and ask help in remaining humble and open when responding to all holy desires in all your choices and actions in life. Then, conclude by praying the Lord's Prayer and allowing these images to o fade from your consciousness.

[5]   Afterward, take 10-15 minutes in a quiet space to reflect on the most significant moments from this time of prayer and record your reflections in your journal.

6.5   A Meditation on Galatians 5:16-25

In this meditation on Galatians 5:16-25, you will see and hear Saint Brigid teaching a crowd how to distinguish between sinful and holy desires.

[1]   Begin by reading the biblical selection and reviewing your notes on it.

[2]   Then, focus on this specific time and place as you allow all other concerns to fall away before considering the people and place in this moment of prayer.

• Allow an image of Brigid to emerge in your imagination, noting her physical characteristics and mannerisms. Look at what she is wearing or carrying. Make a note of whether she is sitting, standing, or walking. Ponder this mental image, allowing any other observations about Brigid to form in your mind.

• Observe the people around Saint Brigid, becoming aware of their appearance and demeanor. Observe whether they are sitting, standing, or walking. Take a moment to ponder this mental image, allowing other impressions of these men and women to form.

• Allow yourself to become aware of the location of this moment of prayer. Observe its physical characteristics and the arrangement of the people in it. Look around the place and notice more details about it – if it is in dim or bright light, if it is still and silent or filled with noise, if it has an unusual smell or not, etc.

• Take a moment to remain in this place with these men and women before allowing these images to fade from your consciousness.

[3]   Become aware of your desires during this moment of prayer. Remember your desire to experience the divine presence all around you and to trust in God's plan for you, asking that all your intentions and actions may be directed purely to the service and praise of God. Recall your desire to understand the precious invitation at the heart of Jesus' call to follow him. Also, ask for the wisdom and strength to remain faithful to Jesus despite the challenges and temptations that might distract you from this desire.

As these desires fill your consciousness, let all other concerns fall aside as you focus on this time and place of prayer.

[4]   Allow the image of Saint Brigid and her disciples to reemerge in your imagination.

- Watch as the group assembles around Brigid. Listen to the sounds of this moment and become comfortable as you prepare to hear Brigid speak. Feel the anticipation of the people around you and share in that enthusiasm.
- As you see Brigid quieting the crowd, ask God to help you share in this experience – either by joining these events or by listening quietly to them. Focus your attention on Saint Brigid, noting her physical appearance and her demeanor.
- Then, watch and listen as Brigid recites the passage from Paul's letter to the Galatians and explains its meaning and importance. You may want to quietly read the passage while remaining prayerfully aware of your mental image or you may choose to stay completely within the imagined realm of your prayer. Whichever you choose, know that God will offer you the words from the biblical passage that you need to hear – even if only in fragments.
- After Brigid finishes speaking, allow her image and this place to fade from your imagination as you become aware of the phrases and images from this moment which touched you most deeply. Recall the emotions and memories – including any sounds or smells – evoked during your prayer. Allow these seminal aspects of your meditation to linger on your mind and in your heart, noting any special feelings evoked by them.

[5] Then, become aware of Jesus' presence with you in this moment and have an open and informal conversation about this prayer period and how the passage from Paul's epistle expresses your own needs or desires – giving space for Jesus to respond or to highlight different aspects from the biblical account and your experiences during this contemplation. Then, gradually allow your thoughts to recede as you focus on God's broader presence in your life and in the world around you.

[6] Conclude by allowing these desires to fade from your consciousness as you offer this traditional Irish prayer:

> *Confirm me in your love divine,*
> *Smooth for my feet life's rugged way;*
> *My will with yours entwine,*
> *Lest evil lead my steps astray.*
> *Be with my still as guard and guide,*
> *Keep me in holy sanctity,*
> *Let my firm faith on you abide,*
> *From fraud and error hold me free. Amen.*

[7]   Afterward, take 10-15 minutes in a quiet space to reflect on the most significant moments from your prayer and record your reflections in your journal.

6.6 An Application of the Senses

[1]   Become aware of your prayerful desires during this day or week. Bring to mind your desire to experience an inner knowledge of Jesus Christ who became human for you so you may better love and follow him. Ask also that you may understand the precious invitation at the heart of your meditations on the Two Standards, the Three Classes of Persons and the Three Modes of Humility.

[2]   When you are ready, call to mind the various prayers of the preceding day or days. Allow the images and words of these prayers to linger and then slowly fade from your consciousness.

• Remember your meditation on the Two Standards from *The Spiritual Exercises of Saint Ignatius*. Consider the images and feelings evoked in you during your prayer, feeling God's presence in these memories and becoming aware of the specific sensations associated with each image.

• Recall your meditation on the Three Classes of Persons from *The Spiritual Exercises of Saint Ignatius*, considering it in the same way as your memories of the Two Standards.

• Review your meditation on the Three Modes of Humility from *The Spiritual Exercises of Saint Ignatius* in the same manner as the previous meditations.

* Reminisce on your mediation on Galatians 5:16-25 in the same manner as the previous meditations.

Make a mental note of which senses are most active. You may see an image or a color, hear a sound or a phrase, or smell a scent or a fragrance. You may even taste a flavor or feel a sensation on your skin.

[3]   Then, relax and allow these various memories and experiences to quietly enter and leave your consciousness without being controlled. Linger on the sensory images and memories being evoked in you – noticing any images or colors, any sounds or phrases, any scents or fragrances, any flavors or physical sensations associated with each prayer.

[4]   When you are ready, become completely still and clear your mind of all thoughts and concerns. Allow an image of a special personal space to form in your imagination. Then, watch as God enters that place and forms a small image or object for you that expresses the thought or awareness that you most need to carry with you into your life.

Reverently pick up the object or image, a reflection of the most important gift you have been given during this time of prayer. Look at it carefully and become aware of the divine presence contained within it. Take a moment to register what it looks like and how it feels in your hand. Then, feel the joy and confidence that comes from touching the presence of God as you accept this gift, offering a short prayer of gratitude while you relax into the pleasure of this moment.

[5]   Then, conclude by allowing these images to fade from your consciousness as you offer this traditional Irish prayer:

> *Confirm me in your love divine,*
> *Smooth for my feet life's rugged way;*
> *My will with yours entwine,*
> *Lest evil lead my steps astray.*
> *Be with my still as guard and guide,*
> *Keep me in holy sanctity,*
> *Let my firm faith on you abide,*
> *From fraud and error hold me free. Amen.*

[6]   While your experiences are still fresh in your mind, record the most significant impressions or sensations from this time of prayer in your journal.

6.7 Review of Prayer

[1] Remember your desires during the preceding day or week of prayer. Become aware of the divine presence all around you, offering you inner knowledge of Jesus Christ who became human for you so you may better love and follow him. Recall your desire to understand the precious invitation at the heart of your meditations on the Two Standards, the Three Classes of Persons and the Three Modes of Humility.

Ask God once again to fulfill these desires in your own life and in your interactions with others.

[2] Then, take a moment to allow the words, thoughts, and feelings from your prayers during the last day or week to linger before asking God to reveal the fulfillment of your deepest desires in these various memories.

• Think about the prayer sequence at the beginning of this day or week. Make a mental note of any words, insights or images that remain particularly significant or meaningful to you.

• Ponder the story, "Brigid and the Two Lepers". Note any words, insights, or images from it that remain particularly significant or meaningful to you.

• Remember your meditation on the Two Standards from *The Spiritual Exercises of Saint Ignatius*.

– Consider the most powerful images, phrases, or feelings from your prayer. Ask yourself what gifts God gave to you through these moments, perhaps offering you new insights or perhaps affirming an important aspect of your faith. Ask yourself how God may be calling you to change through these moments, being as specific as possible.

– Examine your disposition as you prayed, noting whether prayer came easily or with resistance. Recall the easiest moments in your prayer and any moments of joy you may have experienced. Remember also if you encountered any difficulty opening yourself to God or if you felt any sadness as you prayed. Ask God to help you understand why these feelings surfaced.

– Bring to mind any moments when you added personal elements (e.g., familiar places or people from your life) or connected your prayers to other scriptures or spiritual writings. Ask yourself how these additions helped or hindered you as you prayed. Again, if you do not know why this happened, ask God to help you understand.

- Recall your meditation on the Three Classes of Persons from *The Spiritual Exercises of Saint Ignatius*. Then, review your prayer in the same way as your earlier reflection on the Two Standards.
- Review your meditation on the Three Modes of Humility from *The Spiritual Exercises of Saint Ignatius* in the same manner as the previous meditations.
* Reminisce on your mediation on Galatians 5:16-25 in the same manner as the previous meditations.
- Reflect on the ebb and flow of sensory impressions and feelings that marked your application of the senses. Isolate the most memorable moments and sensory impressions from your prayer and reflect on how God used these moments to give you a particular gift.

[3] Finally, ponder the times when images or feelings from the readings of this day or week surfaced outside these prayer periods. Consider those moments or events in which God's presence or guidance was especially strong as well as any moments when you were struggling. Think about the most memorable aspects of these experiences, asking God to explain their significance.

[4] Take a moment to allow the words, thoughts, and feelings of these prayers to linger on your mind and in your heart. Finally, conclude by allowing these desires to fade from your consciousness as you offer this traditional Irish prayer:

> O God, I believe in you; strengthen my belief.
> I trust in you; confirm my trust.
> I love you; double my love.
> I repent that I angered you,
> Increase my repentance.
> Fill you my heart with awe without despair;
> With hope, without over-confidence;
> With piety without infatuation;
> And with joy without excess.
> My God, consent to guide me by your wisdom;
> To constrain me by your right;
> To comfort me by your mercy;
> And to protect me by your power. Amen.

[5] After finishing these prayers, summarize your reflections on the gifts or graces you received during the prayers of this last day or week and record these thoughts in your journal.

7. Following Jesus as a Disciple

7.1a   You Are, O Christ, My Health And Light

a prayer in praise of Jesus' power and majesty

Take a moment to quiet your spirit, becoming completely present to this time and place. Allow all other thoughts and concerns to fall away as you come into the presence of God. Then, when you are ready, begin.

You are, O Christ, my health and light,
The power that glorifies the sun,
    That veils with deepening shades the night,
    And gives each star its course to run.

No wandering thought or vain desire
Be near my soul to soil or stain,
    But kindled by the holy fire
    Of love for you, with you remain.

A Hymn, sung or heard (optional)

O you who seek the Christ to find,
Uplift your eyes on high;
    For lo! to every humble mind
    His glory fills the sky.

His mighty wonders there behold,
In boundless fields of light,
    Sublime, eternal, and as old
    As heaven and ancient night.

Here is the nation's King indeed,
Here Israel's mighty Lord,
    To Abraham promised and his seed,
    Forevermore adored.

To him each prophet did witness,
By word and sign sincere;
    Blessed by the Father, saying in sweetness,
    "Behold, believe and hear!"

To Jesus, who his light displays
To babes, all glory be,
>   To Father and Spirit equal praise
>   For all eternity.

Read or recite Psalm 91.

Holy Lord,
Under my thoughts may I God-thoughts find.
Half of my sins escape my mind.
>   For what I said, or did not say,
>   Pardon me, O Lord, I pray.

Read Luke 18: 35-43, aloud or quietly.

O Lord, Jesus the Christ,
If I were in Heaven my harp I would sound
With apostles and angels and saints all around,
>   Praising and thanking the Son who is crowned,
>   May the poor race of Eve for that heaven be bound!

Holy Lord,
Be my heart and hopes renewed
In light and love and gratitude,
>   So, illumed by you, may my actions
>   Worthily fulfill your loving intentions.

I praise you, Lord, forevermore;
With the Father, who I also adore,
>   And with the Spirit, three in one,
>   Reigning while endless ages run.

O Holy Lord,
>   God with the Father and the Spirit,
For me is many a snare designed,
To fill my mind with doubts and fears;
>   Far from the land of holy saints,
>   I dwell within my vale of tears.
Let faith, let hope, let love –
Traits far above the cold world's way –

With patience, humility, and awe,
Become my guides from day to day.

I acknowledge, the evil I have done.
From the day of my birth till the day of my death,
Through the sight of my eyes,
Through the hearing of my ears,
Through the sayings of my mouth,
Through the thoughts of my heart,
Through the touch of my hands,
Through the course of my way,
Through all I said and did not,
Through all I promised and fulfilled not,
Through all the laws and holy commandments I broke.
I ask even now absolution of you,
For fear I may have never asked it as was right,
And that I might not live to ask it again,

O Holy Lord, my King in Heaven,
May you not let my soul stray from you,
May you keep me in a good state,
May you turn me toward what is good to do,
May you protect me from dangers, small and great.
May you fill my eyes with tears of repentance,
So I may avoid the sinner's awful sentence.
May the Grace of the God for ever be with me,
And whatever my needs, may the Triune God give me.

Select one of the following options for the Lord's Prayer.

Option A

O Jesus Christ,
Lord of heaven and earth,
Help me pray as you yourself taught:
"Our Father in heaven,
hallowed be your name.
Your kingdom come.
Your will be done,
on earth as it is in heaven.

*Give us this day our daily bread.
And forgive us our debts,
as we also have forgiven our debtors.
And do not bring us to the time of trial,
but rescue us from the evil one."
(Matthew 6: 9-13)*
From the foes of my land,
from the foes of my faith,
From the foes who would us dissever,
 O Lord, preserve me, in life and in death,
 With the Sign of the Cross for ever.
 *For the kingdom, the power, and the glory
 are yours now and for ever. Amen.*

Please proceed with "I beseech you, O Lord…," found after Option B.

Option B

O Jesus Christ,
Lord of heaven and earth,
Help me pray as you yourself taught:
 *Our Father in heaven,
 hallowed be your name,
 your kingdom come,
 your will be done,
 on earth as in heaven.
 Give us today our daily bread.
 Forgive us our sins
 as we forgive those who sin against us.
 Lead us not into temptation
 but deliver us from evil.*
From the foes of my land,
from the foes of my faith,
From the foes who would us dissever,
 O Lord, preserve me, in life and in death,
 With the Sign of the Cross for ever.
 *For the kingdom, the power, and the glory
 are yours now and for ever. Amen.*

I beseech you, O Lord.
God in Heaven, unsurpassed in power and might;
> Be behind me, Be on my left,
> Be before me, Be on my right!
Against each danger, you are my help;
In distress, upon you I call.
> In dark times, may you sustain me
> And lift me up again when I fall.
Lord over heaven and of earth,
You know my offenses.
> Yet, listening to my pleadings,
> You guide me away from sinful pretenses.
Lord of all creation and the many creatures,
You bestow on me many earthly treasures.
> Revealing love in each life and season,
> You share with me heavenly pleasures.
May you arouse me
In moments both of joy and of strife;
> Most holy Lord, bring me new life!

A Hymn, sung or heard (optional)

O Jesus Christ,
> Lord of heaven and earth,
> You are my riches, my store, my provision,
My star through the years
When troubles rend me,
> Through times of strife and tears,
> Sweet Jesus, defend me.

O you who seek the Lord, come nigh,
To heaven uplift your reverent eyes,
> The Royal Banner of our God
> Is blazoned on the midnight skies.

O Jesus, to the world revealed!
To you let glory ever be,
> To Father and to Holy Ghost,
> From age to age eternally.

End this time of prayer by taking some time to bring to mind the various ways God shields you from harm or guides you through the world's tumult. Then, when you are ready, conclude by saying:

O Holy Lord, King in Heaven,
I place myself at the edge of your grace,
    On the floor of your house myself I place,
And to banish the sin of my heart away,
    I lower my knee to you this day.
Through life's torrents of pain may you bring me whole,
    And, O Lord Jesus Christ, preserve also my soul. Amen.

7.1b   Preparation for Prayer

Consideration of the Readings

After reciting or prayerfully reading the prayer sequence for this day or week:

- Read about Jesus feeding the five thousand people in Matthew 14:13-21, making a mental note of each person's appearance and actions during the episode as well as the key elements of the story and its setting. Again, consider any aspects of this story that speak strongly to you before recording these observations in your workbook.
- Read about Jesus healing the blind beggar in Luke 18:35-43, noting each person's appearance and actions during the episode as well as the key elements of the story and its setting, including the setting in your workbook. Then, record any aspects of this story that speak strongly to you.
- Read about Jesus' transfiguration in Matthew 17:1-9, noting each person's appearance and actions during the episode as well as the key elements of the story and its setting before recording any aspects of this story that speak strongly to you.
- Read 2 Peter 1:3-11. Again, pay careful attention to any phrases or images that seem particularly meaningful to you. Then, record these highlights in your workbook so you will remember them during this day or week of prayer.

Note: You also should consider any aspect of the prayer sequence from this day or week that seemed particularly significant to you.

Contemplation of Your Needs

When you are ready, allow any distractions to fade from your consciousness as you become aware of your desire to live in God's goodness. Feel yourself yearning to properly use the many gifts God has given you, to experience God's continuing care, and to be open to the immense love God shows for you, then:

- Read "Two Miracles Performed by Brigid" (found on page 313). Allow yourself to linger on any thoughts, phrases or images that

seem particularly meaningful or significant to your earlier preparations or prayer.
  • Pray for your desires in the coming day or week. Ask that the divine presence all around you may be revealed, offering you inner knowledge of Jesus Christ who became human for you so you may better love and follow him. Ask also that you may experience Christ's power and what it means to be a disciple of Jesus.
  • Conclude by praying for support and nourishment as you walk in the presence of the Son of God.
Then, record any significant thoughts, emotions, or reactions from these moments in your workbook.

After this, put your notes aside. Without straining your memory, consider in turn each of the readings for the coming day or week and allow them to take shape in your imagination. Prayerfully ponder how each reading affects you emotionally without overtly thinking about their content, asking God to illuminate the spiritual gifts offered in each reading.

Finally, conclude by offering this prayer:
O God, I believe in you; strengthen my belief.
I trust in you; confirm my trust.
I love you; double my love.
I repent that I angered you,
Increase my repentance.
Fill you my heart with awe without despair;
With hope, without over-confidence;
With piety without infatuation;
And with joy without excess.
My God, consent to guide me by your wisdom;
To constrain me by your right;
To comfort me by your mercy;
And to protect me by your power. Amen.

Allow these words to linger on your mind and in your heart for a few moments and then write the most important thoughts, feelings, and desires in your journal.

7.2 A Contemplation of Matthew 14:13-21

In this contemplation of Matthew 14:13-21, you will see and hear Jesus feeding five thousand people with only two fish and five loaves of bread.

[1] Begin by reading the biblical selection and reviewing your notes on it.

[2] Then, focus on this specific time and place as you allow all other concerns to fall away before considering the people and place in this moment of prayer.

- Allow an image of Jesus to emerge in your imagination, noting his physical characteristics and mannerisms. Look at what he is wearing or carrying. Make a note of whether he is sitting, standing, or walking. Ponder this mental image, allowing any other observations about Jesus to form in your mind.

- Observe the men and women around Jesus, becoming aware of their appearance and demeanor. See if they are sitting, standing, or walking. Look at Jesus' disciples and their actions, toward Jesus and the crowd. Look at the crowd, noting their actions and demeanor. Take a moment to ponder this mental image, allowing other impressions of these people to form.

- Allow yourself to become aware of the location of this moment of prayer. Observe its physical characteristics and the arrangement of the people in it. Look around the place and notice more details about it – if it is overcast or sunny, if it is still and silent or filled with noise, if it has an unusual smell or not, etc.

- Take a moment to remain in this place with these men and women before allowing these images to fade from your consciousness.

[3] Become aware of your desires during this moment of prayer. Remember your desire to experience the divine presence all around you so you may attain a deep "felt knowledge" of Jesus Christ, who became human for you so you may better love and follow him. Recall your desire that in this day or week of prayer, you may experience Christ's power and what it means to be a disciple of Jesus. Also, ask for support and nourishment as you walk in the presence of the Son of

these desires fill your consciousness, let all other concerns ou focus on this time and place of prayer.

[4]   Allow the image of Jesus and the crowd to reemerge in your imagination.
- Watch as the group assembles around Jesus. Listen to the sounds of this moment and become comfortable as you prepare to hear Jesus speak. Feel the anticipation of the people around you and share in that enthusiasm.
- Ask God to help you enter this moment – either by joining these events or by listening quietly to them. Focus your attention on Jesus, noting his physical appearance and his demeanor.
- Then, see and hear Jesus speaking to his disciples before feeding the crowd through this miracle. You may want to quietly read the passage in Matthew's gospel while remaining prayerfully aware of your mental image or you may choose to stay completely within the imagined realm of your prayer. Whichever you choose, know that God will offer you the words from the biblical passage that you need to hear – even if only in fragments.
- As these images fade from your imagination, become aware of the phrases and images from this moment which touched you most deeply. Recall the emotions and memories – including any sounds or smells – evoked during your prayer. Allow these seminal aspects of your meditation to linger on your mind and in your heart, noting any special feelings evoked by them.

[5]   Then, become aware of Jesus' presence with you in this moment and have an open and informal conversation about this prayer period and how the passage from Matthew's gospel expresses your own needs or desires – giving space for Jesus to respond or to highlight different aspects from the biblical account and your experiences during this contemplation. Then, gradually allow your thoughts to recede as you focus on God's broader presence in your life and in the world around you.

[6]   Conclude by offering this prayer:

> *Confirm me in your love divine,*
> *Smooth for my feet life's rugged way;*
> *My will with yours entwine,*
> *Lest evil lead my steps astray.*
> *Be with my still as guard and guide,*
> *Keep me in holy sanctity,*
> *Let my firm faith on you abide,*
> *From fraud and error hold me free. Amen.*

[7] Afterward, take 10-15 minutes in a quiet space to reflect on the most significant moments from your prayer and record your reflections in your journal.

7.3 A Contemplation of Luke 18:35-43

In this contemplation of Luke 18:35-43, you will see and hear Jesus healing a blind man.

[1] Begin by reading the biblical selection and reviewing your notes on it.

[2] Then, focus on this specific time and place as you allow all other concerns to fall away before considering the people and place in this moment of prayer.

- Allow an image of Jesus to emerge in your imagination, noting his physical characteristics and mannerisms. See him walking, observing what he is wearing or carrying. Ponder this mental image, allowing any other observations about Jesus to form in your mind.

- Observe the people around Jesus, becoming aware of their appearance and demeanor. Observe whether they are sitting, standing, or walking. See Jesus' disciples, observing their behavior toward Jesus and each other. See the crowd around Jesus and their various actions as they walk with Jesus. Finally, see the blind beggar sitting alone and observe his actions and demeanor. Take a moment to ponder this mental image, allowing other impressions of these men and women to form.

- Allow yourself to become aware of the location of this moment of prayer. Observe its physical characteristics and the arrangement of the people in it. Look around the place and notice more details about it – if it is still and silent or filled with noise, if it has an unusual smell or not, etc.

- Take a moment to remain in this place with these men and women before allowing these images to fade from your consciousness.

[3] Become aware of your desires during this moment of prayer. Remember your desire to experience the divine presence all around you so you may attain a deep "felt knowledge" of Jesus Christ, who became human for you so you may better love and follow him. Recall your desire that in this day or week of prayer, you may experience Christ's power and what it means to be a disciple of Jesus. Also, ask for support and nourishment as you walk in the presence of the Son of God.

As these desires fill your consciousness, let all other concerns fall aside as you focus on this time and place of prayer.

[4] Allow the image of Jesus and the crowd to reemerge in your imagination.
- Watch as the group assembles around Jesus. Listen to the sounds of this moment and become comfortable in it. Feel the anticipation of the people around you and share in that enthusiasm.
- Ask God to help you enter this moment – either by joining these events or by listening quietly to them. Focus your attention on Jesus, noting his physical appearance and his demeanor.
- Watch and listen as you observe Jesus healing the blind man as well as the various ways that the disciples and people in the crowd behave toward Jesus during and after this miracle. You may want to quietly read the passage in Luke's gospel while remaining prayerfully aware of your mental image or you may choose to stay completely within the imagined realm of your prayer. Whichever you choose, know that God will offer you the words from the biblical passage that you need to hear – even if only in fragments.
- As these images fade from your imagination, become aware of the phrases and images from this moment which touched you most deeply. Recall the emotions and memories – including any sounds or smells – evoked during your prayer. Allow these seminal aspects of your meditation to linger on your mind and in your heart, noting any special feelings evoked by them.

[5] Then, become aware of Jesus' presence with you in this moment and have an open and informal conversation about this prayer period and how the passage from Luke's gospel expresses your own needs or desires – giving space for Jesus to respond or to highlight different aspects from the biblical account and your experiences during this contemplation. Then, gradually allow your thoughts to recede as you focus on God's broader presence in your life and in the world around you.

[6] Conclude by offering this prayer:

Confirm me in your love divine,
Smooth for my feet life's rugged way;
My will with yours entwine,
Lest evil lead my steps astray.
Be with my still as guard and guide,
Keep me in holy sanctity,
Let my firm faith on you abide,
From fraud and error hold me free. Amen.

[7]   Afterward, take 10-15 minutes in a quiet space to reflect on the most significant moments from your prayer and record your reflections in your journal.

7.4 A Contemplation of Matthew 17:1-9

In this contemplation of Matthew 17:1-9, you will see and hear the events surrounding Jesus' transfiguration.

[1] Begin by reading the biblical selection and reviewing your notes on it.

[2] Then, focus on this specific time and place as you allow all other concerns to fall away before considering the people and place of this moment of prayer.

- Allow an image of Jesus to emerge in your imagination, noting his physical characteristics and mannerisms. Look at what he is wearing or carrying. Make a note of whether he is sitting, standing, or walking. Ponder this mental image, allowing any other observations about Jesus to form in your mind.

- Observe the three disciples with Jesus, becoming aware of their appearance and demeanor. See what they are wearing as well as how they behave toward Jesus and each other. Observe Moses and Elijah, noting what they are wearing and how they behave toward Jesus. Take a moment to ponder this mental image, allowing other impressions of these men and women to form.

- Allow yourself to become aware of the location of this moment of prayer. Observe its physical characteristics and the arrangement of the people in it. Look around the place and notice more details about it – if it is overcast or sunny, if it has an unusual smell or not, etc.

- Take a moment to remain in this place with these men and women before allowing these images to fade from your consciousness.

[3] Become aware of your desires during this moment of prayer. Remember your desire to experience the divine presence all around you so you may attain a deep "felt knowledge" of Jesus Christ, who became human for you so you may better love and follow him. Recall your desire that in this day or week of prayer, you may experience Christ's power and what it means to be a disciple of Jesus. Also, ask for support and nourishment as you walk in the presence of the Son of God.

As these desires fill your consciousness, let all other concerns fall aside as you focus on this time and place of prayer.

[4] Allow the image of Jesus and his disciples to reemerge in your imagination.

- Watch as the disciples walk with Jesus. Listen to the sounds of this moment and become comfortable in it. Feel the anticipation of the disciples as they are alone with Jesus and share in their enthusiasm.
- Ask God to help you share in this experience – either by joining these events or by listening quietly to them. Focus your attention on Jesus, noting his physical appearance and his demeanor.
- Then, watch and listen as you observe the events of Jesus' transfiguration and the reactions of the disciples. You may want to quietly read the passage in Matthew's gospel while remaining prayerfully aware of your mental image or you may choose to stay completely within the imagined realm of your prayer. Whichever you choose, know that God will offer you the words from the biblical passage that you need to hear – even if only in fragments.
- As these images fade from your imagination, become aware of the phrases and images from this moment which touched you most deeply. Recall the emotions and memories – including any sounds or smells – evoked during your prayer. Allow these seminal aspects of your meditation to linger on your mind and in your heart, noting any special feelings evoked by them.

[5] Then, become aware of Jesus' presence with you in this moment and have an open and informal conversation about this prayer period and how the passage from Matthew's gospel expresses your own needs or desires – giving space for Jesus to respond or to highlight different aspects from the biblical account and your experiences during this contemplation. Then, gradually allow your thoughts to recede as you focus on God's broader presence in your life and in the world around you.

[6] Conclude by offering this prayer:
> *Confirm me in your love divine,*
> *Smooth for my feet life's rugged way;*
> *My will with yours entwine,*
> *Lest evil lead my steps astray.*
> *Be with my still as guard and guide,*
> *Keep me in holy sanctity,*
> *Let my firm faith on you abide,*
> *From fraud and error hold me free. Amen.*

[7] Afterward, take 10-15 minutes in a quiet space to reflect on the most significant moments from your prayer and record your reflections in your journal.

7.5 A Meditation on 2 Peter 1:3-11

In this meditation on 2 Peter 1:3-11, you will see and hear Saint Brigid teach her disciples how they are transformed through their choice to follow Christ.

[1] Begin by reading the biblical selection and reviewing your notes on it.

[2] Then, focus on this specific time and place as you allow all other concerns to fall away before considering the people and place in this moment of prayer.

- Allow an image of Brigid to emerge in your imagination, noting her physical characteristics and mannerisms. Look at what she is wearing or carrying. Make a note of whether she is sitting, standing, or walking. Ponder this mental image, allowing any other observations about Brigid to form in your mind.
- Observe the people around Saint Brigid, becoming aware of their appearance and demeanor. Observe whether they are sitting, standing, or walking. Take a moment to ponder this mental image, allowing other impressions of these men and women to form.
- Allow yourself to become aware of the location of this moment of prayer. Observe its physical characteristics and the arrangement of the people in it. Look around the place and notice more details about it – if it is in dim or bright light, if it is still and silent or filled with noise, if it has an unusual smell or not, etc.
- Take a moment to remain in this place with these men and women before allowing these images to fade from your consciousness.

[3] Become aware of your desires during this moment of prayer. Remember your desire to experience the divine presence all around you so you may attain a deep "felt knowledge" of Jesus Christ, who became human for you so you may better love and follow him. Recall your desire that in this day or week of prayer, you may experience Christ's power and what it means to be a disciple of Jesus. Also, ask for support and nourishment as you walk in the presence of the Son of God.

As these desires fill your consciousness, let all other concerns fall aside as you focus on this time and place of prayer.

[4] Allow the image of Saint Brigid and her disciples to reemerge in your imagination.

- Watch as the group assembles around Brigid. Listen to the sounds of this moment and become comfortable as you prepare to hear Brigid speak. Feel the anticipation of the people around you and share in that enthusiasm.
- As you hear Brigid invite her companions to pray, ask God to help you share in their prayer – either by joining them or by listening quietly to them. Focus your attention on Saint Brigid, noting her physical appearance and her demeanor.
- Then, watch and listen as Brigid recites the words of Peter's epistle before discussing its meaning and importance. You may want to quietly read the passage while remaining prayerfully aware of your mental image or you may choose to stay completely within the imagined realm of your prayer. Whichever you choose, know that God will offer you the words from the biblical passage that you need to hear – even if only in fragments.
- As these images fade from your imagination, become aware of the phrases and images from this moment which touched you most deeply. Recall the emotions and memories – including any sounds or smells – evoked during your prayer. Allow these seminal aspects of your meditation to linger on your mind and in your heart, noting any special feelings evoked by them.

[5] Then, become aware of Jesus' presence with you in this moment and have an open and informal conversation about this prayer period and how the passage from Peter's epistle expresses your own needs or desires – giving space for Jesus to respond or to highlight different aspects from the biblical account and your experiences during this contemplation. Then, gradually allow your thoughts to recede as you focus on God's broader presence in your life and in the world around you.

[6] Conclude by offering this prayer:
Confirm me in your love divine,
Smooth for my feet life's rugged way;
My will with yours entwine,
Lest evil lead my steps astray.
Be with my still as guard and guide,
Keep me in holy sanctity,
Let my firm faith on you abide,
From fraud and error hold me free. Amen.

[7]   Afterward, take 10-15 minutes in a quiet space to reflect on the most significant moments from your prayer and record your reflections in your journal.

7.6 An Application of the Senses

[1] Become aware of your prayerful desires during this day or week. Bring to mind your desire to experience an inner knowledge of Jesus Christ who became human for you so you may better love and follow him. Ask also that you may experience Christ's power and what it means to be a disciple of Jesus.

[2] Call to mind the various prayers of the preceding day or days. Allow the images and words of these prayers to linger and then slowly fade from your consciousness.

- Remember your imaginative contemplation of Matthew 14:13-21. Consider the images and feelings evoked in you during your prayer, feeling God's presence in these memories and becoming aware of the specific sensations associated with each image.

- Recall your imaginative contemplation of Luke 18:35-43, considering it in the same way as your earlier memories of Matthew 14.

- Review your imaginative contemplation of Matthew 17:1-9 in the same manner as the previous prayers.

- Revisit your meditation on 2 Peter 1:3-11 in the same manner as the previous prayers.

Make a mental note of which senses are most active. You may see an image or a color, hear a sound or a phrase, or smell a scent or a fragrance. You may even taste a flavor or feel a sensation on your skin.

[3] Then, relax and allow these various memories and experiences to quietly enter and leave your consciousness. Linger on the sensory images and memories being evoked in you – noticing any images or colors, any sounds or phrases, any scents or fragrances, any flavors or physical sensations associated with each prayer.

[4] When you are ready, become completely still and clear your mind of all thoughts and concerns. Allow an image of a special personal space to form in your imagination. Then, watch as God enters that place and forms a small image or object for you that expresses the thought or awareness that you most need to carry with you into your life.

Reverently pick up the object or image, a reflection of the most important gift you have been given during this time of prayer. Look at it carefully and become aware of the divine presence contained within it. Register what it looks like and how it feels in your hand. Then, feel the joy and confidence that comes from touching the presence of God

as you accept this gift, offering a short prayer of gratitude while you relax into the pleasure of this moment.

[5]   Then, conclude by offering this prayer:
> *Confirm me in your love divine,*
> *Smooth for my feet life's rugged way;*
> *My will with yours entwine,*
> *Lest evil lead my steps astray.*
> *Be with my still as guard and guide,*
> *Keep me in holy sanctity,*
> *Let my firm faith on you abide,*
> *From fraud and error hold me free. Amen.*

[6]   While your experiences are still fresh in your mind, record the most significant impressions or sensations from this time of prayer in your journal.

7.7 Review of Prayer

[1]   Remember your desires during the preceding day or week of prayer. Become aware of the divine presence all around you, offering you inner knowledge of Jesus Christ who became human for you so you may better love and follow him. Recall your desire to experience Christ's power and what it means to be a disciple of Jesus.

Ask God once again to fulfill these desires in your own life and in your interactions with others.

[2]   Then, take a moment to allow the words, thoughts, and feelings from your prayers during the last day or week to linger before asking God to reveal the fulfillment of your deepest desires in these various memories.

• Think about the prayer sequence at the beginning of this day or week. Make a mental note of any words, insights or images that remain particularly significant or meaningful to you.

• Ponder the story, "Two Miracles Performed by Brigid". Note any words, insights, or images from it that remain particularly significant or meaningful to you.

• Remember your imaginative contemplation of Matthew 14:13-21.

– Consider the most powerful images, phrases, or feelings from your prayer. Ask yourself what gifts God gave to you through these moments, perhaps offering you new insights or perhaps affirming an important aspect of your faith. Ask yourself how God may be calling you to change through these moments, being as specific as possible.

– Examine your disposition as you prayed. Recall the easiest moments in your prayer and any moments of joy you may have experienced. Remember also if you encountered any difficulty opening yourself to God or if you felt any sadness as you prayed. Ask God to help you understand why these feelings surfaced.

– Bring to mind any moments when you added personal elements (e.g., familiar places or people from your life) or connected your prayers to other scriptures or spiritual writings. Ask yourself how these additions helped or hindered you as you prayed. Again, if you do not know why this happened, ask God to help you understand.

• Recall your imaginative contemplation of Luke 18:35-43. Then, review your prayer in the same way as your earlier reflection on Matthew 14.

- Review your imaginative contemplation of Matthew 17:1-9 in the same manner as the previous prayers.
- Reminisce on your meditation on 2 Peter 1:3-11 in the same manner as the same manner as the previous prayers.
- Reflect on the ebb and flow of sensory impressions and feelings that marked your application of the senses. Isolate the most memorable moments and sensory impressions from your prayer and reflect on how God used these moments to give you a particular gift.

[3] Finally, ponder the times when images or feelings from the readings of this day or week surfaced outside these prayer periods. Think about the most memorable aspects of these experiences, asking God to explain their significance.

[4] Take a moment to allow the words, thoughts, and feelings of these prayers to linger on your mind and in your heart. Finally, conclude by offering this prayer:

O God, I believe in you; strengthen my belief.
I trust in you; confirm my trust.
I love you; double my love.
I repent that I angered you,
Increase my repentance.
Fill you my heart with awe without despair;
With hope, without over-confidence;
With piety without infatuation;
And with joy without excess.
My God, consent to guide me by your wisdom;
To constrain me by your right;
To comfort me by your mercy;
And to protect me by your power. Amen.

[5] After finishing these prayers, summarize your reflections on the gifts or graces you received during the prayers of this last day or week and record these thoughts in your journal.

8. Following Jesus as a Companion

8.1a   Oh, Kind Creator Of The Skies
a prayer of Christian fellowship

Take a moment to quiet your spirit, becoming completely present to this time and place. Allow all other thoughts and concerns to fall away as you come into the presence of God. Then, when you are ready, begin.

Oh, kind Creator of the skies,
Eternal light to guide my feet,
    Give ear to my beseeching cries
    And save me in your mercy sweet.

Descending from your throne above,
You strive the sluggish world to win,
    Moved by the power of mighty love,
    Lest earth be lost in death and sin.

A Hymn, sung or heard (optional)

To my Friends, remember what I say,
that in the day of Judgement's shock,
    when all ghosts ambling down the Mount,
    the sheep may count you of their flock.

And narrow though you find the path
To heaven's high wrath, and hard to gain,
    I warn you shun that broad white road
    That leads to the abode of pain.

Not on the world I love bestow,
Passing flowers that blow and die;
    Follow not you the spacious track
    That turns your back to God most high.

And love your neighbor as yourself,
(not for wealth your love should be),
    But a greater love than every love
    Give God above who loves you.

He shall not see the abode of pain
Whose mercies rain on poor folk still:
    Alms, fastings, prayers, must aid the soul;
    your blood control, control your will.

Shun folly, shun greed, shun sensual fires,
(eager desires of those enslaved),
    Anger and pride and hatred shun,
    'Til heaven be won, 'til you be saved.

Read or recite Psalm 107.

Holy Lord,
Under my thoughts may I God-thoughts find.
Half of my sins escape my mind.
    For what I said, or did not say,
    Pardon me, O Lord, I pray.

Read Luke 10: 25-37, aloud or quietly.

O Lord, Jesus the Christ,
If I were in Heaven my harp I would sound
With apostles and angels and saints all around,
    Praising and thanking the Son who is crowned,
    May the poor race of Eve for that heaven be bound!

Holy Lord,
Since hell each soul pursues each day,
Man and woman, 'til life does end,
    Be not deceived, as others may,
    Remember what I say, my Friend.

To him, our King, to Mary's son,
Who did not shun the evil death,
    Since he our goal is, to him alone,
    Commit your soul, your life, your breath.

O Holy Lord,
    God with the Father and the Spirit,
For me is many a snare designed,

To fill my mind with doubts and fears;
> Far from the land of holy saints,
> I dwell within my vale of tears.
Let faith, let hope, let love –
Traits far above the cold world's way –
> With patience, humility, and awe,
> Become my guides from day to day.

I acknowledge, the evil I have done.
From the day of my birth till the day of my death,
> Through the sight of my eyes,
Through the hearing of my ears,
> Through the sayings of my mouth,
Through the thoughts of my heart,
> Through the touch of my hands,
Through the course of my way,
> Through all I said and did not,
Through all I promised and fulfilled not,
> Through all the laws and holy commandments I broke.
I ask even now absolution of you,
> For fear I may have never asked it as was right,
> And that I might not live to ask it again,

O Holy Lord, my King in Heaven,
May you not let my soul stray from you,
May you keep me in a good state,
> May you turn me toward what is good to do,
> May you protect me from dangers, small and great.
May you fill my eyes with tears of repentance,
> So I may avoid the sinner's awful sentence.
May the Grace of the God for ever be with me,
> And whatever my needs, may the Triune God give me.

Select one of the following options for the Lord's Prayer.

Option A

O Jesus Christ,
Lord of heaven and earth,
Help me pray as you yourself taught:

"Our Father in heaven,
hallowed be your name.
Your kingdom come.
Your will be done,
on earth as it is in heaven.
Give us this day our daily bread.
And forgive us our debts,
as we also have forgiven our debtors.
And do not bring us to the time of trial,
but rescue us from the evil one."
(Matthew 6: 9-13)
From the foes of my land,
from the foes of my faith,
From the foes who would us dissever,
> O Lord, preserve me, in life and in death,
> With the Sign of the Cross for ever.
> *For the kingdom, the power, and the glory*
> *are yours now and for ever. Amen.*

Please proceed with "I beseech you, O Lord...," found after Option B.

Option B

O Jesus Christ,
Lord of heaven and earth,
Help me pray as you yourself taught:
> *Our Father in heaven,*
> *hallowed be your name,*
> *your kingdom come,*
> *your will be done,*
> *on earth as in heaven.*
> *Give us today our daily bread.*
> *Forgive us our sins*
> *as we forgive those who sin against us.*
> *Lead us not into temptation*
> *but deliver us from evil.*

From the foes of my land,
from the foes of my faith,
From the foes who would us dissever,

O Lord, preserve me, in life and in death,
With the Sign of the Cross for ever.
*For the kingdom, the power, and the glory
are yours now and for ever. Amen.*

I beseech you, O Lord.
God in Heaven, unsurpassed in power and might;
> Be behind me, Be on my left,
> Be before me, Be on my right!
Against each danger, you are my help;
In distress, upon you I call.
> In dark times, may you sustain me
> And lift me up again when I fall.
Lord over heaven and of earth,
You know my offenses.
> Yet, listening to my pleadings,
> You guide me away from sinful pretenses.
Lord of all creation and the many creatures,
You bestow on me many earthly treasures.
> Revealing love in each life and season,
> You share with me heavenly pleasures.
May you arouse me
In moments both of joy and of strife;
> Most holy Lord, bring me new life!

A Hymn, sung or heard (optional)

O Jesus Christ,
> Lord of heaven and earth,
> You are my riches, my store, my provision,
My star through the years
When troubles rend me,
> Through times of strife and tears,
> Sweet Jesus, defend me.

Hail, heaven's eternal glory, to you I sing
Who unto all the blessed hope did bring.
> Born of the Virgin, chaste and pure,
> And of our Heavenly Father most sure.

Give us your right hand, Lord, that we may rise,
Make clean our hearts and purify our eyes,
> Like blazing torches let our song of praise
> And gratitude ascend against the skies.

End this time of prayer by taking some time to bring to mind the various ways God shields you from harm or guides you through the world's tumult. Then, when you are ready, conclude by saying:

O Holy Lord, King in Heaven,
I place myself at the edge of your grace,
> On the floor of your house myself I place,
And to banish the sin of my heart away,
> I lower my knee to you this day.
Through life's torrents of pain may you bring me whole,
> And, O Lord Jesus Christ, preserve also my soul. Amen.

8.1b Preparation for Prayer

<u>Consideration of the Readings</u>

After reciting or prayerfully reading the prayer sequence for this day or week:
- Read about Jesus' interaction with the sinful woman in Luke 7:36-50. Make a mental note of Jesus' appearance and actions during the episode, the people listening to him, and the key elements of Jesus' message. Then, consider any aspects of this story that speak strongly to you before recording these observations in your workbook.
- Read about Jesus telling the parable of the Good Samaritan in Luke 10:25-37, noting each person's appearance and actions during the episode as well as the key elements of the story and its setting. Then, record any aspects of this story that speak strongly to you.
- Read about Jesus' preaching in Matthew 5:1-16, noting Jesus' appearance and actions during the episode, the people listening to him, and the key elements of Jesus' message. Then, consider any aspects of this story that speak strongly to you before recording these observations in your workbook.
- Read Colossians 3:12-17. Again, pay careful attention to any phrases or images that seem particularly meaningful to you. Then, record these highlights in your workbook so you will remember them during this day or week of prayer.

Note: You also should consider any aspect of the prayer sequence from this day or week that seemed particularly significant to you.

<u>Contemplation of Your Needs</u>

When you are ready, allow any distractions to fade from your consciousness as you become aware of your desire to live in God's goodness. Feel yourself yearning to properly use the many gifts God has given you, to experience God's continuing care, and to be open to the immense love God shows for you, then:
- Read "Brigid and the Silver Chain" (found on page 313). Allow yourself to linger on any thoughts, phrases or images that seem

particularly meaningful or significant to your earlier preparations or prayer.

- Pray for your desires in the coming day or week. Ask that the divine presence all around you may be revealed, offering you inner knowledge of Jesus Christ who became human for you so you may better love and follow him. Ask also that you may experience the compassion that Jesus expresses in his interaction with others and understand what it is to be a companion of Jesus.
- Conclude by praying to be a better companion of Jesus and act in the same manner he demonstrates through his own actions and responses to others.

Then, record any significant thoughts, emotions, or reactions from these moments in your workbook.

After this, put your notes aside. Without straining your memory, consider in turn each of the readings for the coming day or week and allow them to take shape in your imagination. Prayerfully ponder how each reading affects you emotionally without overtly thinking about their content, asking God to illuminate the spiritual gifts offered in each reading.

Finally, conclude by offering this prayer:
O God, I believe in you; strengthen my belief.
I trust in you; confirm my trust.
I love you; double my love.
I repent that I angered you,
Increase my repentance.
Fill you my heart with awe without despair;
With hope, without over-confidence;
With piety without infatuation;
And with joy without excess.
My God, consent to guide me by your wisdom;
To constrain me by your right;
To comfort me by your mercy;
And to protect me by your power. Amen.

Allow these words to linger on your mind and in your heart for a few moments and then write the most important thoughts, feelings, and desires in your journal.

8.2   A Contemplation of Luke 7:36-50

In this contemplation of Luke 7:36-50, you will see and hear Jesus forgive a sinner.

[1]   Begin by reading the biblical selection and reviewing your notes on it.

[2]   Then, focus on this specific time and place as you allow all other concerns to fall away before considering the people and place in this moment of prayer.

• Allow an image of Jesus to emerge in your imagination, noting his physical characteristics and mannerisms. Look at what he is wearing or carrying. Make a note of whether he is sitting, standing, or walking. Ponder this mental image, allowing any other observations about Jesus to form in your mind.

• Observe the people around Jesus, becoming aware of their appearance and demeanor. Observe whether they are sitting, standing, or walking. See Jesus' disciples, observing their behavior toward Jesus and each other. See the crowd around Jesus and their various actions as they are with Jesus. Finally, see the woman accused of adultery and observe her appearance, actions, and demeanor. Take a moment to ponder this mental image, allowing other impressions of these men and women to form.

• Allow yourself to become aware of the location of this moment of prayer. Observe its physical characteristics and the arrangement of the people in it. Look around the place and notice more details about it – if it is in dim or bright light, if it is still and silent or filled with noise, if it has an unusual smell or not, etc.

• Take a moment to remain in this place with these men and women before allowing these images to fade from your consciousness.

[3]   Become aware of your desires during this moment of prayer. Remember your desire to experience the divine presence all around you so you may attain a deep "felt knowledge" of Jesus Christ, who became human for you so you may better love and follow him. Recall your desire that in this day or week of prayer, you may experience the compassion that Jesus expresses in his interactions with others and understand what it is to be a companion of Jesus. Also, ask that you may act in the same manner that Jesus demonstrates through his own actions and responses to others.

As these desires fill your consciousness, let all other concerns fall aside as you focus on this time and place of prayer.

[4]   Allow the image of Jesus and the crowd to reemerge in your imagination.

- Watch as the group assembles around Jesus. Listen to the sounds of this moment and become comfortable as you prepare to hear Jesus speak. Feel the anticipation of the people around you and share in that enthusiasm.

- Ask God to help you share in this experience – either by joining these events or by listening quietly to them. Focus your attention on Jesus, noting his physical appearance and his demeanor.

- Then, watch and listen as Jesus speaks to the crowd before the woman is brought to Jesus and forgiven by him. You may want to quietly read the passage in John's gospel while remaining prayerfully aware of your mental image or you may choose to stay completely within the imagined realm of your prayer. Whichever you choose, know that God will offer you the words from the biblical passage that you need to hear – even if only in fragments.

- As these images fade from your imagination, become aware of the phrases and images from this moment which touched you most deeply. Recall the emotions and memories – including any sounds or smells – evoked during your prayer. Allow these seminal aspects of your meditation to linger on your mind and in your heart, noting any special feelings evoked by them.

[5]   Then, become aware of Jesus' presence with you in this moment and have an open and informal conversation about this prayer period and how the passage from Luke's gospel expresses your own needs or desires – giving space for Jesus to respond or to highlight different aspects from the biblical account and your experiences during this contemplation. Then, gradually allow your thoughts to recede as you focus on God's broader presence in your life and in the world around you.

[6]   Conclude by offering this prayer:

Confirm me in your love divine,
Smooth for my feet life's rugged way;
My will with yours entwine,
Lest evil lead my steps astray.
Be with my still as guard and guide,
Keep me in holy sanctity,
Let my firm faith on you abide,

From fraud and error hold me free. Amen.

[7]   Afterward, take 10-15 minutes in a quiet space to reflect on the most significant moments from your prayer and record your reflections in your journal.

8.3   A Contemplation of Luke 10:25-37

In this contemplation of Luke 10:25-37, you will see and hear Jesus tell the parable of the Good Samaritan.

[1]   Begin by reading the biblical selection and reviewing your notes on it.

[2]   Then, focus on this specific time and place as you allow all other concerns to fall away before considering the people and place in this moment of prayer.

• Allow an image of Jesus to emerge in your imagination, noting his physical characteristics and mannerisms. Look at what he is wearing or carrying. Make a note of whether he is sitting, standing, or walking. Ponder this mental image, allowing any other observations about Jesus to form in your mind.

• Observe the people around Jesus, becoming aware of their appearance and demeanor. Observe whether they are sitting, standing, or walking. See Jesus' disciples, observing their behavior toward Jesus and each other. See the crowd around Jesus and their various actions as they are with Jesus. Take a moment to ponder this mental image, allowing other impressions of these men and women to form.

• Allow yourself to become aware of the location of this moment of prayer. Observe its physical characteristics and the arrangement of the people in it. Look around the place and notice more details about it – if it is in dim or bright light, if it is still and silent or filled with noise, if it has an unusual smell or not, etc.

• Take a moment to remain in this place with these men and women before allowing these images to fade from your consciousness.

[3]   Become aware of your desires during this moment of prayer. Remember your desire to experience the divine presence all around you so you may attain a deep "felt knowledge" of Jesus Christ, who became human for you so you may better love and follow him. Recall your desire that in this day or week of prayer, you may experience the compassion that Jesus expresses in his interactions with others and understand what it is to be a companion of Jesus. Also, ask that you may act in the same manner that Jesus demonstrates through his own actions and responses to others.

As these desires fill your consciousness, let all other concerns fall aside as you focus on this time and place of prayer.

[4]   Allow the image of Jesus and the crowd to reemerge in your imagination.
• Watch as the group assembles around Jesus. Listen to the sounds of this moment and become comfortable as you prepare to hear Jesus speak. Feel the anticipation of the people around you and share in that enthusiasm.
• As you watch Jesus calm the crowd, ask God to help you share in this experience – either by joining these events or by listening quietly to them. Focus your attention on Jesus, noting his physical appearance and his demeanor.
• Then, watch and listen as Jesus speaks to the crowd and tells the parable of the Good Samaritan. You may want to quietly read the passage in John's gospel while remaining prayerfully aware of your mental image or you may choose to stay completely within the imagined realm of your prayer. Whichever you choose, know that God will offer you the words from the biblical passage that you need to hear – even if only in fragments.
• As these images fade from your imagination, become aware of the phrases and images from this moment which touched you most deeply. Recall the emotions and memories – including any sounds or smells – evoked during your prayer. Allow these seminal aspects of your meditation to linger on your mind and in your heart, noting any special feelings evoked by them.
[5]   Then, become aware of Jesus' presence with you in this moment and have an open and informal conversation about this prayer period and how the passage from Luke's gospel expresses your own needs or desires – giving space for Jesus to respond or to highlight different aspects from the biblical account and your experiences during this contemplation. Then, gradually allow your thoughts to recede as you focus on God's broader presence in your life and in the world around you.
[6]   Conclude by offering this prayer:
Confirm me in your love divine,
Smooth for my feet life's rugged way;
My will with yours entwine,
Lest evil lead my steps astray.
Be with my still as guard and guide,
Keep me in holy sanctity,
Let my firm faith on you abide,
From fraud and error hold me free. Amen.

[7]   Afterward, take 10-15 minutes in a quiet space to reflect on the most significant moments from your prayer and record your reflections in your journal.

8.4　A Contemplation of Matthew 5:1-16

In this contemplation of Matthew 5:1-16, you will see and hear Jesus preach to a crowd on the Beatitudes.

[1]　Begin by reading the biblical selection and reviewing your notes on it.

[2]　Then, focus on this specific time and place as you allow all other concerns to fall away before considering the people and place in this moment of prayer.

- Allow an image of Jesus to emerge in your imagination, noting his physical characteristics and mannerisms. Look at what he is wearing or carrying. Make a note of whether he is sitting, standing, or walking. Ponder this mental image, allowing any other observations about Jesus to form in your mind.

- Observe the people around Jesus, becoming aware of their appearance and demeanor. Observe whether they are sitting, standing, or walking. See Jesus' disciples, observing their behavior toward Jesus and each other. See the crowd around Jesus and their various actions as they are with Jesus. Take a moment to ponder this mental image, allowing other impressions of these men and women to form.

- Allow yourself to become aware of the location of this moment of prayer. Observe its physical characteristics and the arrangement of the people in it. Look around the place and notice more details about it – if it is in dim or bright light, if it is still and silent or filled with noise, if it has an unusual smell or not, etc.

- Take a moment to remain in this place with these men and women before allowing these images to fade from your consciousness.

[3]　Become aware of your desires during this moment of prayer. Remember your desire to experience the divine presence all around you so you may attain a deep "felt knowledge" of Jesus Christ, who became human for you so you may better love and follow him. Recall your desire that in this day or week of prayer, you may experience the compassion that Jesus expresses in his interactions with others and understand what it is to be a companion of Jesus. Also, ask that you may act in the same manner that Jesus demonstrates through his own actions and responses to others.

As these desires fill your consciousness, let all other concerns fall aside as you focus on this time and place of prayer.

[4]   Allow the image of Jesus and the crowd to reemerge in your imagination.
- Watch as the group assembles around Jesus. Listen to the sounds of this moment and become comfortable as you prepare to hear Jesus speak. Feel the anticipation of the people around you and share in that enthusiasm.
- Ask God to help you enter this moment – either by joining these events or by listening quietly to them. Focus your attention on Jesus, noting his physical appearance and his demeanor.
- Then, watch and listen as Jesus speaks to the crowd and tells them the Beatitudes. You may want to quietly read the passage in John's gospel while remaining prayerfully aware of your mental image or you may choose to stay completely within the imagined realm of your prayer. Whichever you choose, know that God will offer you the words from the biblical passage that you need to hear – even if only in fragments.
- As these images fade from your imagination, become aware of the phrases and images from this moment which touched you most deeply. Recall the emotions and memories – including any sounds or smells – evoked during your prayer. Allow these seminal aspects of your meditation to linger on your mind and in your heart, noting any special feelings evoked by them.

[5]   Then, become aware of Jesus' presence with you in this moment and have an open and informal conversation about this prayer period and how the Beatitudes express your own needs or desires – giving space for Jesus to respond or to highlight different aspects from the biblical account and your experiences during this contemplation. Then, gradually allow your thoughts to recede as you focus on God's broader presence in your life and in the world around you.

[6]   Conclude by offering this prayer:

Confirm me in your love divine,
Smooth for my feet life's rugged way;
My will with yours entwine,
Lest evil lead my steps astray.
Be with my still as guard and guide,
Keep me in holy sanctity,
Let my firm faith on you abide,
From fraud and error hold me free. Amen.

[7]   Afterward, take 10-15 minutes in a quiet space to reflect on the most significant moments from your prayer and record your reflections in your journal.

8.5   A Meditation on Colossians 3:12-17

In this meditation on Colossians 3:12-17, you will see and hear Saint Brigid teach her disciples how to express the Beatitudes through their lives.

[1]   Begin by reading the biblical selection and reviewing your notes on it.

[2]   Then, focus on this specific time and place as you allow all other concerns to fall away before considering the people and place in this moment of prayer.

• Allow an image of Brigid to emerge in your imagination, noting her physical characteristics and mannerisms. Look at what she is wearing or carrying. Make a note of whether she is sitting, standing, or walking. Ponder this mental image, allowing any other observations about Brigid to form in your mind.

• Observe the people around Saint Brigid, becoming aware of their appearance and demeanor. Observe whether they are sitting, standing, or walking. Take a moment to ponder this mental image, allowing other impressions of these men and women to form.

• Allow yourself to become aware of the location of this moment of prayer. Observe its physical characteristics and the arrangement of the people in it. Look around the place and notice more details about it – if it is in dim or bright light, if it is still and silent or filled with noise, if it has an unusual smell or not, etc.

• Take a moment to remain in this place with these men and women before allowing these images to fade from your consciousness.

[3]   Become aware of your desires during this moment of prayer. Remember your desire to experience the divine presence all around you so you may attain a deep "felt knowledge" of Jesus Christ, who became human for you so you may better love and follow him. Recall your desire that in this day or week of prayer, you may experience the compassion that Jesus expresses in his interactions with others and understand what it is to be a companion of Jesus. Also, ask that you may act in the same manner that Jesus demonstrates through his own actions and responses to others.

As these desires fill your consciousness, let all other concerns fall aside as you focus on this time and place of prayer.

[4]   Allow the image of Saint Brigid and her disciples to reemerge in your imagination.

- Watch as the group assembles around Brigid. Listen to the sounds of this moment and become comfortable as you prepare to hear Brigid speak. Feel the anticipation of the people around you and share in that enthusiasm.
- As you hear Brigid invite her companions to listen, ask God to help you enter this moment – either by joining these events or by listening quietly to them. Focus your attention on Saint Brigid, noting her physical appearance and her demeanor.
- Then, watch and listen as Brigid speaks to her disciples about Paul's letter to the Colossians and its importance. You may want to quietly read the passage while remaining prayerfully aware of your mental image or you may choose to stay completely within the imagined realm of your prayer. Whichever you choose, know that God will offer you the words from the biblical passage that you need to hear – even if only in fragments.
- As these images fade from your imagination, become aware of the phrases and images from this moment which touched you most deeply. Recall the emotions and memories – including any sounds or smells – evoked during your prayer. Allow these seminal aspects of your meditation to linger on your mind and in your heart, noting any special feelings evoked by them.

[5] Then, become aware of Jesus' presence with you in this moment and have an open and informal conversation about this prayer period and how the Beatitudes expresses your own needs or desires – giving space for Jesus to respond or to highlight different aspects from the biblical account and your experiences during this contemplation. Then, gradually allow your thoughts to recede as you focus on God's broader presence in your life and in the world around you.

[6] Conclude by offering this prayer:

> *Confirm me in your love divine,*
> *Smooth for my feet life's rugged way;*
> *My will with yours entwine,*
> *Lest evil lead my steps astray.*
> *Be with my still as guard and guide,*
> *Keep me in holy sanctity,*
> *Let my firm faith on you abide,*
> *From fraud and error hold me free. Amen.*

[7] Afterward, take 10-15 minutes in a quiet space to reflect on the most significant moments from your prayer and record your reflections in your journal.

8.6 An Application of the Senses

[1] Become aware of your prayerful desires during this day or week. Bring to mind your desire to experience an inner knowledge of Jesus Christ who became human for you so you may better love and follow him. Ask also that you may experience the compassion that Jesus expresses in his interaction with others and understand what it is to be a companion of Jesus.

[2] Call to mind the various prayers of the preceding day or days. Allow the images and words of these prayers to linger and then slowly fade from your consciousness.

- Remember your imaginative contemplation of Luke 7:36-50. Consider the images and feelings evoked in you during your prayer, feeling God's presence in these memories and becoming aware of the specific sensations associated with each image.
- Recall your imaginative contemplation of Luke 10:25-37, considering it in the same way as your memories of Luke 7.
- Review your imaginative contemplation of Matthew 5:1-16 in the same manner as the previous prayers.
- Revisit your mediation on Colossians 3:12-17 in the same manner as the previous prayers.

Make a mental note of which senses are most active. You may see an image or a color, hear a sound or a phrase, or smell a scent or a fragrance. You may even taste a flavor or feel a sensation on your skin.

[3] Then, relax and allow these various memories and experiences to quietly enter and leave your consciousness. Linger on the sensory images and memories being evoked in you – noticing any images or colors, any sounds or phrases, any scents or fragrances, any flavors or physical sensations associated with each prayer.

[4] When you are ready, become completely still and clear your mind of all thoughts and concerns. Allow an image of a special personal space to form in your imagination. Then, watch as God enters that place and forms a small image or object for you that expresses the thought or awareness that you most need to carry with you into your life.

Reverently pick up the object or image, a reflection of the most important gift you have been given during this time of prayer. Look at it carefully and become aware of the divine presence contained within it. Register what it looks like and how it feels in your hand. Then, feel the joy and confidence that comes from touching the presence of God

as you accept this gift, offering a short prayer of gratitude while you relax into the pleasure of this moment.

[5]   Then, conclude by offering this prayer:

> *Confirm me in your love divine,*
> *Smooth for my feet life's rugged way;*
> *My will with yours entwine,*
> *Lest evil lead my steps astray.*
> *Be with my still as guard and guide,*
> *Keep me in holy sanctity,*
> *Let my firm faith on you abide,*
> *From fraud and error hold me free. Amen.*

[6]   While your experiences are still fresh in your mind, record the most significant impressions or sensations from this time of prayer in your journal.

8.7　Review of Prayer

[1]　Remember your desires during the preceding day or week of prayer. Become aware of the divine presence all around you, offering you inner knowledge of Jesus Christ who became human for you so you may better love and follow him. Recall your desire to experience the compassion that Jesus expresses in his interaction with others and understand what it is to be a companion of Jesus.

Ask God once again to fulfill these desires in your own life and in your interactions with others.

[2]　Then, take a moment to allow the words, thoughts, and feelings from your prayers during the last day or week to linger before asking God to reveal the fulfillment of your deepest desires in these various memories.

• Think about the prayer sequence at the beginning of this day or week. Make a mental note of any words, insights or images that remain particularly significant or meaningful to you.

• Ponder the story, "Brigid and the Silver Chain". Note any words, insights, or images from it that remain particularly significant or meaningful to you.

• Remember your imaginative contemplation of Luke 7:36-50.

– Consider the most powerful images, phrases, or feelings from your prayer. Ask yourself what gifts God gave to you through these moments, perhaps offering you new insights or perhaps affirming an important aspect of your faith. Ask yourself how God may be calling you to change through these moments, being as specific as possible.

– Examine your disposition as you prayed. Recall the easiest moments in your prayer and any moments of joy you may have experienced. Remember also if you encountered any difficulty opening yourself to God or if you felt any sadness as you prayed. Ask God to help you understand why these feelings surfaced.

– Bring to mind any moments when you added personal elements (e.g., familiar places or people from your life) or connected your prayers to other scriptures or spiritual writings. Ask yourself how these additions helped or hindered you as you prayed. Again, if you do not know why this happened, ask God to help you understand.

• Recall your imaginative contemplation of Luke 10:25-37. Then, review your prayer in the same way as your earlier reflection on Luke 7.

- Review your imaginative contemplations of Matthew 5:1-16 in the same manner as the previous prayers.
- Reminisce on your meditation on Colossians 3:12-17 in the same manner as the same manner as the previous prayers.
- Reflect on the ebb and flow of sensory impressions and feelings that marked your application of the senses. Isolate the most memorable moments and sensory impressions from your prayer and reflect on how God used these moments to give you a particular gift.

[3] Finally, ponder the times when images or feelings from the readings of this day or week surfaced outside these prayer periods. Think about the most memorable aspects of these experiences, asking God to explain their significance.

[4] Take a moment to allow the words, thoughts, and feelings of these prayers to linger on your mind and in your heart. Finally, conclude by offering this prayer:

O God, I believe in you; strengthen my belief.
I trust in you; confirm my trust.
I love you; double my love.
I repent that I angered you,
Increase my repentance.
Fill you my heart with awe without despair;
With hope, without over-confidence;
With piety without infatuation;
And with joy without excess.
My God, consent to guide me by your wisdom;
To constrain me by your right;
To comfort me by your mercy;
And to protect me by your power. Amen.

[5] After finishing these prayers, summarize your reflections on the gifts or graces you received during the prayers of this last day or week and record these thoughts in your journal.

9. Following Jesus as a Friend

9.1a   To The Fount Of Life Eternal
a prayer of praise and gratitude for Christ's love

Take a moment to quiet your spirit, becoming completely present to this time and place. Allow all other thoughts and concerns to fall away as you come into the presence of God. Then, when you are ready, begin.

To the fount of life eternal
Longs my thirsting soul to rise,
Longs to break the carnal prison
      Where the darkness holds its eyes,
      Weeps and wanders like an exile,
      Yearning for its native skies.

O, when bowed beneath the burdens
And the labors of the day,
      Comes the dream of one's lost glory
      Shining sweet with heavenly ray,
Present grief but swells the longing
      For the blessings cast away.

A Hymn, sung or heard (optional)

To you, O Christ, my prayers shall rise,
With tears of sorrow blending;
      Come to my help, O you Holy One,
      On my dark night descending.

My heart shall in you find its rest,
And e'en in dreams shall praise your love;
      And with each rising of the sun,
      New songs shall raise to you above.

Impart a noble life, and may
My spirit's warmth be heightened.
      Bid night depart, and with your love,
      O, may my life be brightened.

In hymns I pay my vows to you:

At every hour to you I pray,
    Erase the many sins I have made
    And allow me with you to stay.

You are my Lord, ever most high,
You guide my path by your grace.
    May I always serve your intentions
    And your desires fully embrace.

Read or recite Psalm 15.

Holy Lord,
Under my thoughts may I God-thoughts find.
Half of my sins escape my mind.
    For what I said, or did not say,
    Pardon me, O Lord, I pray.

Read John 15:12-17, aloud or quietly.

O Lord, Jesus the Christ,
If I were in Heaven my harp I would sound
With apostles and angels and saints all around,
    Praising and thanking the Son who is crowned,
    May the poor race of Eve for that heaven be bound!

Holy Lord,
A reckoning-day for my actions comes,
The winnowing day of the wheat and chaff,
    I must account for each pledge and promise
    Of my living and labouring on your behalf.

Not with flattery, not with lies,
Not with pride nor haughty tone,
    Is it right for me to become Christ's friendship
    With but the love of God alone.

O Holy Lord,
    God with the Father and the Spirit,
For me is many a snare designed,
To fill my mind with doubts and fears;

    Far from the land of holy saints,
    I dwell within my vale of tears.
Let faith, let hope, let love –
Traits far above the cold world's way –
    With patience, humility, and awe,
    Become my guides from day to day.

I acknowledge, the evil I have done.
From the day of my birth till the day of my death,
    Through the sight of my eyes,
Through the hearing of my ears,
    Through the sayings of my mouth,
Through the thoughts of my heart,
    Through the touch of my hands,
Through the course of my way,
    Through all I said and did not,
Through all I promised and fulfilled not,
    Through all the laws and holy commandments I broke.
I ask even now absolution of you,
    For fear I may have never asked it as was right,
    And that I might not live to ask it again,

O Holy Lord, my King in Heaven,
May you not let my soul stray from you,
May you keep me in a good state,
    May you turn me toward what is good to do,
    May you protect me from dangers, small and great.
May you fill my eyes with tears of repentance,
    So I may avoid the sinner's awful sentence.
May the Grace of the God for ever be with me,
    And whatever my needs, may the Triune God give me.

Select one of the following options for the Lord's Prayer.

Option A

O Jesus Christ,
Lord of heaven and earth,
Help me pray as you yourself taught:
    "Our Father in heaven,

> *hallowed be your name.*
> *Your kingdom come.*
> *Your will be done,*
> *on earth as it is in heaven.*
> *Give us this day our daily bread.*
> *And forgive us our debts,*
> *as we also have forgiven our debtors.*
> *And do not bring us to the time of trial,*
> *but rescue us from the evil one."*
> *(Matthew 6: 9-13)*

From the foes of my land,
from the foes of my faith,
From the foes who would us dissever,
> O Lord, preserve me, in life and in death,
> With the Sign of the Cross for ever.
> *For the kingdom, the power, and the glory*
> *are yours now and for ever. Amen.*

Please proceed with "I beseech you, O Lord…," found after Option B.

Option B

O Jesus Christ,
Lord of heaven and earth,
Help me pray as you yourself taught:
> *Our Father in heaven,*
> *hallowed be your name,*
> *your kingdom come,*
> *your will be done,*
> *on earth as in heaven.*
> *Give us today our daily bread.*
> *Forgive us our sins*
> *as we forgive those who sin against us.*
> *Lead us not into temptation*
> *but deliver us from evil.*

From the foes of my land,
from the foes of my faith,
From the foes who would us dissever,
> O Lord, preserve me, in life and in death,

With the Sign of the Cross for ever.
*For the kingdom, the power, and the glory
are yours now and for ever. Amen.*

I beseech you, O Lord.
God in Heaven, unsurpassed in power and might;
    Be behind me, Be on my left,
    Be before me, Be on my right!
Against each danger, you are my help;
In distress, upon you I call.
    In dark times, may you sustain me
    And lift me up again when I fall.
Lord over heaven and of earth,
You know my offenses.
    Yet, listening to my pleadings,
    You guide me away from sinful pretenses.
Lord of all creation and the many creatures,
You bestow on me many earthly treasures.
    Revealing love in each life and season,
    You share with me heavenly pleasures.
May you arouse me
In moments both of joy and of strife;
    Most holy Lord, bring me new life!

A Hymn, sung or heard (optional)

O Jesus Christ,
    Lord of heaven and earth,
    You are my riches, my store, my provision,
My star through the years
When troubles rend me,
    Through times of strife and tears,
    Sweet Jesus, defend me.

O Most Holy Lord,
Happy is that blessed spirit
Who beholds its maker nigh,
    Sees the Ruler of creation
    On the throne of majesty,
Marshalling the stars and planets

In their courses through the sky.

Fill my soul with strength and vigor
In my warfare here below;
>	Be your name to me a bulwark
>	In my struggle with the foe;
And your sweet reward hereafter
On my soul, dear Lord, bestow.

End this time of prayer by taking some time to bring to mind the various ways God shields you from harm or guides you through the world's tumult. Then, when you are ready, conclude by saying:

O Holy Lord, King in Heaven,
I place myself at the edge of your grace,
>	On the floor of your house myself I place,
And to banish the sin of my heart away,
>	I lower my knee to you this day.
Through life's torrents of pain may you bring me whole,
>	And, O Lord Jesus Christ, preserve also my soul. Amen.

9.1b   Preparation for Prayer

Consideration of the Readings

After reciting or prayerfully reading the prayer sequence for this day or week:

- Read about Jesus telling his disciples they are now his friends in John 15:12-17. Make a mental note of any phrases or images that seem particularly meaningful to you. Then, record these seminal aspects of the reading in your workbook so you will remember them during this day or week of prayer.

- Read about the death of Lazarus in John 11:1-37. Again, note each person's appearance and actions during the episode as well as the key elements of the story and its setting, including the setting in your workbook. Then, record any aspects of this story that speak strongly to you.

- Read about the resurrection of Lazarus in John 11:38-45, noting each person's appearance and actions during the episode as well as the key elements of the story and its setting before recording any aspects of this story that speak strongly to you.

- Read 1 Corinthians 13:1-13 and Brigid's prayer, "The Things Brigid Wished For" or "I would wish for a great lake of ale for the King of Kings" (found on page 314). Again, pay careful attention to any phrases or images that seem particularly meaningful to you. Then, record these highlights in your workbook so you will remember them during this day or week of prayer.

<u>Note:</u> You also should consider any aspect of the prayer sequence from this day or week that seemed particularly significant to you.

Contemplation of Your Needs

When you are ready, allow any distractions to fade from your consciousness as you become aware of your desire to live in God's goodness. Feel yourself yearning to properly use the many gifts God has given you, to experience God's continuing care, and to be open to the immense love God shows for you, then:

• Read "Brigid Discusses a Vision with Patrick" (found on page 314). Allow yourself to linger on any thoughts, phrases or images that seem particularly meaningful or significant to your earlier preparations or prayer.

• Pray for your desires in the coming day or week. Ask that the divine presence all around you may be revealed, offering you inner knowledge of Jesus Christ who became human for you so you may better love and follow him. Ask also that you may open yourself to the love that Jesus has for those with whom he is most intimately associated.

• Conclude by praying that you may experience that love and be a true friend of Jesus, reflecting that love in your interactions with others and in your interior choices.

Then, record any significant thoughts, emotions, or reactions from these moments in your workbook.

After this, put your notes aside. Without straining your memory, consider in turn each of the readings for the coming day or week and allow them to take shape in your imagination. Prayerfully ponder how each reading affects you emotionally without overtly thinking about their content, asking God to illuminate the spiritual gifts offered in each reading.

Finally, conclude by offering this prayer:
O God, I believe in you; strengthen my belief.
I trust in you; confirm my trust.
I love you; double my love.
I repent that I angered you,
Increase my repentance.
Fill you my heart with awe without despair;
With hope, without over-confidence;
With piety without infatuation;
And with joy without excess.
My God, consent to guide me by your wisdom;
To constrain me by your right;
To comfort me by your mercy;
And to protect me by your power. Amen.

Allow these words to linger on your mind and in your heart for a few moments and then write the most important thoughts, feelings, and desires in your journal.

9.2   A Contemplation of John 15:12-17

In this contemplation of John 15:12-17, you will see and hear Jesus tell his disciples they are his friends.

[1]   Begin by reading the biblical selection and reviewing your notes on it.

[2]   Then, focus on this specific time and place as you allow all other concerns to fall away before considering the people and place in this moment of prayer.

• Allow an image of Jesus to emerge in your imagination, noting his physical characteristics and mannerisms. Look at what he is wearing or carrying. Make a note of whether he is sitting, standing, or walking. Ponder this mental image, allowing any other observations about Jesus to form in your mind.

• Observe the disciples around Jesus, becoming aware of their appearance and demeanor. Observe how act toward Jesus and each other. Take a moment to ponder this mental image, allowing other impressions of these men and women to form.

• Allow yourself to become aware of the location of this moment of prayer. Observe its physical characteristics and the arrangement of the people in it. Look around the place and notice more details about it – if it is in dim or bright light, if it is still and silent or filled with noise, if it has an unusual smell or not, etc.

• Take a moment to remain in this place with these men and women before allowing these images to fade from your consciousness.

[3]   Become aware of your desires during this moment of prayer. Remember your desire to experience the divine presence all around you so you may attain a deep "felt knowledge" of Jesus Christ, who became human for you so you may better love and follow him. Recall your desire that in this day or week of prayer, you may open yourself to the love that Jesus has for those with whom he is most intimately associated. Also, ask that you may experience that love and be a true friend of Jesus, reflecting that love in your interactions with others and in your interior choices.

As these desires fill your consciousness, let all other concerns fall aside as you focus on this time and place of prayer.

[4]   Allow the image of Jesus and the crowd to reemerge in your imagination.

- Watch as the disciples assemble around Jesus. Listen to the sounds of this moment and become comfortable as you prepare to hear Jesus speak. Feel the anticipation of the people around you and share in that enthusiasm.
- Ask God to help you enter this moment – either by joining these events or by listening quietly to them. Focus your attention on Jesus, noting his physical appearance and his demeanor.
- Then, watch and listen as Jesus tells the disciples they are his friends and the significance of this statement. You may want to quietly read the passage in John's gospel while remaining prayerfully aware of your mental image or you may choose to stay completely within the imagined realm of your prayer. Whichever you choose, know that God will offer you the words from the biblical passage that you need to hear – even if only in fragments.
- As these images fade from your imagination, become aware of the phrases and images from this moment which touched you most deeply. Recall the emotions and memories – including any sounds or smells – evoked during your prayer. Allow these seminal aspects of your meditation to linger on your mind and in your heart, noting any special feelings evoked by them.

[5] Then, become aware of Jesus' presence with you in this moment and have an open and informal conversation about this prayer period and how becoming Jesus' friend fulfills your own needs or desires – giving space for Jesus to respond or to highlight different aspects from the biblical account and your experiences during this contemplation. Then, gradually allow your thoughts to recede as you focus on God's broader presence in your life and in the world around you.

[6] Conclude by offering this prayer:

> *Confirm me in your love divine,*
> *Smooth for my feet life's rugged way;*
> *My will with yours entwine,*
> *Lest evil lead my steps astray.*
> *Be with my still as guard and guide,*
> *Keep me in holy sanctity,*
> *Let my firm faith on you abide,*
> *From fraud and error hold me free. Amen.*

[7] Afterward, take 10-15 minutes in a quiet space to reflect on the most significant moments from your prayer and record your reflections in your journal.

9.3 A Contemplation of John 11:1-37

In this contemplation of John 11:1-37, you will see and hear Jesus as he responds to the death of Lazarus.

[1]   Begin by reading the biblical selection and reviewing your notes on it.

[2]   Then, focus on this specific time and place as you allow all other concerns to fall away before considering the people and place in this moment of prayer.

- Allow an image of Jesus to emerge in your imagination, noting his physical characteristics and mannerisms. Look at what he is wearing or carrying. Make a note of whether he is sitting, standing, or walking. Ponder this mental image, allowing any other observations about Jesus to form in your mind.

- Observe the people around Jesus, becoming aware of their appearance and demeanor. Observe whether they are sitting, standing, or walking. See Jesus' disciples, observing their behavior toward Jesus and each other. See the crowd around Jesus and their various actions as they are with Jesus. Take a moment to ponder this mental image, allowing other impressions of these men and women to form.

- Allow yourself to become aware of the location of this moment of prayer. Observe its physical characteristics and the arrangement of the people in it. Look around the place and notice more details about it – if it is still and silent or filled with noise, if it has an unusual smell or not, etc.

- Take a moment to remain in this place with these men and women before allowing these images to fade from your consciousness.

[3]   Become aware of your desires during this moment of prayer. Remember your desire to experience the divine presence all around you so you may attain a deep "felt knowledge" of Jesus Christ, who became human for you so you may better love and follow him. Recall your desire that in this day or week of prayer, you may open yourself to the love that Jesus has for those with whom he is most intimately associated. Also, ask that you may experience that love and be a true friend of Jesus, reflecting that love in your interactions with others and in your interior choices.

As these desires fill your consciousness, let all other concerns fall aside as you focus on this time and place of prayer.

[4]   Allow the image of Jesus and the crowd to reemerge in your imagination.
- Watch as the group assembles around Jesus. Listen to the sounds of this moment and become comfortable as you prepare to hear Jesus speak. Feel the anticipation of the people around you and share in that enthusiasm.
- Ask God to help you share in this experience – either by joining these events or by listening quietly to them. Focus your attention on Jesus, noting his physical appearance and his demeanor.
- Then, watch and listen as Jesus hears about the death of Lazarus and pay special attention to his response after hearing this news. You may want to quietly read the passage in John's gospel while remaining prayerfully aware of your mental image or you may choose to stay completely within the imagined realm of your prayer. Whichever you choose, know that God will offer you the words from the biblical passage that you need to hear – even if only in fragments.
- As these images fade from your imagination, become aware of the phrases and images from this moment which touched you most deeply. Recall the emotions and memories – including any sounds or smells – evoked during your prayer. Allow these seminal aspects of your meditation to linger on your mind and in your heart, noting any special feelings evoked by them.

[5]   Then, become aware of Jesus' presence with you in this moment and have an open and informal conversation about this prayer period and how the passage from John's gospel expresses your own needs or desires – giving space for Jesus to respond or to highlight different aspects from the biblical account and your experiences during this contemplation. Then, gradually allow your thoughts to recede as you focus on God's broader presence in your life and in the world around you.

[6]   Conclude by offering this prayer:

Confirm me in your love divine,
Smooth for my feet life's rugged way;
My will with yours entwine,
Lest evil lead my steps astray.
Be with my still as guard and guide,
Keep me in holy sanctity,
Let my firm faith on you abide,
From fraud and error hold me free. Amen.

[7] Afterward, take 10-15 minutes in a quiet space to reflect on the most significant moments from your prayer and record your reflections in your journal.

9.4 A Contemplation of John 11:38-45

In this contemplation of John 11:38-45, you will see and hear Jesus as he raises Lazarus from the dead.

[1] Begin by reading the biblical selection and reviewing your notes on it.

[2] Then, focus on this specific time and place as you allow all other concerns to fall away before considering the people and place in this moment of prayer.

- Allow an image of Jesus to emerge in your imagination, noting his physical characteristics and mannerisms. Look at what he is wearing or carrying. Make a note of whether he is sitting, standing, or walking. Ponder this mental image, allowing any other observations about Jesus to form in your mind.
- Observe the people around Jesus, becoming aware of their appearance and demeanor. Observe whether they are sitting, standing, or walking. See Jesus' disciples, observing their behavior toward Jesus and each other. See the crowd around Jesus and their various actions as they are with Jesus. Take a moment to ponder this mental image, allowing other impressions of these men and women to form.
- Allow yourself to become aware of the location of this moment of prayer. Observe its physical characteristics and the arrangement of the people in it. Look around the place and notice more details about it – if it is still and silent or filled with noise, if it has an unusual smell or not, etc.
- Take a moment to remain in this place with these men and women before allowing these images to fade from your consciousness.

[3] Become aware of your desires during this moment of prayer. Remember your desire to experience the divine presence all around you so you may attain a deep "felt knowledge" of Jesus Christ, who became human for you so you may better love and follow him. Recall your desire that in this day or week of prayer, you may open yourself to the love that Jesus has for those with whom he is most intimately associated. Also, ask that you may experience that love and be a true friend of Jesus, reflecting that love in your interactions with others and in your interior choices.

As these desires fill your consciousness, let all other concerns fall aside as you focus on this time and place of prayer.

[4]   Allow the image of Jesus and the crowd to reemerge in your imagination.
- Watch as the group assembles around Jesus. Listen to the sounds of this moment and become aware of the behavior of the men and women in it. Feel the anticipation of the people around you and share in those feelings.
- Ask God to help you share in this moment – either by joining these events or by listening quietly to them. Focus your attention on Jesus, noting his physical appearance and his demeanor.
- Then, watch and listen as Jesus comes to Bethany and raises Lazarus from the dead. You may want to quietly read the passage in John's gospel while remaining prayerfully aware of your mental image or you may choose to stay completely within the imagined realm of your prayer. Whichever you choose, know that God will offer you the words from the biblical passage that you need to hear – even if only in fragments.
- As these images fade from your imagination, become aware of the phrases and images from this moment which touched you most deeply. Recall the emotions and memories – including any sounds or smells – evoked during your prayer. Allow these seminal aspects of your meditation to linger on your mind and in your heart, noting any special feelings evoked by them.

[5]   Then, become aware of Jesus' presence with you in this moment and have an open and informal conversation about this prayer period and how the passage from John's gospel expresses your own needs or desires – giving space for Jesus to respond or to highlight different aspects from the biblical account and your experiences during this contemplation. Then, gradually allow your thoughts to recede as you focus on God's broader presence in your life and in the world around you.

[6]   Conclude by offering this prayer:

Confirm me in your love divine,
Smooth for my feet life's rugged way;
My will with yours entwine,
Lest evil lead my steps astray.
Be with my still as guard and guide,
Keep me in holy sanctity,
Let my firm faith on you abide,
From fraud and error hold me free. Amen.

[7]   Afterward, take 10-15 minutes in a quiet space to reflect on the most significant moments from your prayer and record your reflections in your journal.

9.5 A Meditation on 1 Corinthians 13:1-13

In this meditation on 1 Corinthians 13:1-13, you will see and hear Saint Brigid teach her disciples that friendship with Christ requires love.

[1] Begin by reading the biblical selection and reviewing your notes on it.

[2] Then, focus on this specific time and place as you allow all other concerns to fall away before considering the people and place in this moment of prayer.

- Allow an image of Brigid to emerge in your imagination, noting her physical characteristics and mannerisms. Look at what she is wearing or carrying. Make a note of whether she is sitting, standing, or walking. Ponder this mental image, allowing any other observations about Brigid to form in your mind.

- Observe the people around Saint Brigid, becoming aware of their appearance and demeanor. Observe whether they are sitting, standing, or walking. Take a moment to ponder this mental image, allowing other impressions of these men and women to form.

- Allow yourself to become aware of the location of this moment of prayer. Observe its physical characteristics and the arrangement of the people in it. Look around the place and notice more details about it – if it is in dim or bright light, if it is still and silent or filled with noise, if it has an unusual smell or not, etc.

- Take a moment to remain in this place with these men and women before allowing these images to fade from your consciousness.

[3] Become aware of your desires during this moment of prayer. Remember your desire to experience the divine presence all around you so you may attain a deep "felt knowledge" of Jesus Christ, who became human for you so you may better love and follow him. Recall your desire that in this day or week of prayer, you may open yourself to the love that Jesus has for those with whom he is most intimately associated. Also, ask that you may experience that love and be a true friend of Jesus, reflecting that love in your interactions with others and in your interior choices.

As these desires fill your consciousness, let all other concerns fall aside as you focus on this time and place of prayer.

[4] Allow the image of Saint Brigid and her disciples to reemerge in your imagination.

- Watch as the group assembles around Brigid. Listen to the sounds of this moment and become comfortable as you prepare to hear Brigid speak. Feel the anticipation of the people around you and share in that enthusiasm.
- As you hear Brigid invite her companions to listen, ask God to help you share in this experience – either by joining these events or by listening quietly to them. Focus your attention on Saint Brigid, noting her physical appearance and her demeanor.
- Then, see and hear Brigid speaking to her disciples about Paul's letter to the Corinthians and its importance. You may want to quietly read the passage while remaining prayerfully aware of your mental image or you may choose to stay completely within the imagined realm of your prayer. Whichever you choose, know that God will offer you the words from the biblical passage that you need to hear – even if only in fragments.
- Afterward, watch and listen as Brigid recites her prayer of holy friendship, "The Things Brigid Wished For" or "I would wish a great lake of ale for the King of Kings" (found on page 314). Again, read the prayer while retaining your mental image of being with Brigid and her disciples. As you read the prayer, allow its words to evoke images and feelings from the days or weeks of this retreat – as well as from your life before it and your hopes after it is ended.
- After Saint Brigid finishes praying, allow these images to fade from your imagination, become aware of the phrases and images from this moment which touched you most deeply. Recall the emotions and memories – including any sounds or smells – evoked during your prayer. Allow these seminal aspects of your meditation to linger on your mind and in your heart, noting any special feelings evoked by them.

[5] Then, become aware of Jesus' presence with you in this moment and have an open and informal conversation about this prayer period and how the passage from Paul's epistle expresses your own desires about how wish to live as his friend and disciple – giving space for Jesus to respond or to highlight different aspects from the biblical account and your experiences during this contemplation. Then, gradually allow your thoughts to recede as you focus on God's broader presence in your life and in the world around you.

[6] Conclude by offering this prayer:
Confirm me in your love divine,
Smooth for my feet life's rugged way;

> *My will with yours entwine,*
> *Lest evil lead my steps astray.*
> *Be with my still as guard and guide,*
> *Keep me in holy sanctity,*
> *Let my firm faith on you abide,*
> *From fraud and error hold me free. Amen.*

[7] Afterward, take 10-15 minutes in a quiet space to reflect on the most significant moments from your prayer and record your reflections in your journal.

9.6 An Application of the Senses

[1] Become aware of your prayerful desires during this day or week. Bring to mind your desire to experience an inner knowledge of Jesus Christ who became human for you so you may better love and follow him. Ask also that you may open yourself to the love that Jesus has for those with whom he is most intimately associated.

[2] Call to mind the various prayers of the preceding day or days. Allow the images and words of these prayers to linger and then slowly fade from your consciousness.

- Remember your imaginative contemplation of John 15:12-17. Consider the images and feelings evoked in you during your prayer, feeling God's presence in these memories and becoming aware of the specific sensations associated with each image.
- Recall your imaginative contemplation of John 11:1-37 considering it in the same way as your memories of John 15.
- Review your imaginative contemplations of John 11:38-45 in the same manner as the previous prayers.
- Revisit your mediation on 1 Corinthians 13:1-13 (including Brigid's prayer at its conclusion) in the same manner as the previous prayers.

Make a mental note of which senses are most active. You may see an image or a color, hear a sound or a phrase, or smell a scent or a fragrance. You may even taste a flavor or feel a sensation on your skin.

[3] Then, relax and allow these various memories and experiences to quietly enter and leave your consciousness. Linger on the sensory images and memories being evoked in you – noticing any images or colors, any sounds or phrases, any scents or fragrances, any flavors or physical sensations associated with each prayer.

[4] When you are ready, become completely still and clear your mind of all thoughts and concerns. Allow an image of a special personal space to form in your imagination. Then, watch as God enters that place and forms a small image or object for you that expresses the thought or awareness that you most need to carry with you into your life.

Reverently pick up the object or image, a reflection of the most important gift you have been given during this time of prayer. Look at it carefully and become aware of the divine presence contained within it. Register what it looks like and how it feels in your hand. Then, feel the joy and confidence that comes from touching the presence of God

as you accept this gift, offering a short prayer of gratitude while you relax into the pleasure of this moment.

[5]   Then, conclude by offering this prayer:
>   *Confirm me in your love divine,*
>   *Smooth for my feet life's rugged way;*
>   *My will with yours entwine,*
>   *Lest evil lead my steps astray.*
>   *Be with my still as guard and guide,*
>   *Keep me in holy sanctity,*
>   *Let my firm faith on you abide,*
>   *From fraud and error hold me free. Amen.*

[6]   While your experiences are still fresh in your mind, record the most significant impressions or sensations from this time of prayer in your journal.

9.7 Review of Prayer

[1] Remember your desires during the preceding day or week of prayer. Become aware of the divine presence all around you, offering you inner knowledge of Jesus Christ who became human for you so you may better love and follow him. Recall your desire to open yourself to the love that Jesus has for those with whom he is most intimately associated.

After bringing these thoughts and desires into your consciousness, ask God once again to fulfill these desires in your own life and in your interactions with others.

[2] Then, take a moment to allow the words, thoughts, and feelings from your prayers during the last day or week to linger – on your mind and in your heart – before asking God to reveal the fulfillment of your deepest desires in these various memories.

• Think about the prayer sequence at the beginning of this day or week. Make a mental note of any words, insights or images that remain particularly significant or meaningful to you.

• Ponder the story, "Brigid Discusses a Vision with Patrick". Note any words, insights, or images from them that remain particularly significant or meaningful to you.

• Remember your imaginative contemplation of John 15:12-17.

– Consider the most powerful images, phrases, or feelings from your prayer. Ask yourself what gifts God gave to you through these moments, perhaps offering you new insights or perhaps affirming an important aspect of your faith. Ask yourself how God may be calling you to change through these moments, being as specific as possible.

– Examine your disposition as you prayed, noting whether prayer came easily or with resistance. Recall the easiest moments in your prayer and any moments of joy you may have experienced. Remember also if you encountered any difficulty opening yourself to God or if you felt any sadness as you prayed. Ask God to help you understand why these feelings surfaced.

– Bring to mind any moments when you added personal elements (e.g., familiar places or people from your life) or connected your prayers to other scriptures or spiritual writings. Ask yourself how these additions helped or hindered you as you prayed. Again, if you do not know why this happened, ask God to help you understand.

- Recall your imaginative contemplation of John 11:1-37. Then, review your prayer in the same way as your earlier reflection on John 15.
- Review your imaginative contemplations of John 11:38-45 in the same manner as the previous prayers.
- Reminisce on your meditation on 1 Corinthians 13:1-13 (including Brigid's prayer at its conclusion) in the same manner as the same manner as the previous prayers.
- Reflect on the ebb and flow of sensory impressions and feelings that marked your application of the senses. Isolate the most memorable moments and sensory impressions from your prayer and reflect on how God used these moments to give you a particular gift, perhaps offering you new insights or changing you in some way.

[3] Finally, ponder the times when images or feelings from the readings of this day or week surfaced outside these prayer periods. Consider those moments or events in which God's presence or guidance was especially strong as well as any moments when you were struggling. Think about the most memorable aspects of these experiences, asking God to explain their significance.

[4] Take a moment to allow the words, thoughts, and feelings of these prayers to linger on your mind and in your heart. Finally, conclude by offering this prayer:

> O God, I believe in you; strengthen my belief.
> I trust in you; confirm my trust.
> I love you; double my love.
> I repent that I angered you,
> Increase my repentance.
> Fill you my heart with awe without despair;
> With hope, without over-confidence;
> With piety without infatuation;
> And with joy without excess.
> My God, consent to guide me by your wisdom;
> To constrain me by your right;
> To comfort me by your mercy;
> And to protect me by your power. Amen.

[5] After finishing these prayers, summarize your reflections on the gifts or graces you received during the prayers of this last day or week and record these thoughts in your journal.

Embracing the Adventure of Jesus' Friendship

Embracing the Adventure of Jesus' Friendship

During these last days or weeks of prayer, you traveled with Jesus Christ through your prayerful encounters with his early life in public ministry – experiencing both his human and divine nature. You received an invitation to struggle under the standard of Christ in the cosmic struggle between God's desires and those forces (both cosmic and personal) that would undermine God's activity in the world around you. You observed Christ performing miracles, displaying compassion to those in need, and demonstrating deep in human friendships. During this spiritual journey, you deepened in your relationship with Jesus – first approaching him as a disciple before becoming his companion and now recognizing that you may even become his friend.

During this spiritual adventure, you were invited to the frontiers of human existence and offered an opportunity to serve under the standard of Christ in the cosmic struggle to redeem creation. Your contemplations of the gospel were more than pleasant stories or fantasies. Through your participation in the life and ministry of Jesus, God actively reached out to you and aroused in you greater and more specific desires to participate in the earthly and cosmic mission of Jesus Christ. These moments with Jesus also clarified – and purified – these aspirations in you so you might more fully offer yourself to God in service.

While this might seem daunting, your intimate experiences with Jesus during these last days or weeks transformed you and given you the ability to walk with Jesus as his friend. Your desire to serve God through Jesus Christ no longer relies on your gratitude for what God has done in your past. Instead, your relationship with Jesus now focuses on how you may serve him in the future with love and devotion. You are beginning to participate in the communion of saints, drawing strength and clarity of thought from those men and women who preceded you in befriending Jesus Christ. Still, all these thoughts and feelings are just beginning to clarify in you, and you must rely on your friendship with Jesus Christ for guidance.

In his *Spiritual Exercises*, Saint Ignatius declares this openness to God's desires and guidance requires what he called "indifference" – behaving "as though at the center of a pair of scales, ready to follow the direction... perceived to be more to the glory and praise of God our Lord (*Sp.Ex.* #179)". This also is the spirit of availability demonstrated by the ancient Celtic saints who devoted their lives to monastic service or later embraced God's call to leave these communities on pilgrimages into the unknown. These men and women completely trusted the friend they discovered in Jesus Christ – as well as the joy experienced in his service – and their example should give you confidence to embrace the adventure of your own friendship with Jesus Christ.

A Contemplation of the Friendship of Jesus Christ

So, through the following exercise, consider the qualities of Jesus Christ that would lead you to embrace him as a friend:

Note: This exercise is an adaptation of the "Consideration of Christ's Kingdom" in The Spiritual Exercises of Saint Ignatius. *You may want to read the text of this exercise as Ignatius presented it (see page 299) since this might offer different perspectives on various aspects of this exercise, illuminate your reflections, and open you to a broader awareness of God's activity during your prayers. However, you should feel free to ignore this suggestion if it distracts you from your prayers.*

[1]   Focus on this specific time and place as you allow all other concerns to fall away. As you become still, become aware of your desires during this moment of prayer. Ask of Jesus Christ that you may not be deaf to his offer of friendship but alert and eager to fulfill his most holy will to the best of your ability. Ask also that you might fully understand the qualities of Jesus, the King of Heaven, which attract you to him as a friend.

As these desires fill your consciousness, let all other concerns fall aside as you focus on this specific time and place of prayer.

[2]   Then, slowly and deliberately, consider the invitation of Jesus Christ to become his friend.

•   In your imagination, allow yourself to see your closest and most loyal friend. Take a moment to look at this person, making a mental note of his or her physical appearance and demeanor. Visualize your time together, both in good times and in bad. Watch and listen as your friend consoles you during difficult moments in your life, putting aside his or her needs or desires to support you. See the sacrifices your friend makes on your behalf. Hear your friend counsel you, often knowing you better than you know yourself. Feel the pleasure your friend experiences when you are doing well as well as the sorrow he or she experiences as you struggle.

Linger for a time in this moment, becoming aware of all the emotions and thoughts evoked in you. Then, allow this moment to fade from your consciousness while retaining an awareness of the feelings evoked in you by this invitation and the challenges opposed to accepting this invitation through your frail human nature.

- When you are ready, allow yourself to see Jesus Christ standing in front of you. Note his physical appearance and demeanor. In your imagination, visualize the various ways Jesus has cared for you in both good times and bad. Watch and listen as Jesus consoles you during difficult times in your life and lifts various burdens from you (including your sins). See the sacrifices Jesus makes on your behalf. Hear Jesus counsel you, knowing you better than you know yourself. Feel the pleasure Jesus experiences when you are doing well as well as the sorrow he experiences when you struggle – always offering you his unconditional love and support.

Again, linger in this moment and become aware of all the emotions and thoughts evoked in you. Then, allow this moment to fade from your consciousness while retaining an awareness of the feelings evoked in you by this invitation and the sense of liberation you have been offered in this moment.

- Afterward, allow the various words and images of your prayer to flow freely in your consciousness without being controlled. Become aware of those aspects of your prayer that arouse holy desires in you, toward God and toward others (including nonhuman creatures). Become aware of those aspects of your prayer that make you feel shame for those times you fall short of these holy aspirations.

- Gradually allow these thoughts and images to fade from your consciousness and become aware of the return of Jesus, standing, or sitting with you in this moment. Then, have open and informal conversation about your experiences during this meditation. Speak about how these experiences express your own desires and fears, giving space for Jesus to explain the love at the heart of your relationship. At the end of this conversation, ask Jesus to help you reform those aspects of your personality and life that impede your ability to respond to his friendship.

- Then, gradually allow your thoughts to recede as you focus on Jesus' continuing presence in your life and in the world around you.

[3] Conclude by offering this prayer adapted from a Christian song collected in Daniel Joseph Donahoe's *Early Christian Hymns (Series II)*:

> *O Christ, my everlasting Light,*
> *You the glory of the starry sky,*
> *Illume the darkness of my night,*
> *Quicken my breast and purify.*
> *O, save me from insidious snares,*
> *Protect me from the dangerous foe,*
> *Guard, lest I stumble unawares,*
> *And let my sleep no evil know.*
> *Keep you my heart forever pure,*
> *Increase my faith, my will with you combine.*
> *Be with me, your protection sure,*
> *Save by your power and love divine. Amen.*

[4] Afterward, take 10-15 minutes in a quiet space to reflect on the most significant moments from your prayer and record your reflections in your journal.

Living as a Citizen of Heaven

Introduction

Just as you did after completing your retreat in *From Loss to Love*, you should take some time after this retreat to review the spiritual gifts you received during it. Remember that you are being transformed into an instrument of God's love and that this transformation requires time and further prayer to become fully realized in your life. Remember as well that the challenges and demands of daily life may impede your ability to sustain or realize the holy desires that emerged during your retreat.

Nourishing the Gifts of the Retreat

Therefore, you need to remain aware of God's loving activity in your life – nourishing the received during your retreat and nourishing the holy desires evoked in you during this period of intense prayer. As with your early retreat, you need to maintain the spirit of generosity that you displayed during your retreat while also being careful to remain vigilant for any distractions or temptations which might undermine God's continuing activity in your life. So, once again, you spend the first three months after your retreat:

- Reviewing your thoughts and feelings by making at least one examen daily, paying particular attention to those moments in your day when you t=found yourself thinking about some aspect of your retreat.
- Repeating at least once every week a significant contemplation or meditation from your retreat.
- Considering once every week a specific "memento of grace" you received during the retreat – a particular moment of prayer or an insight that had a transformative effect on how you approached God and others.

<u>Note:</u> Approach these prayers as an opportunity to re-engage the seminal aspects of your retreat. Remember they are opportunities for personal and spiritual growth, not a burden or obligation.

After three months of prayer, you may begin considering changes to your life that reflect the holy desires of your retreat. Remember to approach these spiritual leadings with the same spirit of generosity and openness that you displayed during your retreat, knowing you are being transformed into an instrument of God's love.

Resources for Prayer and Reflection

The resources in this section are designed to help you cultivate this holistic approach to your spiritual life by providing materials for prayer and reflection related to each of these aspects of spirituality. This includes reflections, prayer materials and spiritual exercises intended to foster but a deeper spiritual life that also embraces sacred citizenship and articulate witness.

The materials related to spiritual practices include:
- A collection of traditional Irish prayers used in the development of the prayer sequences for this retreat and scriptural citations related to the themes of your most recent retreat.
- A consideration of the meaning and significance of the ideal of soul friendship, a core practice of early Celtic Christianity developed from the desert tradition of the Third and Fourth Centuries.
- "Laments, Litanies and Loricas", an exercise designed to help you understand and develop prayers in response to world around you.

The resources related to sacred citizenship focus on the social dimensions of Saint Brigid's life and ministry. This includes reflection questions on the readings concerning Saint Brigid intended help you extend your own spiritual life outward towards others in the service of God's creation.

Finally, the materials focusing on articulate witness explore the process of discovering the styles of public witness most appropriate to your passions. These reflections also address the on-going process of discerning God's desires for you and the public manifestations of your faith.

Spiritual Practices

Traditional Prayers

The following early Christian hymns and traditional Irish prayers were woven into the fabric of the prayer sequences introducing the themes of your most recent retreat. Individually, they offer a treasury of spiritual insight and devotion. By using them alone or by integrating them into your existing prayers, you should draw upon these ancestral voices to enrich and extend your spiritual vocabulary.

Short Prayers

> Let thanks arise on every side
> To Christ my help, my God of Might,
> Who has my body glorified
> And raised it to the throne of light.
> Then let my heart with love o'erflow
> My word and deeds be all of light,
> That when I leave these walks below,
> My soul shall climb the heavenly height.
>
> Source:
> *Early Christian Hymns*, Series 2

> Your name is power; I call out "Save me!",
> And lo, your glory shines aflame,
> While heaven and hell with trembling knee
> Bow down before your holy name.
> To you I come, to you I cry,
> O ruler of the judgment day;
> Defend me by your grace, lest I
> With powers of gloom be cast away.
>
> Source:
> *Early Christian Hymns*

> Gentle Jesus, fount of healing,
> Solace unto souls appealing
> By the mildness of your grace,
> Calm my restless mind, and render

Soothing thoughts therein and tender;
Pride and bitterness efface.
By your fostering care provided
All my life shall thus be guided,
Safe in faith, from evil free ;
Kindled by your kindness, never
From your love my soul shall sever,
All my desires in you shall be.

> Source:
> *Early Christian Hymns*, Series 2

Dear Redeemer, loved and loving,
All my faith I place in you;
your undying truths you teach,
With unfailing force to me,
Come in tender love, my Saviour;
Fill with faith the fragile breast;
Lift my spirit to your comfort,
Let me find in you sweet rest.
O my loving Lord, I love you
And in all, your love I see;
Let me cleave to you forever
And, dear Lord, cleave you to me.

> Source:
> *Early Christian Hymns*, Series 2

The Victor, Christ, with flag unfurled
Brings triumph o'er the sinful world,
The king of darkness quells, and opes
The gates of heaven to human hopes.
Dear Jesus, bring us purity,
That you our paschal joy may be;
Be with us always; let your love
Illume our spirits from above.

> Source:
> *Early Christian Hymns*

Hear me, Christ, my King,
Hear you the praise I bring,
And lead me on;

In tender mercy bend,
My soul from harm defend,
And let my hopes ascend
Unto your throne.
Upon the road of life
Keep me from stain and strife
In your sweet care;
Extend your right hand, Lord,
your gracious aid afford,
Be you my watch and ward;
Lord, hear my prayer.

> Source:
> *Early Christian Hymns*, Series 2

Be you my lasting joy, O Lord,
My love on earth, my high reward;
Kind Ruler of the world, inspire
My longing soul with holy fire.
To you I bow my heart in prayer,
Lord, keep me from the tempter's snare;
Lift up my soul with heavenly grace,
And fit me for your dwelling-place.

> Source:
> *Early Christian Hymns*

You are, O Christ, my health and light,
The power that glorifies the sun,
That veils with deepening shades the night,
And gives each star its course to run.
No wandering thought or vain desire
Be near my soul to soil or stain,
But kindled by the holy fire
Of love for you, with you remain.

> Source:
> *Early Christian Hymns*, Series 2

Be my heart and hopes renewed
In light and love and gratitude,
So, illumed by you, may my actions
Worthily fulfill your loving intentions.

I praise you, Lord, forevermore;
With the Father, who I also adore,
And with the Spirit, three in one,
Reigning while endless ages run.

Source:
Early Christian Hymns

Oh, kind Creator of the skies,
Eternal light to guide my feet,
Give ear to my beseeching cries
And save me in your mercy sweet.
Descending from your throne above,
You strive the sluggish world to win,
Moved by the power of mighty love,
Lest earth be lost in death and sin.

Source:
Early Christian Hymns

Long Prayers

Ancient of days, enthroned on high!
The Father unbegotten He,
Whom space contains not, nor time,
Who was and is and shall be:
And one-born Son, and Holy Ghost,
Who co-eternal glory share:
One only God, of Persons Three,
We praise, acknowledge, and declare.
Christ the Most High from heaven descends,
The Cross his sign and banner bright.
The sun in darkness shrouds His face,
The moon no more pours forth her light:
The stars upon the earth shall fall
As figs drop from the parent tree,
When earth's broad space is bathed in fire,
And men to dens and mountains flee.

Zeal of the Lord, consuming fire,
Shall 'whelm the foes, amazed and dumb,
Whose stony hearts will not receive
That Christ hath from the Father come:
But I shall soar my Lord to meet,
And so with him shall ever be,
To reap the due rewards amidst
The glories of Eternity.

Source:
The Story of Iona

My God, my life, my love, my light,
My strength, my joy, my treasure,
Let it be my thought both day and night
In you to take my pleasure.
Increase my love, my sighs, my groans
My careless lips to move it,
And let my thoughts be fixed alone
On right living, with all sins abhorred.
Blot out my crimes and me forgive,
O Lord do not deny me,
And grant my thoughts for ever be
On Jesus Crucified.
In honour of your passion's sake,
This new year's gift bestow me,
That I into protection take
Sweet Jesus, my King and Lord.
To God the Father glory be,
For his mercy still I crave,
And to His Son who died for me
Who spilt his blood to me save.
And to the Holy Ghost all three.
They on us bestow gifts and grace,
And should our thoughts for ever be
That the Godhead's love we embrace.

Source:
The Religious Songs of Connacht, Volume 1

Jesus, our heavenly Lord and King,
You did the world's salvation bring,

And by your death upon the tree,
Did out of bondage make us free.
Hear now our prayers, O Son of God,
Preserve the gifts your hand bestowed,
Unto your love all nations draw,
And bring mankind to know your law.
The tongues of all creation call
And hail your name as Lord of all:
Their life arose from God's command,
Their living hope, from your right hand.
The Father's luminous thrones above,
With beating wings and words of love,
The cherubim and seraphim,
Sing out to you their ceaseless hymn.
They sing to you in sweet accord,
Their, "Holy, holy, holy Lord";
Great God of hosts and victories,
your glory fills the earth and skies.

Source:
Early Christian Hymns, Series 2

To you, O Christ, my prayers shall rise,
With tears of sorrow blending;
Come to my help, O you Holy One,
On my dark night descending.
My heart shall in you find its rest,
And e'en in dreams shall praise your love;
And with each rising of the sun,
New songs shall raise to you above.
Impart a noble life, and may
My spirit's warmth be heightened.
Bid night depart, and with your love,
O, may my life be brightened.
In hymns I pay my vows to you:
At every hour to you I pray,
Erase the many sins I have made
And allow me with you to stay.
You are my Lord, ever most high,
You guide my path by your grace.
May I always serve your intentions

And your desires fully embrace.

Source:
Hymns of the Early Church

Meeting a Soul Friend

One of the most well-known stories about Saint Brigid involves a conversation with one of her foster-sons recorded in *The Martyrology of Oengus the Culdee*:

> *A young cleric of the community of Ferns, a foster-son of Brigid's, used to come to her with wishes. He was with her in the refectory, to partake of food. Once after coming to communion, she strikes a clapper. "Well, young cleric there," says Brigid, "hast thou a soul friend?" "I have," replied the young cleric. "Let us sing his requiem," says Brigid, "for he has died. I saw when half thy portion had gone, that thy quota was put into thy trunk, and thou without any head on thee, for thy soul friend died, and anyone without a soul friend is a body without a head; and eat no more till thou gettest a soul friend."*

This story highlights the importance of soul friendship in the world of the ancient Celtic saints and invites further reflection on its significance.

Some scholars point to examples in both the Old and New Testaments (i.e., David and Jonathan, Paul and Barnabas, etc.) as demonstrations of the ancient roots of soul friendship. However, the beliefs and practices shaping this special relationship emerged during the period of the Desert Fathers and Mothers in the Third and Fourth Centuries. Usually living alone in the desert, these ascetics would welcome others into their small cells in an open-ended act of hospitality which made a place for the visitor in the home and consciousness of the host.

This act of sharing the hermit's cell involved more than physical hospitality and care. It established a spiritual bond between the host and the visitor that invited a mutual sharing of their innermost secrets and desires. It created a balance between the joy of encountering God in solitude and the very different joy offered by being able to share that experience with another person. Finally, it provided an opportunity for each person to validate or challenge the spiritual leadings and temptations they experienced while alone with God through a generous and honest dialogue with their soul friend.

As the hermits of the desert began to gather into larger communities, the practice of spiritual friendship became a vital aspect of monastic life. Most of the time, and certainly in the many monastic communities of the Celtic saints, a monastic soul friend was usually an elder who was wiser, holier, and more experienced in the ways of God. This person became a teacher and a spiritual guide for a younger member of the community as he or she deepened in their own spiritual life.

However, soul friendship acquired a special status among the ancient Celtic saints and developed practices that echoed back to the earlier experiences the hermits and ascetics of the desert tradition. In the Celtic tradition, the hierarchies established in monasteries did not necessarily define soul friendship. Soul friendships developed between men and women of equivalent age and spiritual maturity. Men and women also could be soul friends, and there are many stories of soul friendships between Celtic saints of both genders. For the ancient Celtic saints, soul friendship was an act of communion – a gift of God mirroring the cosmic communion of angels and saints.

Still, while the ancient Celtic saints believed a person could have many soul friends and receive the benefits of learning through the mutual sharing of each person's experiences of God (including through brief encounters), it was important to have one specific soul friend nurturing the moral and spiritual growth of the other. It was to this soul friend that a person made confession before being assigned an appropriate penance (often specified a penitential manual) and receiving absolution. It also was this soul friend who offered guidance when a person needed to make major life choices, engaging together in the process of mutual discernment of God's will.

Whether in a life-long friendship or one lasting only a few days, the qualities of a soul friend remain the same. He or she must be open to the transformational possibilities of a conversation devoted to discerning God's will, trusting in each new revelation while remaining vigilant for self-deception. Yearning for God's presence deep within their own solitude and in dialogue with another person, a soul friend lives a humble life of faithful righteousness marked by trust in a God that permeates every aspect of creation – and sharing that knowledge in intimate mutual expirations of the mind and heart of God.

For these reasons, Saint Brigid could say, "Anyone without a soul friend is a body without a head".

☧

With these thoughts in mind, consider the following questions:

[1]   Have you ever experienced a sense of spiritual communion with another person?

    • If so, what were the most rewarding and memorable aspects of this experience. What were the most challenging aspects?

    • If not, does the thought of this experience excite you? Why? Does it intimidate or frighten you? Why?

[2]   What aspect(s) of your personality limit or inhibit your ability enter the spiritual communion of a soul friendship? How may they be repaired or reformed?

Bring your answers to these questions to God in prayer, either in a sequence of petitions or a conversation. Then, record your thoughts in your retreat workbook.

☧

    Separately, on another day or in a different prayer session, conduct the following imaginative exercise:

[1]   Focus your attention on the present moment. Allow your thoughts to subside as you become still. Notice your emotions as you begin this exercise, taking a moment to recognize each before allowing them to fade away.

[2]   In your imagination, see saint Brigid sitting at a table. Notice her physical appearance and demeanor, seeing what she is wearing as well as what she is doing. Look around the room and observe its physical characteristics – whether it is brightly lit or dim, whether it is constructed of wood or stone, etc. Look at the table in front of Brigid, noticing its construction and the objects on it. Look around the room again, noting any other people in the room with Brigid as well as their physical appearance. Then, allow these images to fade from your imagination.

[3]   When you are ready, place yourself at the table with Brigid. She is seated near you and looks at you with love and concern. Open yourself to feel these emotions as she begins to talk with you about your life. In this moment, notice for gentleness and how she feels at ease

speaking with you about deeply personal matters. Observe your own sense of comfort in her presence. Linger in this gentle moment as you talk about recent events in your life.

[4]   Notice Brigid becoming more serious as she begins speaking about your need for soul friend. Allow the conversation to be shaped by random thoughts emerging from the questions she asks you, such as:

- What qualities in a friend make you more comfortable with him or her?
- Have you already had a soul friend relationship? What was it like?
- Has your personality or spiritual life changed in any way since that friendship?
- What are the qualities you desire and a soul friend now?
- How are these different from the soul friend from your past?

As you speak with her, answering her questions, take time to notice her responses as well as the feelings evoked in you through her questions.

[5]   Become aware as the conversation shifts from your desires to a consideration of your needs as Brigid begins to ask questions such as:

- Have you resisted God's help in the past, in private prayer or through others?
- What caused these different types of resistance in the past?
- Do you still experience these fears and impediments in the present?
- What are your strengths and weaknesses as you confront these challenges?
- How will a soul friend help you address these issues at this time in your life?

Again, take time to notice Brigid's responses as well as the feelings evoked in you through her questions.

[6]   Then, when you are ready, allow this conversation to fade from your imagination. Feel God's presence all around you and ask that you may better understand any aspects of your personality or spiritual life that need correction or repair. Request that you may be open to these transformations and be led to a soul friend able to guide you while confronting these challenges.

[7]   Conclude this exercise by saying this traditional Irish prayer:

Help me, O God, no evil do,
'Til fades in dusk the sunset flame,
That I unstained may come to you

> *And sing the glories of your name.*
> *Eternal Triune Deity, your word*
> *Made all the spheres that roll above,*
> *You are the everlasting Lord,*
> *The fount of everlasting love. Amen.*

[8]   Afterward, compare your experience in this exercise with your earlier observations in this section and record your thoughts on soul friendship (especially your concerns, needs and desires concerning this type of relationship) in your workbook or journal.

Laments, Litanies and Loricas

An excerpt from* Nurturing the Courage of Pilgrims, *with additions and minor adjustments.

This subsection explores the relationships between three forms a prayer familiar to the ancient Celtic saints: the lament, the litany and the lorica. Each of these types of prayer serves a unique purpose, so take your time exploring them and the ways in which they might help you in your own unique spiritual journey.

The Lament

Part One

The lament is a prayer of loss, sorrow, mourning and even anger. There are many laments found in the Bible, especially among the psalms. Most of these reflect a person's pain or grief (the "individual" psalms of lament) but some also share communal sorrows (the "national" psalms of lament).

These laments, like others found in the Bible (e.g., Ezekiel 33:1-20, Jeremiah 20:7-18, Matthew 3:1-12, etc.) usually follow a similar pattern. They begin by expressing suffering and even a sense of abandonment, often giving a list of events or circumstances causing this pain, before asking for God's help in restoring order. While laments may seem to be complaints, they express the very human struggles of faithful men and women.

Consider, for example, Psalm 12:

> Help, O Lord, for there is no longer anyone who is godly;
>   the faithful have disappeared from humankind.
> They utter lies to each other;
>   with flattering lips and a double heart they speak.
> May the Lord cut off all flattering lips,
>   the tongue that makes great boasts

those who say, "With our tongues we will prevail;
> our lips are our own – who is our master?"
"Because the poor are despoiled, because the needy groan,
> I will now rise up," says the Lord;
> "I will place them in the safety for which they long."
The promises of the Lord are promises that are pure,
> silver refined in a furnace on the ground,
> purified seven times.
You, O Lord, will protect us;
> you will guard us from this generation forever.
On every side the wicked prowl,
> as vileness is exalted among humankind.
>> Psalm 12: 1-8.

After reflecting on this psalm, prayerfully engage it through an imaginative contemplation in which either Brigid or Jesus shares the psalm with others. Then, speak with Jesus in your imagination about the meaning of the psalm and how it might connect to your life. Write your observations from this period of prayer in your journal.

Part Two

After finishing your reflections on Psalm 12 – and on a separate day – consider an unjust personal or social issue directly involving you and/or the people in your community. Think about the various elements shaping this issue and your reasons for feeling concerned about this issue. Then…

[1]   On separate sheets of paper (or pages in your notebook), write each concern you listed about the topic you have selected. Be as specific as possible, separating each topic into as many distinct and self-contained concerns as possible.

[2]   Reflecting on each issue and its related concerns individually, ask…
- Why was this topic not properly addressed?
- Was it because of the actions of individual people or groups?
- Were you part of the reason it was not addressed?
- What efforts in the past, either by others or by you, sought to solve the problem but proved inadequate?
- What needs to happen if the problem is to be solved or eliminated?

[3]   Again, on separate pages, group your answers from the individual issues into a single list of concerns. This should include the following groupings:
    (a)   the reasons why a topic was not properly addressed.
    (b)   the actions of people or groups that impeded the resolution of this problem.
    (c)   your culpability in Impeding the resolution of this problem.
    (d)   the actions by you and others, the sought – but failed – to solve or eliminate the problem.
    (e)   future actions needed to solve or eliminate the problem.
[4]   In your imagination, prayerfully present these lists to Jesus and discuss them in as much detail as possible. Make certain to note the emotions evoked by each specific issue or response from your lists. When you have finished praying, be certain to include these emotional responses next to each topic for concern.

Part Three

Before writing your lament, take some time to remember:
[1]   A lament is a statement of faith in which you expect God to hear you and respond to your needs. You should begin by calling out to God and asking to be heard. Express (or list) the various complaints you have about the failure to resolve the issue at the center of your lament. You should also be able to express your criticism Of God and of those around you in failing to address this issue before.
[2]   At the same time, a lament is a statement of pain, suffering, grief and even anger. You are coming before a God who knows every aspect of you, so there is nothing that you are able – or should want – to hide. Present your deepest and truest feelings about this topic as directly and honestly as possible.
[3]   Finally, a lament is an affirmation of an existing relationship of love. You have a history of God's loving care and part of the lament should serve as a reminder of the ways in which God has helped you in the past and of your expectation that God will offer loving support for your needs in the present (and the future).

After taking some time reflecting on how these elements of a lament might shape the presentation of the concerns you have, write your prayer. It should include:
- a direct appeal to God had its beginning.
- a description of the situation, issues or problems which have brought you sorrow or grief.
- a specific set of petitions that you are asking God to address.
- an affirmation of your trust in God's help (based on your personal or communal history).
- a concluding statement of praise.

<u>Note:</u> *The form of your lament should be entirely your own. While the psalms and other laments in the Bible are often poems or songs, you should feel free to use whatever style you like. Remember, this is a direct communication between you and a God who knows you better then you know yourself. The words that you share with God should reflect that intimacy.*

<u>Part Four</u>

Now, take your lament to prayer. After taking the time you need to focus on the present moment, begin by reading your lament slowly and deliberately. Allow each word and phrase to rest gently in your consciousness and feel the emotions evoked in your reading as you allow yourself to focus entirely on your experiences in the moment. Also, if something does not feel right about your lament (e.g., the wording seems too vague, you find some aspect of a problem out of place, etc.), take the time to rewrite that portion of your prayer.

After prayerfully reading your lament, put all other thoughts out of your consciousness and become as still as possible. Then, return to your lament and read it aloud at the speed that seems most appropriate to the emotions you are trying to convey. Allow yourself to feel the fullness of your grief, sorrow, or anger as you speak to God about your needs and desires. When you are finished, imagine Jesus sitting in front of you and speak with him about the specific issues of your lament. As always, make certain to give space for Jesus to respond.

After you have finished these prayers, review your lament and revise any aspects of it that you feel need to be clarified. Then, record your lament and any other significant observations from your prayers in your journal.

The Litany

<u>Part One</u>

Unlike the lament, the litany is a prayer of joyful affirmation. It proclaims the gifts of God's presence in a person's life through a sequence of almost identical statements of faith and gratitude. The repetitive nature of this prayer reaffirms the all-pervasive relationship between God and his creatures by highlighting the various manifestations of God's activity in the life of the person or group praying the litany.

Consider, for example, this litany from the 9th Century *Book of Cerne*:

> *Be my helper.*
> *In the name of the holy Trinity.*
> *Holy Trinity,*
> *you are my true God,*
> *you are my holy Father,*
> *you are my faithful Lord,*
> *you are my great King,*
> *you are my just Judge,*
> *you are my greatest teacher,*
> *you are my ready helper,*
> *you are my powerful physician,*
> *you are the most excellent of men,*
> *you are my living bread,*
> *you are my priest forever,*
> *you are my leader to the homeland,*
> *you are my true light,*
> *you are my sweet holiness,*
> *you are my perfect patience,*

> *you are my pure simplicity,*
> *you are my complete unity,*
> *you are my peaceful concord,*
> *you are my total care,*
> *you are my safe harbor,*
> *you are my never-ending salvation,*
> *you are my great compassion,*
> *you are my valiant endurance,*
> *you are my spotless offering,*
> *you are my completed redemption,*
> *you are my future hope,*
> *you are my perfect charity,*
> *you are my eternal life, to you I pray,*
> *and ask that I may walk with you*
> *when I rest in you,*
> *and when I rise again before you.*
> *Hear me, O Lord,*
> *who lives and reigns,*
> *now and forever. Amen.*

Take a moment to remember Jesus' admonition In Matthew 6:7 that, "When you are praying, do not heap up empty phrases…". Then, reflect on the simplicity of the litany's language and structure. Repetitive spiritual practices may be found in all major religions to achieve various goals, but in the Abrahamic faiths (and certainly among the ancient Celtic saints) the repetitive prayers like the litany must express a person's deepest needs and desires for the prayers to be effective.

After reflecting on this litany, prayerfully engage it in the same manner that you approached your lament – slowly and deliberately at first as you allow each word or phrase to settle into your consciousness and then at the speed that seems most appropriate to the emotions it evokes. Then, add the phrase "to you I pray," to every line that begins "you are my…" and say the litany again at the speed that seems most appropriate to you. Take some time to consider the various emotions and spiritual qualities the litany evokes in you and write your observations in your journal.

<u>Part Two</u>

Then, on a separate day from your reflections on the litany, consider a personal or social issue in your life that you were able to resolve. Think about the various elements shaping this issue and your reasons for feeling concerned about this issue. You also should reflect on the various ways you and other people were able to effectively solve or eliminate this problem. Then...

[1]   On separate sheets of paper (or pages in your notebook), write each concern you listed about the topic you have selected. Be as specific as possible, separating each topic into as many distinct and self-contained concerns as possible.

[2]   Reflecting on each issue and its related concerns individually, ask...
- How was this topic addressed or resolved?
- Was it because of the actions of individual people or groups?
- Were you part of the reason it was addressed or resolved?
- What efforts in the past, either by others or by you, sought to solve the problem but proved inadequate?
- What needs to happen if the problem is to be solved or eliminated?

Note: Group these achievements according to their degree of effectiveness and separate them according to whether they were addressed by individuals or groups. Again, be as specific as possible about the actions that were needed to achieve these results and the people involved in successfully addressing them.

You may find it helpful to think about these solutions and achievements in terms of their degree of completion. In this way, there are certain aspects of them for which you can express clear gratitude and others that will be brought to prayer as petitions for the future.

[3]   Reflecting on each issue and its related concerns individually, ask...
- What aspect of God's activity in the world helped achieve each of these victories?
- To whom did God offer protection, guidance or initiative in addressing these problems?
- What more does God need to do who completely solve the problems and concerns found on your lists?

- What attributes of God will be necessary for these future victories to be achieved?

[4]   Then, develop your lists of individual achievements into two lists: one that shows things that have already been achieved and the other activities that need support in the future. Next to each item on each list, write the human quality (e.g., wisdom, courage, patience, etc.) needed for that item either to have been achieved or to be achieved in the future.

[5]   In your imagination, prayerfully present these lists and notes to Jesus, discussing them in as much detail as possible. Make certain to note the emotions evoked by each specific issue or response from your lists. When you have finished praying, be certain to include these emotional responses next to each topic for concern.

[6]   At the end of your prayer, decide the phrase (or phrases) that you will choose to repeat during your litany. For example, you may decide to use the phrase (e.g., "Lord, source of...", "Grant me...", etc.) followed by each hopefully qualities you needed to successfully address the problems and issues from "Circles of Compassion and Action".

Part Three

Before writing your litany, take some time to remember:

[1]   Like the lament, a litany is a statement of faith in which you expect God to hear you and respond to your needs. You should begin by calling out to God and asking to be heard. Then, recognize that God is the source of all your strengths and capabilities by listing them in a repetitive manner (with or without a responsive phrase). Then, conclude with a simple expression of gratitude or acknowledgement for God's presence in your life.

[2]   Also, the litany has tremendous flexibility. For example, you can divide the repetitive strophes into actions or qualities experienced in different times (i.e., past, present and future) with each of these divisions using different invocational phrases. You also have the freedom to include or exclude responses to your invocational phrases (see the final paragraph of Part One of this consideration of the litany).

[3]   Finally, as with all prayer, a litany affirms an existing relationship of love. You have a history of God's loving care and part of the lament should serve as a reminder of the ways in which God has

helped you in the past and of your expectation that God will offer loving support for your needs in the present (and the future).

After taking some time reflecting on how these elements of a litany might shape the presentation of the concerns you have, write your prayer. It should include:
- a direct appeal to God had its beginning.
- the invocational phrase (or phrases) that you will choose to repeat during your litany. For example, you may decide to use the phrase (e.g., "Lord, source of...", "Grant me...", etc.) followed by each hopefully qualities you needed to successfully address the problems and issues from "Circles of Compassion and Action".
- responsive phrase(s) to your invocations, if you choose to include any. These could be a single repeated phrase (e.g., "Grant us your grace", Help us", etc.) or phrases that respond specifically to the attribute mentioned in the invocation. (e.g., "courage... Grant us bravery", wisdom... Grant us insight", etc.)
- a concluding statement of praise.

Part Four

Now, take your litany to prayer. After taking the time you need to focus on the present moment, begin by reading your litany slowly and deliberately. Allow each word and phrase to rest gently in your consciousness and feel the emotions evoked in your reading as you allow yourself to focus entirely on your experiences in the moment. Also, if something does not feel right about your litany (e.g., the wording seems too vague, you find some aspect of a problem out of place, etc.), take the time to rewrite that portion of your prayer.

After prayerfully reading your litany, put all other thoughts out of your consciousness and become as still as possible. Then, return to your lament and read it aloud at the speed that seems most appropriate to the emotions you are trying to convey. Allow yourself to feel the fullness of your joy as you invoke God's presence by speaking of how the various divine attribute have fulfilled (and will fulfill) your various needs and desires.

After you have finished these prayers, review your litany and revise any aspects of it that you feel need to be clarified. Then, record your lament and any other significant observations from your prayers in your journal.

The Lorica

Part One

Often referred to in the Celtic tradition as a breastplate, the lorica is a prayer of protection. It very directly and deliberately asks for gods care and shielding in a world which can be hostile both to God's desires and to those who seek to serve God in the world. It is a highly personal prayer, so it can take depending upon the person invoking it.

Consider, for example, this anonymous lorica found in a 10th Century manuscript:

> *May our Lord Jesus Christ*
> *be near you to defend you,*
> *within you to refresh you,*
> *around you to preserve you,*
> *before you to guide you,*
> *behind you to justify you,*
> *above you to bless you;*
> *who lives and reigns*
> *with the Father and the Holy Spirit,*
> *one God, now and forever.*

This lorica is a caim, also called an "encircling prayer". In this case, the prayer is being said as a blessing upon another person as it asks God to protectively surround that person in a dangerous world. However, the caim also may be used to invoke God's protection for the person saying the prayer or for significant objects or events.

Now, consider the 7th Century Lorica of St. Fursa (Fursey):

> *May the guiding hands of God be on my shoulders,*
> *may the presence of the Holy Spirit be on my head,*
> *may the sign of Christ be on my forehead,*
> *may the voice of the Holy Spirit be in my ears,*
> *may the smell of the Holy Spirit be in my nose,*
> *may the sight of the company of heaven be in my eyes,*
> *may the speech of the company of heaven be in my mouth,*
> *may the work of the church of God be in my hands,*
> *may the serving of God and my neighbor be in my feet,*
> *may God make my heart his home,*
> *and may I belong to God, my Father, completely.*

In this case, the lorica (which you may recognize since it was used incorporated into the morning and evening prayers of the second section) blesses the person with God's protection using language that mirrors the anointing an individual would receive when going out into the world on mission. So, it is not surprising this lorica amplifies this liturgical imagery by using a repetitive pattern very much like the litany.

> <u>Note:</u> *You also may find it useful to consider the most famous Celtic lorica: Saint Patrick's Breastplate, also known as "The Deer's Cry" (which you prayed during your retreat in* From Loss to Love*). Much longer than the examples presented above, it incorporates many different types of Celtic prayer in a single statement of faith as it invokes God's protection at the beginning of the day. Many translations (including a particularly eloquent one by Kuno Meyer) are available online.*

After considering these prayers, take time to prayerfully engage each of them in turn on separate days. On each day, begin by saying the lorica slowly and deliberately, allowing each word and phrase to settle to settle into your consciousness. Then, reread the prayer again at the speed that seems most appropriate to you. Afterward, take time to reflect on the dynamics of this prayer in relation to your own spiritual needs and prayer style. Finally, share your reflections in an imaginary conversation with Jesus and write your observations in your journal.

<u>Part Two</u>

After these considerations, prepare a lorica of your own by considering the challenges that you are confronting that require God's protection and the style a prayer that best suits your temperament.

[1]   Begin by considering your personal or social situation. Ask...

• What are the various ways that you need God's protection, both in your daily life and in moments of stress?

• Do you feel especially threatened by any circumstances in your life? Are there specific men or women That you feel are trying to harm you?

• If so, what are they doing and how can God protect you from these actions?

• How might you be harming yourself and how might God protect you from these actions?

[2]   Then, decide on the style of your lorica. Take a moment to consider how you experience God's presence in your life and think of the prayer style that comes closest to mirroring your encounters with God.

• If you experience God as a pervasive presence that takes form according to the specific needs of the moment, then you might consider a litany.

• If you feel particularly threatened, you might consider modeling your lorica on a lament.

Note: If you feel God embracing you in moments of crisis, you might want to prepare a caim (an encircling prayer), using the morning examen from this retreat series as a model.

[3]   Finally, write your lorica. Decide if any of the various examples of prayer described in this subsection inspire you, even going online to research them in more detail if necessary. Also, think about any personally significant biblical verses that you might be able to adapt into a lorica. Allow your mind to freely play with the styles of prayer as they interact with the needs you have for God's protection. Then, finally, write the lorica that seems best suited to you, your personal needs and your temperament.

Whether it is long or short, it should be something that you want to pray on a daily basis – at least until your circumstances change.

Part Three

Now, take your lorica to prayer. After taking the time you need to focus on the present moment, begin by reading your lorica slowly and deliberately. Allow each word and phrase to rest gently in your consciousness and feel the emotions evoked in your reading as you allow yourself to focus entirely on your experiences in the moment. Also, if something does not feel right about your prayer (e.g., the wording seems too vague, you find some aspect of a problem out of place, etc.), take the time to rewrite that portion.

After prayerfully reading your lorica, put all other thoughts out of your consciousness and become as still as possible. Then, return to your prayer and read it aloud at the speed that seems most appropriate to the emotions you are trying to convey. Allow yourself to feel the fullness of your joy as you invoke God's presence and protection.

After you have finished these prayers, review your lorica and revise any aspects of it that you feel need to be clarified. Then, record your lament and any other significant observations from your prayers in your journal.

Sacred Citizenship

Brigid of Kildare – The Flame of Justice

In this excerpt from *A Passion for Justice: Social Ethics in the Celtic Tradition* (2008), Johnston McMaster explores the hallmarks of Saint Brigid's life as a "citizen of heaven".

Active Compassion for the Poor

Kildare is reputed to have been known as the "City of the Poor". If we are to judge by the Life by Cogitosus, it is a reputation well deserved. Compassion is a major theme in the Life with twenty-three of thirty-two chapters in Cogitosus' hagiography dealing with Brigid's concern for friends and strangers, the marginalized and guests, including lepers – a widespread disease in Ireland at the time: "One day, when a certain person came asking for salt, just as other poor and destitute people and countless numbers were accustomed to come to her seeking their needs, the most Blessed Brigid supplied an ample amount." The poor and strangers were drawn from every quarter "by the reputation of her great deeds and the excess of her generosity". Kildare was also described as "the safest place of refuge among all the towns of the whole land of the Irish, with all their fugitives."

The transformation of water into the best beer story is in response to lepers. These were social outcast, the most avoided and dreaded people in six-century Ireland. Compassion is the key virtue in Brigid's life as she responds to the poor, the fugitives and the untouchables. Not only do they reflect the Jesus story and his preferential option for the poor and marginalized, but they are also a reminder that religious worship and prayer and social justice are indivisible. Spirituality is inseparable from active solidarity with the poor, the nobodies, the abused and the marginalized ...

Concern in Animal Welfare

Cogitosus has a number of animal stories. Brigid is frequently portrayed as practicing prayer: in one story she is in a trance, "her soul and celestial meditation." She put a large quantity of bacon down beside her dog and a month later found it intact! The dog emerges as a hero! In another story a hunted wild boar joins her herd. She blessed it and it served her tamely and humbly.

Wolves act as swineherds for her, a wild fox is produced to take the place of the king's pet and saves the life of a poor man who killed the king's fox, and wild ducks came to her. Indeed, "Brigid felt the tenderness for some ducks."

Brigid, according to Cogitosus, had a close relationship with animals. this animal kinship is a familiar theme in the Lives of all Celtic saints. Wild animals become friends. Again the theomythical point Cogitosus is making is about the importance of compassion towards all life, human and animate. The story of the wild fox combines both the man sentenced to execution and the fox as recipients of Brigid's compassion. She is concerned for the welfare and the well-being of all life.

An anthropocentric view of life assumes that humans are in every way superior to all other forms of life and that animals only exist to serve the needs and pleasures of humans. This worldview frequently leads to abuse of animals and cruelty, justified by human superiority and the right to dominate. Cogitosus' theomythical stories are the reminder that humans are not at the center of the world for at the top of the bioladder, and that they have ethical responsibilities to care for the animal world. The praxis of spirituality is about friendship and partnership with all creation.

Living Beyond Patriarchy

There is no evidence that any hagiographer was a woman, even though there were communities of women and double communities, both of which were places of learning. Brigid is a significant leader in the early Celtic communities. But there is no surviving document that has been signed off *by a woman*. Even though the large numbers of women committed themselves to the monastic life, the surviving Lives are mostly male. Given that the Lives were written later – Brigid's Life by Cogitosus about 100-150 years later – the lack of women may reflect the growing patriarchy of the Irish church as well as beyond Ireland. "Patriarchal attitudes which negated the value of women's lives and leadership came to dominate much of the Western church, and this too contributed to the scarcity of stories about female saints."...

The Lives do portray Brigid in a struggle with patriarchy. "Issues of sexual politics raise their head several times in Bridget's relationship with the male saints Patrick and Brendan." There is no historical basis for their ever meeting one another, yet the hagiography does have them meet "outside" history and are making a significant point. Reflected in the stories our struggles, not only over primacy and therefore ecclesial politics but also over gender struggles and therefore useful insights into sexual politics and the sexual dynamics of the time.

After one of his voyages when sea monsters attacked his boat, Brendan discovered that invocation of his name and that of Patrick had no effect but the naming of Brigid did subdue the monsters. He arrived to meet Brigid and immediately told her to make confession. Bridget responded by telling him to make his confession first! Brendan responded by suggesting that the sea monsters were right to honor her! In another version of the story Bridget hangs her cloak on a sunbeam but when Brendan tries to do the same his cloak falls in the mud. The hagiographer obviously wanted Brendan to look foolish and Brigid to appear superior. The story reflects sexual politics and Brigid's unwillingness to submit to patriarchy.

The other remarkable story about Brigid is that of her ordination as bishop. Cogitosus does not tell the story but the Irish of Life of Brigid does. Both Cogitosus and the Irish Life tell the story of MacCaille, a pupil of bishop Mel, placing the veil on Brigid's head and how she held the ash beam that supported the altar. The wood was not consumed by fire. What happened next has been denied or repressed, reflecting again the power of patriarchy.

The bishop, being intoxicated with the grace of God there, did not know what he was reciting from his book, for he consecrated Brigid with the orders of a bishop. "Only this virgin in the whole of Ireland will hold episcopal ordination," said Mel. While she was being consecrated a fiery column ascended from her head.

An intoxicated Bishop, not aware of what he was doing and limiting episcopal ordination to Brigid only, indicates an uneasiness with the practice...

Gender equality has always been difficult to achieve in the church in society. Patriarchy is an institutional ethos and is a structural injustice. Whatever other peace factors are required, world peace also depends on peace between the sexes and a justice ethic demands living beyond patriarchy.

The flame of justice, symbolized by the fiery column ascending from Brigid's head following her episcopal ordination, is both a sign of rigid solidarity with the poor and her struggle to overcome patriarchy.

Anamchara

The hagiographers were aware that the role of the anamchara, or soul friend, was central to spirituality in the Irish/Celtic tradition, so they sought to present these saints as real spiritual mentors and soul friends. When Cogitosus wrote his Life of Brigid, she was long dead but in a real sense was very much alive in the theomyth and could accompany another in their struggle to live faithfully and ethically in the world. Hagiographers portray her as being consulted by many laypeople and spiritual leaders. She is consulted by Finian of Clonard, Brendan of Clonfert and Kevin of Glendalough, even though in reality they never met and were not of the exact same era. The point is the power of Brigid as pastor, confessor, mentor and sole friend.

Another story tells of her encounter with a young cleric from a community in Ferns, "a foster-son of Brigid who used to come to her with wishes". Being a foster-son in the Celtic tradition meant that he had spent some of his younger life with Brigid, who had responsibility for his educational and spiritual formation. On this visit she asked him if he had a soul friend. He replied in the affirmative, but the truth was that he had had died. "For your soul friend has died, and anyone without a soul friend is like a body without a head."

The tradition of anamchara/soul friend is closely associated with the Celtic tradition, and Brigid in particular. She was a wise soul friend who was a mentor, guide and companion to many on their life journey. The soul friend was considered indispensable. The young Ferns cleric was told: "Eat no more until you get a soul friend."

A life journey is a spiritual one. It is a journey of faith seeking understanding, a pilgrimage of living theology. Every life story has sacred and mysterious dimensions and it is not a story that can be woven in isolation or alone. Understanding the dimensions, making sense out of life commitments, and life praxis, unraveling ambiguity and struggle with loss and suffering, requires a body with a head, a wise, open, perceptive and often wounded soul friend. Such was Brigid, and the soul friend is a strong insight from her Lives and from the Celtic tradition.

Before proceeding to the next section, ask yourself the following questions:
1. Does a particular part of this excerpt stand out for you? Why? Does it relate to a particular concern in your life or in your interactions with others?
2. Does any aspect of the excerpt relate to your experiences of prayer during your retreat? If so, which?
3. What does the excerpt tell you about Saint Brigid? How does this help you in your own spiritual life? How does this challenge your beliefs about spirituality?
4. How does this excerpt help you understand your calling to become a "citizen of heaven"?

Selections from Cogitosus' *Life of Saint Brigid*

An excerpt from *Saint Patrick's World* (1999), with translations and commentaries by Liam de la Paor.

After reading each of the following sections of Cogitosus' *Life of Saint Brigid*, ask yourself the following questions:
1. What is the most important aspect of the selection? Why?
2. Were there any parts of the selection that you found challenging?
3. Were there any parts of the selection that you found comforting?
4. How will you bring these challenging or comforting aspects of the selection before God in prayer?
5. What is the grace you will ask from God in your prayer regarding these issues?
6. How does the selection help you better understand your relationship with God and with others?
7. What does this selection say to you about your life choices in the past?
8. What does this selection say to you about your desires for the future?

In answering these questions, be specific in your responses and focus on the concrete actions you feel drawn to pursue either in the present or in the future. If a particular question provokes a significant response, record these insights in your retreat journal.

1. She turns water into beer.

On another extraordinary occasion, this venerable Brigid was asked by some lepers for beer, but had none. She noticed water that had been prepared for baths. She blessed it, in the goodness of her abiding faith, and transformed it into the best beer, which she drew copiously for the thirsty. It was indeed He Who turned water into wine in Cana of Galilee who turned water into beer here, through this most Blessed woman's faith.

2. Wolves act as swineherds for her.

Among the many people who offered her gifts was a man who came once from a distant territory. He said that he would give her fat pigs, but asked that she send some of her people with him back to his farm to collect the pigs. The farm was far away, situated at the space of three or four days' journey. She sent some of her workers with him as traveling companions; but they had in fact gone fairly a day's journey (as far as the mountain known as Grabor, which forms a territorial boundary) when they saw his pigs, which they had thought to be in distant parts, coming towards them on the road, driven by wolves which had carried them off. As soon as he realized what had happened, the man recognized them as his pigs. Truly, the wild wolves, because of their enormous reverence for the Blessed Brigid, had left the great forest in the wide plains to work at herding and protecting the pigs. Now, on the arrival of the people she had sent – who were astonished to see such swineherds – the wolves, leaving the pigs there, gave up their unnatural activity. The next day, those who had been sent to collect the pigs gave an account of the marvelous event and return to their homes.

3. A wild fox takes the place of the king's pet.

On another day, a certain person, not knowing the circumstances, saw the king's fox walking into the royal palace, and ignorantly thought it to be a wild animal. He did not know that it was a pet, familiar with the Kings Hall, which entertain the king and his companions with various tricks that it had learned – requiring both intelligence and nimbleness of body. He killed the fox in the view of a large crowd. Immediately, he was seized by the people who had seen the deed. He was accused and brought before the king. When the king heard the story he was angry. He ordered that, unless the man could produce a fox with all the tricks that his fox had had, he and his wife and sons should be executed and all his household be committed to servitude.

When the venerable Brigid heard this story, she was moved to such pity and tenderness that she ordered her chariot to be yoked. Grieving in the depths of her heart for the unhappy man who had been so unjustly judged, and offering prayers to the Lord, she traveled across the plain and took the road which led to the royal palace. And the Lord, instantly, heard her outpoured prayers. He directed one of his wild foxes to come to her. It immediately made all speed, and when it arrived at the most Blessed Brigid's chariot it sprang aboard and sat quietly beside Brigid under her mantle.

As soon as she arrived in the king's presence, she began imploring that unfortunate man, who had not understood the situation and was held prisoner as a victim of his own ignorance, should be set free and released from his chains. But the king would not heed her prayers. He affirmed that he would not release the man unless he could produce another fox with the same tricks as his, that had been killed. In the middle of this she introduced her fox. And, in the presence of the king and of the crowd, it went through all the tricks that the other fox had performed, and amuse the crowd in exactly the same way. The king was satisfied, his nobles, and the great applauding crowd wondered at the marble that had been worked. The king ordered that the man who had been under sentence of death should be set free. Not long after St. Brigid had procured that man's release and had returned home, the same fox, bothered by the crowds, skillfully contrived a safe escape. It was pursued by large numbers of riders and hounds, but made fools of them, fled through the plains and went into the waste and wooded places and so to its den.

4. A band of murderers is deceived by a miracle of glamour.

Once, as was her custom, she was spreading abroad among everyone the seed of the Lord's word, when she observed nine men belonging to a certain peculiarly vain and diabolical cult. They were deceived and corrupted in mind and soul, and at the instigation of the ancient Enemy who ruled among them, they had bound themselves – since they thirsted for the spilling of blood – and resolved with evil vows and oaths to commit murder before the beginning of the forthcoming month of July. The most revered and kindly Brigid preached to them in many gentle phrases, urging them to abandon their mortal errors, to humble their hearts and through true penance to renounce their sinfulness. But they were profane of mind, they had not fulfilled their wicked vow, and they continued their ways, resisting her appeal, and in spite of the abundant prayers which the virgin had poured out to God in her desire (following her Lord) that all should be saved and know the truth.

The criminals went on their way, and met with what they thought was the man they had to kill. They pierced him with their spears and beheaded him with their swords, and were seen by many to return with bloody weapons, as if they had destroyed their adversary. Here was the miracle: they had killed nobody – although it seemed to them that they had fulfilled their vows. When, however, no person was missing in that territory in which they thought they had triumphed, the fullness of the divine favor granted through the most holy Brigid became known to all. And they who had formerly been murderers were now turned back to God through penance.

5. Through the miraculous recovery of a brooch she vindicates a woman accused of theft.

There was a certain nobleman, with the deviousness of a man of the world, who lusted after a particular woman. He exercised his cunning on ways to seduce her. He entrusted a silver brooch to her safe-keeping; then deviously filched it from her without her knowledge and threw it into the sea. This meant that, when she was unable to produce it on demand, she would be forfeit to him as his slave, and so must submit to his embraces to be used as he wished. He contrived this evil for no other reason than to be in a position to demand this ransom. If the silver brooch were not returned, the woman herself must be given to him instead in servitude, because of her failure, to be subject to his wicked lust.

This chaste woman fled in fear to St. Brigid, as she would fly to the safest city of refuge. When Bridget learned what had happened, and how and why; almost before she had heard the story out she summoned a certain person who had fish that had been caught in the river. The fishes' bellies were cut and opened, and there in the middle of one of them was revealed the silver brooch which that most cruel man had thrown into the sea.

Then, easy in her mind, she took along the silver brooch and went with that infamous man to the assembly of the people for the case to be heard. She showed the assembly the brooch, and many witnesses gave testimony, people who were able to identify the brooches the same one that was concerned in this accusation. Brigid took the chaste woman into her own company, and freed her from the clutches of that most cruel tyrant. Indeed he afterwards confessed his fault to St. Brigid and submissively prostrated himself before her. Everyone admired her for the performance of this great miracle, and she gave thanks to God (or whose glory she had done everything) and went home.

6. She divides a silver dish exactly into three.

Three lepers came, asking for alms of any kind, and she gave them a silver dish. So that this would not cause discord and contention among them when they came to share it out, she spoke to a certain person expert in the weighing of gold and silver, and asked him to divide it among them in three parts of equal weight. When he began to excuse himself, pointing out that there was no way he could divided up so that the three parts would weigh exactly the same, the most Blessed Brigid herself took the silver dish and struck it against the stone, breaking it into three parts as she had wished. Marvelous to tell, when the three parts were tested on the scales, not one part was found to be heavier or lighter by a breath than any other. So the three poor people left with their gift and there was no cause for envy or grudging between them.

7. She receives a bishop's vestments from Christ in place of those she had given to the poor.

She followed the example of the most blessed Job and never allowed a poor person to leave empty-handed. Indeed, she gave away to the poor the foreign and exotic robes of the illustrious bishop Conlaeth, vestments he wore in the course of the liturgy of the Lord and the apostolic vigils. When in due course the time for the solemnities came round, the high priest of the people wish to change into his vestments. It was to Christ – in the form of a poor person – that St. Brigid had given the bishop's clothing. Now she handed to the Bishop another set of vestments, similar in all details of texture and color, which she had received at that very moment (draped over a two-wheeled chariot) from Christ, whom, as a beggar, she had clad. She had freely given the other clothes to the poor. Now, at the right moment, she received these instead. For, as she was the living and most blessed instrument of the sublime, she had power to do what she wished.

Articulate Witness

Defining Your Style

The call to articulate witness poses a daunting challenge. It is an invitation to share your innermost experience of God's loving presence – a deeply personal and highly treasured gift – in a public setting where it may not be received with the love and respect you have for it. Yet, since your acts of witness allows you to participate in God's redemption of creation through actions unique to you, you must learn to cherish the gifts of God's love you have received and prepare to proclaim that love to others with courage and confidence.

Slowly and deliberately, consider the words of 1 Corinthians 12:4-13:

> *There are varieties of gifts, but the same Spirit; and there are varieties of services, but the same Lord; and there are varieties of activities, but it is the same God who activates all of them in everyone. To each is given the manifestation of the Spirit for the common good. To one is given through the Spirit the utterance of wisdom, and to another the utterance of knowledge according to the same Spirit, to another faith by the same Spirit, to another gifts of healing by the one Spirit, to another the working of miracles, to another prophecy, to another the discernment of spirits, to another various kinds of tongues, to another the interpretation of tongues. All these are activated by one and the same Spirit, who allots to each one individually just as the Spirit chooses.*
>
> *For just as the body is one and has many members, and all the members of the body, though many, are one body, so it is with Christ.*

Now, ask yourself the following questions:

1. How do you experience God in your life?
   - Do you experience God in distinct moments separate from one another?
   - Are your experiences of God part of a predictable pattern? If so, what is the nature of that pattern?

2. What are the gifts of God that you have experienced in your life?
- Do these gifts feel separate or connected in your consciousness? How?
- How do you respond when God offers you a gift?
- Does this response change according to the nature of the gift?

3. How do your gifts invite you into the service of God?
- What type of service do you want to give to God?
- How does this service reflect the gifts that you have been given by God?
- Are the forms of service you wish to offer to God differ from those of other people?
- Are the forms of service you wish to offer to God solitary in nature?
- Do the forms of service you wish to offer to God connect you to other people? How?

4. How does your experience of God shape your day-to-day activities?
- Are you always aware of God's presence shaping and guiding you in your daily activities?
- Does your awareness of God's guiding presence occur in special moments of grace?
- Are there are recognizable or consistent patterns of God's presence in your day-to-day activities?

5. Do you recognize God's presence in the activities of other people?
- How does this recognition change your faith and experience of God?
- How does this recognition change your relationship to these other people?

After answering these questions, take some time to review your responses in more detail. Register which of the questions evoke the strongest emotional responses and consider the significance of these questions. Also, observe which questions offered you the most creative or intellectual clarity, looking for patterns of thought that will help you decide how to best define your style of articulate witness. Then, record these reflections in your workbook.

Part 1

While the discovery of your passions emerges from a unique experience of God, the definition of your individual style often involves a challenging (yet also consoling) recognition that the expression of your passions in the world is distinctive without necessarily being unique. As you explore different ways to express yourself, you will find there are other people using similar tools to the ones which you find attractive. So, it is important to take time to learn from others – and their experiences, both positive and negative – as you discern the tools which best serve your invitation to articulate witness.

Defining your style is a human activity requiring practicality as you rationally consider your own interests and capabilities as well as contemplate (and hopefully learn from) the experiences of other people. It involves careful reflection on the creative or social resources you will need to express yourself, your ability to use these tools effectively and the receptivity of others to what you have to say or offer. In this way, the definition of your personal style makes you more fully human as it heightens your awareness of your own identity and of the society around you.

However, since your goal remains to express the presence of God to others, defining your style also must involve a prayerful process of reflection and service. Every choice and action should serve the desires of God revealed in prayer, making the definition of your personal style an act of ongoing discernment as you seek to love and serve God. It is a personal journey of faith that transforms you into an instrument of God's desires for creation and human society.

With these thoughts in mind, the definition of your form(s) of articulate witness should involve an active process of learning from the experience and expression of other people. As noted above, your choice of style will make you distinctive but this does not mean you are unique. You may find other people have traveled similar paths of self-exploration and self-expression, so you should begin your own journey by learning of those who preceded you.

If your form of articulate witness involves creative expression, you should seek out similar creative voices and learn from them.
- Begin by reading literary works, listening to musical compositions, or engaging visual representations that you find emotionally compelling. At this point, avoid any form of criticism regarding the type of creative expression that interest you. Instead, take time to enjoy your experiences and note which aspects of these creative works affect you most deeply on an emotional level.

Note: During this initial period of exploration, you will find it helpful to take short breaks from the work that you most enjoy by engaging other creative works that you consider less enjoyable. This will both heighten those aspects of creativity you most enjoy and suggest alternative approaches you might want to incorporate into your eventual creative activities.

- After becoming familiar with the various aspects of the creative works you find most enjoyable, expand your exploration to include an awareness of the creative process that shaped the artist(s) self-expression. This may include reading letters by the artist(s) or memoirs about his or her creative journey and/or discussions of a particular work of art. Avoid biographies and other critical works since these resources will take you away from your emotional engagement with the form(s) of expression attracting you.
- Gradually, when you become comfortable with the "interior life" of the artistic work, you should begin reading criticism and technical studies of the artist(s) and creative expression you find attractive. It is important to remember during this period of critical thinking that these viewpoints remain educated opinions and do not necessarily define your own thoughts or feelings regarded the artwork(s).
- When you feel ready emotionally and creatively, incorporate the things you have learned in your own artistic work. You should remember that this is both a moment of fragility that needs to be protected and a moment of revelation that needs to be honored. You will need to create a safe space in which you can share your creativity with others who understand your spiritual and creative journey.

If your form of articulate witness involves social activity, you should strive to understand the nuances of the issue(s) that concern you.

• Begin by listening to those individuals you find most compelling. Read any articles, books or interviews listen to them as they explain their reasons for pursuing their passions. Also, follow their activities to learn the details of their work as well as the organizational structures supporting their activities. While doing these things, consider the aspects of thought and activity you find attractive as well as those which you find unattractive, deciding which you might wish to emulate or avoid.

Note: After you become familiar with the style of the person(s) or approach(es) you find attractive, you may find it helpful to listen to more critical voices. This will help you better understand your interests as well as suggest alternative methods you might choose to employ in your own form of articulate witness.

• After becoming familiar with the approach(es) you find most emotionally engaging, you should explore the the resources and social networks used by the people or organizations you find attractive. In many cases, this information will be available directly from the individual(s) or organization(s) that interests you. at this point, you should focus your attention on the goals and methods you seek to emulate.

• Once you become comfortable with your knowledge of the approach(es) to the social issue or concern you wish to engage, you should consider critical or opposing opinions. It is important that you not approach this process as a debate. Instead, listen to each alternative thought or method with the intent of finding an aspect in each capable of enriching your own approach to the issue(s) concerning you.

Note: Whether approaching the creative expression or social action of others, you need to remember you are on the journey of self-realization. You should not be afraid to disagree or separate yourself from the models you find attractive or compelling.

However, you need to maintain a humble attitude that recognizes the achievements of others while at the same time understanding that they do not necessarily define you.

During this initial period of exploration, you should maintain an attitude of careful reflection and open prayer.

- You will find it helpful to keep a journal dedicated to documenting your observations and insights concerning the evolution of your vocation to articulate witness. This journal should begin with the summary of the insights you gained during the exercises presented earlier in *From Loss to Love* as well as a personal statement about your hopes for the future. Then, as you proceed through the process of defining your style and discovering your voice, record the events and thoughts which you find most seminal during your journey.

- You should find or create a small circle of intimate friends with whom you can share your ideas openly and without criticism. It is important that you do not to allow this group of friends to inordinately affect you as you engage in the issues surrounding your form of articulate witness. So, you will find it helpful to ask these friends to focus on how your ideas affect them and not how your ideas could be improved.

- At every stage in this process, you will find it helpful to review your thoughts and actions using the "Rules for Discernment" presented in *The Spiritual Exercises of St. Ignatius*. Specifically, should use the rules for discernment presented during the first week of the Ignatian exercises (found in *From Loss to Love*) when encountering an idea or event discreetly or for the first time and use the rules for discernment presented during the second week (found on page 305) when considering the history of an idea or activity.

Part 2

With time and effort, as well as through reflection and prayer, you will become confident in the validity of your own personal style – whether it engages creative expression or social action – and need to test your creative and social concerns in more challenging situations. While it is important in this moment to avoid overconfidence, you need to be careful to make certain that your fears and uncertainties do not undermine your vocation to articulate witness. So, approach this time with courage and with faith in God's continuing presence as you move forward.

If your form of articulate witness involves creative expression, look for opportunities to present your work to others. Initially, you may want to participate in activities that are more supportive (e.g., a writers' or artists' group, an "open microphone" event for new writers, exhibitions for new artists, etc.). However, as your confidence grows, you may find yourself drawn to entering artistic competitions or submitting your work or presentation by others (e.g., performance organizations, publishers, galleries, etc.).

Note: During this process of sharing your creative work with others more broadly, it is important that you remain comfortable at each stage of greater sharing. Do not feel compelled to share beyond the level of comfort provided to you through prayer.

If your form of articulate witness involves social activity, find opportunities to participate in organizations or activities related to your concerns. This may involve doing volunteer work with an organization engaged in the activities that you seek to pursue or going to protests or demonstrations related to your area of concern. You should listen to the people already involved in these activities and learn the reasons that shape their own involvement as well as the activities of the organizations to which they contribute.

Note: This involvement in activities defined by others may lead you to see new issues or activities you want to pursue on your own (possibly in your own organization) or to suggest to the leadership of the organization in which you are participating. As these moments occur, engage them thoughtfully and prayerfully before choosing how to act.

In all these activities, maintain an attitude of humble prayer. As in your earlier explorations, you will find it useful to use the "Rules for Discernment" presented in *The Spiritual Exercises of St. Ignatius* to maintain your awareness of the activity of God underlying your own choices. Again, you should use the rules presented during the first week of the Ignatian exercises when approaching a new event or decision and rely upon the rules presented by Ignatius during the second week when considering the history of an idea or activity.

Part 3

As with the earlier exploration of your passions, take your insights and concerns to prayer on a regular basis. Imagine yourself sitting with Jesus in a comfortable space and tell him about your most intimate experiences of God and how you feel they lead to specific forms of public witness. Listen as Jesus asks you questions about these matters and make a mental note about your reactions to Jesus' questions and observations. Then, explain both your willingness and your reluctance to share these experiences with others in some way. Again, listen to Jesus' response before asking for his continued support as you move forward.

Afterward, take some time to answer the following questions:
- What aspects of your style excite you and leave you without any doubt about using them?
- What emotions make you uncertain about your style choices?
- What are you willing to sacrifice as God asks you to share your deepest spiritual experiences with others?

Part 4

It is important that you remember your style will emerge from practice, reflection, and revision. Over time, you will learn about yourself from consideration of the thoughts and activities of other people while you shape your own creative and social style.

However, the result of this process is not preordained, and you should not hold too tightly to any idea or activity until it becomes clear to you through prayer that it fulfills God's desires for you and the world around you. From experience, you know God is shaping and guiding you through love, and you need to remain open to that loving presence as you develop your own style of speaking to others on God's behalf.

So, you should give yourself permission to experiment with different methods and approaches. Some of these experiments will fail, so learn from them and ask God to help you understand the hidden value of these "noble failures". Other insights will seem essential to your self-understanding in the beginning but lose luster over time.

In these moments of change, approach God and humbly ask to explain their significance and to guide you forward as you continue defining your style – trusting God's promise in Isaiah 41:13:
Do not fear, for I am with you,
do not be afraid, for I am your God;
I will strengthen you, I will help you,
I will uphold you with my victorious right hand.
do not fear, for I am with you,
do not be afraid, for I am your God;
I will strengthen you, I will help you,
I will uphold you with my victorious right hand.

Textual Resources

From Saint Ignatius' *Spiritual Exercises*

Excerpts from *The Spiritual Exercises of Saint Ignatius of Loyola*, edited by Charles Seager.

<u>A Contemplation of the Kingdom of Jesus Christ (91-98)</u>

91. **A contemplation of the kingdom of Jesus Christ, from the likeness of an earthly king calling out his subjects to war...**

The first prelude for the construction of the place will now be, to imagine that we see the synagogues, villages, and towns, through which Christ passed preaching; and so concerning other places.

The second, relating to the obtaining of grace, will here be, to ask of God that we may not be deaf when Christ calls us; but be ready to follow and obey.

92. Let the first point be, to place before my eyes a human king, chosen of God, whom all Christian princes and people are bound to reverence and obey.

93. The second, to imagine that I hear that king speaking to all his subjects: I propose to subject to my power all the countries of the unbelievers. Whosoever, therefore, chooses to follow me, let him be prepared to use no other food, clothing, or other things, than what he sees me use.

He must also persevere in the same labours, watchings, arid other difficulties with me, that each may partake of the victory and felicity in proportion as he shall have been a companion of the labours and troubles;

94. The third is, to consider what his faithful subjects ought to answer this most loving and liberal king, and how promptly to offer themselves prepared for all his will. And, on the other hand, if any one did not hearken, of how great reproach he would be worthy among all men, and how worthless a soldier he would have to be accounted.

95. The second part of this exercise, consists in drawing a comparison between the said king and our Lord Jesus Christ, concerning these three points:

First, we shall thus apply the example: if that earthly king, with his warlike calling forth, is worthy to receive attention and obedience, how much more worthy is Christ, the Eternal King, and conspicuous to the whole world, Who invites each to Himself in these words: "This is My most just will, to claim to Myself the dominion of the whole world, to conquer all My enemies, and so to enter into My Father's glory.

Whoever then desires to come thither with Me, he must needs labour with Me; for the reward will be according to the labour."

96.   The second, we shall reason, that there will be no one of a sound mind, who will not most eagerly offer and dedicate himself entire to the service of Christ.

97.   Thirdly, it must be judged, that they who shall think good to be altogether subjected to the obedience of Him, will offer, not merely themselves for the endurance of labours, but also some greater and more illustrious offerings, conquering the rebellion of the flesh, of the senses, and of the love of self and the world whence each; will answer to the following effect:

98.   "Behold, Supreme King and Lord of all things, I, though most unworthy, yet, relying on Thy grace and help, offer myself altogether to Thee, and submit to Thy will all that is mine; testifying before Thine infinite goodness, as also in the sight of Thy glorious Virgin Mother, and of the whole court of heaven, that this is my mind, this my desire, this my most certain determination, that (so it turn to the greater advancement of Thy praise and my obedience) I may follow Thee as closely as possible, and imitate Thee in bearing all injuries and adversities with the true poverty, both of spirit, and also of goods; if (I say) it please Thy most holy Majesty to choose and receive me to such a state of life."

A Meditation on the Incarnation (101-108)

101.   **The First Meditation of the First Day will be concerning the Incarnation of Christ; containing three preludes, and three points, with one colloquy...**

102.   The first prelude is, to bring forward the history of the matter to be contemplated; which will here be, how the three Divine Persons looking upon the whole surface of the earth covered with men, who were descending into Hell, decree in the eternity of their God-head, that, for the salvation of the human race, the Second Person should assume the nature of man; whence, the pre-determined time arriving, the Archangel Gabriel is appointed a messenger to the blessed Virgin Mary, as will be said below in the Mysteries of the Life of Christ.

103.   The second relates to the composition of the place, which will be an imaginary vision, as if the whole circuit of the earth, inhabited by so many different nations, lay open before the eyes. Then in one particular part of the world, let the cottage of the blessed Virgin, situated at Nazareth, in the province of Galilee, be beheld.

104. The third contains the asking of grace, that I may know intimately how the Son of God became man for my sake, that I may love Him the more ardently, and henceforth follow Him the more carefully.

105. It must be noted here, that as well the preparatory prayer as the three preludes are made in like manner through the whole week, and the following weeks which remain; the preludes only being varied [in form] according to the difference of the subjects.

106. The first point is, that I view all the persons concerned; and first, the human beings living on the face of the earth, so different in manners, gestures, and actions; some white, and others black; some enjoying peace, and the rest disturbed by wars; this one weeping, and that one laughing; one well, another ill, many being born, and many, on the other hand, dying; with other varieties almost innumerable. Next must be contemplated the three Divine Persons, from Their royal throne, looking upon all the races of men, living as blind on the surface of the earth, and descending to Hell. Afterwards, we shall consider the Virgin Mary with the Angel saluting her; always applying something thence to our selves, that from such consideration we may derive some fruit.

107. The second point is, to perceive by the inward hearing what all the Persons are saying, as what the men are saying, who on earth are conversing together, blaspheming, reviling each other; what the Divine Persons are saying, Who, in Heaven are speaking to each other concerning the redemption of the human race; what the Virgin and the Angel are saying, who; in a little cell, are conversing on the Mystery of the Incarnation. By reflecting on all which things, or making some application of them to myself, I shall study to gather some fruit from each.

108. The third, following naturally, will be, to consider at the same time the actions also of the persons; as, for instance, how mortal men are treating one another with enmity and violence, killing one another, and all rushing to Hell; how the Most Holy Trinity is performing the work of the Incarnation; how, also, the Angel is executing his commission, and the blessed Virgin, bearing herself most humbly, is giving thanks to the Divine Majesty. From which things, applied by reflection, as has been said, to ourselves, we must gather fruit as we go on.

The Two Standards (136-147)

136. **A meditation concerning Two Standards: one that of Jesus Christ, our most excellent General; the other that of Lucifer, the most capital enemy of men...**

137. The first prelude will be a certain historical consideration of Christ on the one part, and Lucifer on the other, each of whom is calling all men to him, to be gathered together under his standard.

138. The second is, for the construction of the place, that there be represented to us a most extensive plain around Jerusalem, in which our Lord Jesus Christ stands as the Chief-General of all good people. Again, another plain in the country of Babylon, where Lucifer presents himself as the captain of the wicked and [God's] enemies.

139. The third, for asking grace, will be this, that we ask to explore and see through the deceits of the evil captain, invoking at the same time the Divine help in order to avoid them; and to know, and by grace be able to imitate, the sincere ways of the true and most excellent General, Christ.

140. The first point is, to imagine before my eyes, in the Babylonian plain, the captain of the wicked, sitting in a chair of fire and smoke, horrible in figure, and terrible in countenance.

141. The second, to consider how, having assembled a countless number of demons, he disperses them through the whole world in order to do mischief; no cities or places, no kinds of persons, being left free.

142. The third, to consider what kind of address he makes to his servants, whom he stirs up to seize, and secure in snares and chains, and so draw men (as commonly happens) to the desire of riches, whence afterwards they may the more easily be forced down into the ambition of worldly honour, and thence into the abyss of pride.

Thus, then, there are three chief degrees of temptation, founded in riches, honours, and pride; from which three to all other kinds of vices the downward course is headlong.

143. In like manner, on the opposite side, must be considered our most exalted and excellent Leader and Commander, Christ.

144. The first point will be, to see Christ in a pleasant plain by Jerusalem; placed, indeed, in lowly state, but very beautiful in form, and in appearance supremely worthy of love.

145. The second is, to consider how He, the Lord of the whole world, sends His chosen Apostles, Disciples, and other Ministers through the world, to impart to every race, state, and condition of men, His sacred and saving doctrine.

146. The third, to hear the exhortatory speech of Christ to all His servants and friends destined to such a work, wherein He bids them study to help all, and first to take care to lead them to the spiritual affection of poverty; and moreover (if the course of duty to God, and the choice of heaven leads that way) to real and actual poverty; then to draw them to the desire of reproach and contempt, from which [whence] springs the virtue of humility. And thus there arise three degrees of perfection; namely, poverty, self-abasement, and humility; which are diametrically opposed to riches, honour, and pride, and introduce at once to all virtues.

147. A colloquy is afterwards to be made to the Blessed Virgin, and grace is to be implored through her from her Son, that I may be received and remain under His standard; and that, first by poverty, either that which is only spiritual, or further, that which consists in the loss of one's goods (if indeed He shall vouchsafe to call and admit me thereto); then by contempt or ignominy also, I may imitate Him the more closely, praying however against others being in fault, lest the contempt of me turn both to the damage of some other, and to the offence of God. This first colloquy will be terminated by *Ave Maria* [Hail Mary].

The second colloquy is directed to Jesus Christ, that He would gain for me that same from the Father; and the prayer *Anima Christi* [Soul of Christ] will be added at the end.

The third to the Father, that He would grant the petition, with *Pater noster* [Our Father/The Lord's Prayer].

<u>Anima Christi</u>
Soul of Christ, sanctify me.
Body of Christ, save me.
Blood of Christ, inebriate me.
Water of the side of Christ, wash me.
Passion of Christ, strengthen me.
O good Jesu, hear me:
Within Thy wounds hide me:
Permit me not to be separated from Thee
From the malignant enemy defend me:
In the hour of my death call me,
And bid me come to Thee,
That with Thy Saints I may praise Thee
For ever and ever. Amen.

The Three Classes of Persons (149-157)

149. **A meditation concerning three classes or differences of persons, that we may choose the better part.**

150. Let the first prelude be made by setting before us, to serve as the history, three distinct classes of men and women, each of which has acquired ten thousand ducats with some other aim than that of the service and love of God; but now desires to pacify God and be saved, getting rid somehow or other of the hurtful love of property, as being a hindrance to salvation.

151. The second is an imaginary construction of a certain place, in which I may see myself standing with perseverance before God and all the Saints, with the desire of knowing how I may best please God Himself.

152. The third is to ask the thing I desire, namely, grace to choose that which will be both most acceptable to God and most conducive to my own salvation.

153. The first class, then, desire indeed to get rid of the love of the property they have acquired, in order that they may be reconciled to God; but do not apply the means and due helps during the whole time of life.

154. The second desire, in like manner, to put away the inordinate affection, but at the same time to hold fast the property, and rather draw God to their own wish, than forsake their hindrance and move towards Him by means of the more conducive state.

155. Lastly, the third, while they desire to cast away the worldly affection, are also equally prepared either to part with or to keep the property itself; whichever they shall perceive, either by the Divine motion, or by the dictates of reason, to be more conducive to the service of God; and in the meantime, leaving all as it is, turn over and examine that question only, and admit no other cause of leaving or retaining the property acquired, except the consideration and desire of the Divine glory, that that glory may be the greatest possible.

156. Three colloquies will follow, as they were made a little above concerning the Standards.

157. It must be observed here, that when we perceive that the affection is opposed to the perfect poverty, which consists both in the spirit, and in the renunciation of property, and that it inclines rather to riches; it is very profitable, in order to the striking out of such affection, to ask of God, even though the flesh resist, that [our Lord] would choose us to poverty of this kind: we shall preserve, however, in the meantime,

the liberty of our desire, whereby it may be lawful to us to go the way which is the more suitable to the service of God.

Three Modes of Humility (165-168)

165.   The first Mode of Humility is this, which is necessary for salvation, that I altogether subject myself to the observance of the law of God, and that, not even on the dominion of the whole world being offered me, or the utmost danger of life set before me, I transgress deliberately any divine or human command, which binds us under the penalty of mortal sin.

166.   The second belongs to a greater perfection, namely, that with a fixed mind I be equally inclined towards riches and poverty, honour and ignominy, shortness and length of life, where the opportunity of the praise of God and of my own salvation is equal; and that by the setting before me of no condition, either of human felicity ever so great, or of my own death, I be ever induced to decide to commit a sin, although only venial.

167.   The third mode belongs to the most perfect humility, namely, that, having already attained to the two former, although without anything superadded, the glory of God should be equal, yet, for the sake of the greater imitation of Christ, I choose rather with Him, who was poor, despised, and mocked, to embrace poverty, contempt, and the reputation of folly, than wealth, honours, and the estimation of wisdom.

168.   Moreover, for the attainment of this degree of humility, it will afford a great help to use the preceding threefold colloquy concerning the Standards, asking suppliantly (if it please the Divine good ness) to be brought to such an election, whether the result to be gained in my service towards God, and in the Divine glory, be greater or equal.

Rules for Discernment of Spirits, Week 2

328.   Other Rules useful for the fuller discerning of spirits and suitable more especially for the Second Week.

329.   The first is, that it is the property of God, and of every good Angel, to pour into the mind true spiritual joy, which they cause by taking away all that sad ness arid disturbance of mind which the demon has thrown in; whereas he, on the contrary, is accustomed by certain sophistical arguments bearing before them the appearance of truth, to attack that joy found in the soul.

330. The second, it belongs to God alone to console the soul without any preceding cause of consolation, it being peculiar to the Creator to enter His creature, and turn, draw, and change it altogether to the love of Himself. And we then say that no cause precedes, when neither to our senses, nor to our understanding, nor to our will there is presented anything which can of itself be the cause of such consolation.

331. The third, when a cause of consolation has preceded, as well the bad as the good Angel may be its author; but they aim at contrary ends; the good, that the soul may advance farther in the knowledge and practice of good; the bad, that she may do badly and perish.

332. The fourth, it is the custom of the malignant spirit, to transfigure himself into an Angel of light, and, having known the pious desires of the soul, first to second them, then soon after to entice her to his own perverse wishes. For he puts on the appearance at first of following up and encouraging the person's good and holy thoughts; and then, gradually drawing him into the secret nooses of his deceits, ensnares him.

333. The fifth, our thoughts must be diligently and accurately examined as to their beginning, middle, and end; and if these three be right, it is a sign of the good Angel, suggesting those thoughts; but if in the course of the ideas anything is presented, or follows, which is bad of itself, or calls away from good, or impels to a less good than the soul in searching before had determined to follow, or produces lassitude in her, taking away the peace and tranquillity which she had before, it will then be an evident sign, that the author of such thought is the malignant spirit, as being always opposed to our advantage.

334. The sixth, as often as it happens that the enemy is discovered by his serpentine tail, that is, the evil end, which he always seeks to insinuate into us, it is then a great help to go over the whole series of ideas, and mark what web of good thought he at first wove before him, and how he endeavoured gradually to remove the preceding sweetness of spiritual taste, and to infuse his own venom in order that his deceits, known by means of an experience of this kind, may the more easily be guarded against for the future.

335. The seventh, into the minds of those who are advancing in the blessing of salvation, the two spirits infuse themselves in different ways; the good one gently, placidly, and sweetly, like a drop of water entering into a sponge; but the evil one roughly, unplacidly, and violently, with a kind of noise, as a shower falling down on a rock: but to those who go on daily from bad to worse, the direct opposite happens. Of which

difference the reason is, the proportion in which the disposition of the soul itself is like or unlike to either Angel. For if either spirit finds her contrary to him, he joins himself to her with a noise and pushing which may easily be perceived; but if conformable, he enters quietly, as into his own house with the door open.

336.   The eighth, as often as without any previous cause, consolation is present to us, although, it being sent from God, there can be under it, as has been said above, no deceit, we ought nevertheless attentively and carefully to distinguish the time when the consolation is present from that which follows next, in which the soul is still fervent, and feels the remains of the Divine favour lately received. For in this latter time it often happens that, either from one's own habit, course of thoughts, and judgment, or from the suggestion of the good or evil spirit, we feel or resolve on things which, not proceeding immediately from God, have need of diligent examination, before being assented to or put in practice.

From Celtic Sources

1. A Description of Saint Brigid from *Lives of Saints from The Book of Lismore*, edited by Whitley Stokes.

For everything that Brigid would ask of the Lord was granted her at once. For this was her desire: to satisfy the poor, to expel every hardship, to spare every miserable man. Now there never hath been anyone more bashful, or more modest, or more gentle, or more humble, or sager, or more harmonious than Brigid... She was abstinent, she was innocent, she was prayerful, she was patient: she was glad in God's commandments she was firm, she was humble, she was forgiving, she was loving: she was a consecrated casket for keeping Christ's Body and his Blood: she was a temple of God. Her heart and her mind were a throne of rest for the Holy Ghost. She was simple [towards God]: she was compassionate towards the wretched: she was splendid in miracles and marvels: wherefore her name among created things is Dove among birds. Vine among trees. Sun among stars.

2. Stories about Saint Brigid from *Three Middle-Irish homilies on the lives of Saints Patrick, Brigit and Columba*, edited by Whitley Stokes.

<u>A Prophecy about the Unborn Brigid</u>
Dubthach bought a bondmaid, named Broicsech. Dubthach united himself in wedlock to her, and she became pregnant by him. Thereafter Dubthach's consort grew jealous of the bondmaid and the queen said "unless thou sellest this bondmaid in far-off lands, I will demand my dowry of thee, and I will go from thee."

Dubthach did not at all desire to sell the bondmaid.

So, he went, and his bondmaid along with him, in a chariot, past the house of a certain wizard named Maithgen. When the wizard heard the noise of the chariot, this he said: "See, O gillie, who is in the chariot, for this is the noise of a chariot under a king." Said the gillie, "Dubthach is therein." Then the wizard went to meet the chariot, and he asked of the woman who was biding in the chariot. Said Dubthach, "That is a bondmaid of mine," quoth he. The wizard asked by whom the bondmaid was pregnant. "By Dubthach," says the bondmaid. Said the wizard, "Marvellous will be the offspring, the like of her will not be in (all) the lands." Said Dubthach, "My consort did not allow me not to sell this bondmaid."

Said the wizard through his gift of prophecy, "Thy wife's seed shall serve this bondmaid's seed, for the bondmaid will bring forth a daughter, noble, revered, before the men of the earth. As sun shineth among stars, (so) will shine the maiden's deeds and merits."

Dubthach and the bondmaid rejoiced thereat, (and) Dubthach said, "Since I have (already) sons, I should like to have a daughter."

Then Dubthach went (back) to his house and his bondmaid with him. The wife however was still jealous of the bondmaid.

The Birth of Brigid

Great was the honour in which God held this girl. For two bishops of the Britons came to her from Alba to prophesy of her and to sanctify her…

After these words there came to Dubthach's house another wizard who had been gathering treasures. Now when the wizard knew that the bondmaid was the cause of the anger of Dubthach's wife, he said, "Wilt thou sell the bondmaid?" "I will sell her," saith Dubthach. However quoth the bishops, "Sell the bondmaid, but sell not the child that is in her womb." This Dubthach did. So, the wizard went forth and the bondmaid with him to his house. Later, a certain poet came out of the province of Conaille to the house of the wizard in order to buy a slave or a bondmaid. The wizard sold him the bondmaid, but sold him not the offspring.

Then it came to pass that the wizard made a great feast, and bade the king of Conaille to the feast, and it was then the time for the king's wife to bear a child. There was a prophet along with the king, and a friend of the king's asked him what hour would be lucky for the queen to bring forth the royal offspring. Saith the prophet, "The child that shall be brought forth to-morrow at sunrise shall overtop every birth in Ireland." Now the queen's travail came on before that hour, and she brought forth a dead son. Then the poet asked the prophet what hour would be lucky for the bondmaid to bring forth. Said the poet, "The child that shall be brought forth to-morrow at sunrise, and neither within house nor without, shall surpass every child in Ireland."

On the morrow, at sunrise, when the bondmaid was going with a vessel full of milk in her hand, and when she put one foot over the threshold of the house inside and the other foot outside, then did she bring forth the girl, to wit, Brigid. The maid-servants washed the girl with the milk that was in her mother's hand. Now that was in accord with the merits of Saint Brigid, to wit, with the brightness and sheen of her chastity. On a Wednesday and in the eighth moon was Brigid born and the girl was taken straightway after her birth to the queen's dead son, and when Brigid's breath came to him he swiftly arose out of death.

Then the wizard and the bondmaid with her daughter went into the province of Connacht since her mother (was) of Connaught and her father out of Munster. One day after she was there, the bondmaid went to her island and covered up her daughter in her house. Certain neighbours saw the house all ablaze wherein was the girl, so that a flame of fire was made of it from earth to heaven. But when they went to rescue the house, the fire appeared not and the girl was full of the Holy Spirit.

Brigid Returns to Her Father

Brigid was minded to go and watch over her fatherland. And the wizard sent messengers to Dubthach, that he might come for his daughter. The messengers declared unto Dubthach the maiden's miracles and many wonders. Then Dubthach came and the wizard bade him welcome and gave him his daughter free.

Then they went to their country, Dubthach and his daughter Brigid and there did Brigid work a wondrous miracle, to wit, her foster-mother was in weakness of disease, and the foster-mother sent the holy Brigid and another maiden with her to the house of a certain man named Boetherni, to ask him for a draught of ale. He refused Brigid. Then Brigid filled a vessel out of a certain well, and blessed it, and (the water) was turned into the taste of ale, and she gave it to her foster-mother, who straightway became whole thereby. Now when Boetherni and his guests went to drink at the banquet not a drop thereof was found.

Brigid's Father Attempts to Sell Her

Dubthach and his consort were minded to sell holy Brigid into bondage; for Dubthach liked not his cattle and his wealth to be dealt out to the poor, and that is what Brigid used to do. So Dubthach fared in his chariot, and Brigid along with him. Said Dubthach to Brigid: "Not for honour or reverence to thee art thou carried in a chariot, but to take thee and sell thee, and to grind the quern for Dunlang MacEnda, King of Leinster."

When they came to the King's fortress, Dubthach went in to the King and Brigid remained in her chariot at the fortress door. Dubthach had left his sword in the chariot near Brigid. A leper came to Brigid to ask an alms. She gave him Dubthach's sword. Saith Dubthach to the King: "Wilt thou buy a bondmaid, namely, my daughter?" Dunlang asketh, "Why sellest thou thine own daughter?" Saith Dubthach, "She stayeth not from selling my wealth and giving it to the poor" Respondeth the King, "Let the maiden come into the fortress." Dubthach went for Brigid and was enraged against her, because she had given his sword to the poor man.

So, when Brigid came into the King's presence, the King said to her: "Since it is thy father's wealth that thou takest, much more, if I buy thee, wilt thou take *my* wealth and *my* cattle and give them to the poor?" Saith Brigid, "The Son of the Virgin knoweth if I had thy might with (all) Leinster, and with all thy wealth I would give (them) to the Lord of the Elements." Said the King to Dubthach: "Thou art not fit on either hand to bargain about this maiden, for her merit is higher before God than before men" And the King gave Dubthach for her an ivory-hilted sword.

Brigid and the Religious Scholar

Brigid was once journeying in Mag Laigen, and she saw running past her a student, namely, Ninnid the scholar.

"What art thou doing, O Sage!" saith Brigid, "and whither art thou wending (so) quickly?"

"To heaven," saith the scholar.

"The Son of the Virgin knoweth," saith Brigid, "that I would fain fare with thee!"

Saith the scholar: "O nun," saith he, "hinder me not from my road; or, if thou hinderest, beseech the Lord with me that the journey to heaven may be happy, and I will beseech God with thee that it may be easy for thee, and that thou mayst bring many thousands with thee to heaven."

Brigid repeated a Paternoster with him, and he was pious thenceforward; and Brigid said that neither gallows nor punishment would be for him; and he it is that afterwards administered communion and sacrifice to Brigid.

Brigid and the Two Lepers

One time came two lepers unto Brigid to be healed. Said Brigid to one of the two lepers: "Wash thou the other." Thus was it done, and he was quite sound forthwith. Said Brigid to the sound leper: "Bathe and wash thy comrade even as we did service unto thee." "Besides the time that we have [already] come together," says he, "we will never come together, for it is not fair for thee, O nun, (to expect) me, a sound man with fresh limbs and fresh clean raiment, to wash that loathsome leper there, with his livid limbs falling out of him." However, Brigid herself washed the poor, lowly leper. The haughty leper who had been washen first, then spake, "Meseems," saith he, "that sparks of fire are breaking through my skin." Swifter than speech he was straightway smitten with leprosy from the crown of his head to his soles, because of his disobedience to Brigid.

Two Miracles Performed by Brigid

This (was another) of Brigid's miracles: while she was herding Dubthach's swine, there came two robbers and carried off two boars of the flock. They fared over the plain, and Dubthach met them and fined them for the cost of his swine. Said Dubthach to Brigid, "Is the herding of the swine good, my girl?" saith he. Respondeth Brigid to Dubthach, "Count thou the swine." Dubthach counted the swine, and not one of them was wanting.

Guests, then, came to Dubthach who had sundered a gammon of bacon into five pieces and left them with Brigid to be boiled. And a miserable, greedy hound came into the Brigid. Brigid out of pity gave him the fifth piece. When the hound had eaten that piece Brigid gave another piece to him. Then Dubthach came and said to Brigid: "Hast thou boiled the bacon, and do all the portions remain?" "Count them," saith Brigid. Her father counted them, and none of them was wanting. The guests declared unto Dubthach what Brigid had done. "Abundant," saith Brigid's father, "are the miracles of that maiden." Now the guests ate not the food, for they were unworthy (thereof), but it was dealt out to the poor and to the needy of the Lord.

Brigid and the Silver Chain

Once upon a time the Queen of Cremthan came and brought a chain of silver to Brigid as an offering. The semblance of a human shape was at one of its ends, and an apple of silver on the other end. Brigid gave it to her virgins; they stored it up without her knowledge, for greatly was Brigid used to taking her wealth and giving it to the poor. Before long, a leper came to Brigid and, without her virgins' knowledge, she went to the chain and gave it unto him. When the virgins knew this, they said, with much angry bitterness and wrath,

"Little good have we from thy compassion to every one" say they, "and we ourselves in need of food and raiment." "Ye are sinning," saith Brigid: "Go ye into the church: the place wherein I make prayer, there will ye find your chain" They went at Brigid's word. But, though it had been given to the poor man, the virgins found their chain therein.

Brigid Discusses a Vision with Patrick

Brigid went to converse with Patrick in Mag Lemne while he was preaching the gospel. And Brigid fell asleep at the preaching. Saith Patrick: "Wherefore has thou slept?" Brigid bent her knees thrice and said: "I saw a vision," quoth she. Saith Patrick: "Tell us the vision." "I saw," quoth she, "four ploughs in the south-east, and they ploughed the whole island, and before the sowing was finished the harvest grew up, and clear well-springs and shining streams came out of the furrows, and white garments were round the sowers and the ploughmen. I beheld four other ploughs in the north, and they ploughed the island athwart, and before the harvest came again, the oats which they had sown grew up at once and ripened, and black streams came out of the furrows, and black garments were on the sowers and on the ploughmen. And I am sorrowful thereat," quoth Brigid.

Saith Patrick: "Be not in sadness, for good is that which thou beheldest. The first four ploughs which thou beheldest, those are I and thou. We sow the four books of the gospel with seed of faith and confession. The harvest which appeared to thee, that is the perfect faith of those men-folk. The four other ploughs, those are the false teachers and the liars, and they will overturn the teachings that we sow, and those we shall not uplift. But we, I and thou, shall then be in the presence of the Creator."

3. "The Things Brigid Wished For" or "A great lake of ale for the King of Kings" from *A book of saints and wonders put down here by Lady Gregory according to the old writings and the memory of the people of Ireland* (1907), edited by Lady Augusta Gregory.

These were the wishes of Brigid:

"I would wish a great lake of ale for the King of Kings;
"I would wish the family of Heaven to be drinking it through life and time.
"I would wish the men of Heaven in my own house;

"I would wish vessels of peace to be giving to them.
"I would wish vessels full of alms to be giving away;
"I would wish ridges of mercy for peace-making.
"I would wish joy to be in their drinking;
"I would wish Jesus to be here among them.
"I would wish the three Mary's of great name;
"I would wish the people of Heaven from every side.
"I would wish to be a rent-payer to the Prince; the way if I was in trouble he would give me a good blessing."

Whatever, now, Brigid would ask of the Lord, he would give it to her on the moment. And it is what her desire was, to satisfy the poor, to banish every hardship, and to save every sorrowful man.

About the Author

A former Jesuit, **Timothy J. Ray** brings a diverse background in creative writing, cultural studies, theology, and the history of ideas to his work in spiritual direction and formation. He received his Bachelor of Arts, *magna cum laude*, in a multi-disciplinary program focused on the cultural history of law, economics and politics from Niagara University before earning, with distinction, both his Master of Fine Arts in Dramaturgy and Dramatic Criticism from Yale University and his Master of Letters in Theology from the University of Saint Andrews.

In addition to this Celtic journey through *The Spiritual Exercises of Saint Ignatius of Loyola*, he has published *The Carmichael Prayerbook*, *A Journey to the Land of the Saints* and *A Pilgrimage to the Land of the Saints, Nurturing the Courage of Pilgrims* and *Seeking our Place of Resurrection*.

For more information about Timothy and his activities, please visit http://www.silentheron.net.

Printed in Great Britain
by Amazon